Gourmet's
HOLIDAYS
AND
CELEBRATIONS

Gourmet's
HOLIDAYS
AND
CELEBRATIONS

FROM THE EDITORS OF GOURMET

CONDÉ NAST BOOKS • RANDOM HOUSE, NEW YORK

Copyright © 1992 Condé Nast Books
All rights reserved under International and Pan-American
Copyright Conventions. Published in the United States by
Random House, Inc., New York, and simultaneously in
Canada by Random House of Canada Limited, Toronto.

LIBRARY OF CONGRESS CATALOGING-IN-PUBLICATION
DATA
Gourmet's holidays and celebrations/
the editors of Gourmet.
    p. cm.
    ISBN 0-679-41767-2
    1. Holiday cookery. 2. Entertaining.
    3. Menus. I. Gourmet.
    TX739.G65 1992   642'.4—dc20   92-50206

Most of the recipes in this work were previously
published in *Gourmet* Magazine.

Manufactured in the United States of America

98765432   24689753   23456789
First Edition

Grateful acknowledgment is made to the following
writers for their permission to reprint recipes previously
published in *Gourmet* Magazine:

Alice S. R. Gochman: "Hamantaschen (Tri-Cornered
Cookies)" (page 42); "Prune or Apricot Filling" (page 42);
"Chocolate-Dipped Fruit Balls" (page 42).

Kathryn Livingston: "Hungarian Mixed Vegetable Salad"
(page 142); "Mixed Pickled Mushroom Salad" (page 142);
"Hungarian Dill Pickles" (page 143).

At the time this book went into production, salmonella
was a concern in certain parts of the United States when
handling raw poultry and cooking with raw or
undercooked eggs. In the event that this is still a concern,
please beware of the problem. Also, over the past few
years many cases of food poisoning have been linked to
raw and undercooked shellfish in certain parts of the
United States. Please beware that this may be a problem
in your area.

For Condé Nast Books

Jill Cohen, Director
Ellen Maria Bruzelius, Direct Marketing Manager
Kristine Smith-Cunningham,
    Advertising Promotion Manager
Mary Ellen Kelly, Fulfillment Manager
Lisa Faith Phillips, Direct Marketing Associate
Diane Pesce, Composition Production Manager
Serafino J. Cambareri, Quality Control Manager

For *Gourmet* Books

Diane Keitt, Editor
Judith Tropea, Associate Editor

For *Gourmet* Magazine

Gail Zweigenthal, Editor-in-Chief

Zanne Early Zakroff, Executive Food Editor
Kemp Miles Minifie, Senior Food Editor
Alexis M. Touchet, Associate Food Editor
Leslie Glover Pendleton, Food Editor
Amy Mastrangelo, Food Editor
Kathleen Nilon Atencio, Food Editor
Elizabeth S. Imperatore, Food Editor

Romulo A. Yanes, Photographer
Marjorie H. Webb, Stylist
Nancy Purdum, Stylist

Produced in association with
Media Projects Incorporated

Carter Smith, Executive Editor
Lelia Wardwell, Project Editor
Anne B. Wright, Assistant Project Editor
Marilyn Flaig, Indexer
Lydia Link, Designer

The text of this book was set in Berkeley Old Style by the
Composition Department of Condé Nast Publications,
Inc. The four-color separations were done by The Color
Company. The book was printed and bound at R. R.
Donnelley and Sons. Text paper is Citation Web Gloss.

Front Jacket: "Curried Butternut Squash and Apple Soup"
(page 131).

Back Jacket: "Hanukkah Jelly Donuts" (page 175); "Hot
Cranberry Apple Cider" (page 174); "Orange-Flavored
Chicken Breasts with Bacon" (page 83); "Vegetable
Brochettes" (page 85); "Tea Sandwiches in a Bread
Basket" (page 136).

Frontispiece: "Fajitas with Peppers and Red Onions"
(page 106); "Flour Tortillas" (page 107); "Chunky
Guacamole" (page 107); "Fresh Tomato Salsa" (page
107).

Acknowledgments

Holizzz *Holidays and Celebrations* has been in the making for several years, and the editors of *Gourmet Books* would like to thank all those who contributed their skills and ideas: Evie Righter, the editor of the original manuscript; Georgia Chan Downard, our recipe development coordinator; Elizabeth R. Pearce, who helped develop the manuscript; Mary Goodbody, our writer; Lori Longbotham, our microwave recipe evaluator; and Toni Rachiele, who proofread the galleys. We would like to thank Rochelle Udell for her conceptual design of this book.

Also, we would like to give special thanks to our *Gourmet* colleagues, particularly Zanne Early Zakroff, Food Department Director, who made the time to edit recipes and answer our many questions; to Kemp Miles Minifie, Alexis M. Touchet, Leslie Glover Pendleton, Amy Mastrangelo, Kathleen Nilon Atencio, and Elizabeth S. Imperatore, members of the *Gourmet* Food Department, who prepared dishes for photography; and to Romulo Yanes, photographer, and Marjorie Webb and Nancy Purdum, prop stylists, for the care and attention that they gave to each new photograph. And, thank you to Randi Barritt for her creative styling of the front jacket. Thanks to Gerald Asher, *Gourmet*'s wine editor, who selected beverages for the menus.

Finally, we would like to thank Lydia Link, our book designer, not only for her sense of style but also for her dedication to this project.

Contents

Introduction 9

FALL 101

WINTER 149

Introduction

There is something special about this cookbook. Just by leafing through its colorful pages you will be reminded of those wonderful days each year when family and friends are gathered around your table to celebrate joyous occasions and the rush and worries of the workaday world seem far, far away. Such days are cherished ones; after all, what could be more important than spending time with those closest to you? Naturally, celebrations such as these call for just the right menus, and here you will find *Gourmet*'s tried and true favorites.

Holidays and Celebrations offers a delightful variety of seasonal menus for *all* your special occasions, and we were sure to include those dishes that your family waits for all year: a bubbly Spiced Apple Pie to conclude A Victorian Thanksgiving; an aromatic Crown Roast of Lamb as centerpiece of An Elegant Easter Dinner; tasty Beer Ribs for a Memorial Day Picnic; a tempting Glazed Virginia Ham for a New Year's Open House; a plate of warm, soft jelly doughnuts to end a Latkes Party for Hanukkah . . . shall I go on? And, because life can be hectic, we have included make-ahead information and microwave instructions whenever we thought they would be helpful. Now all you need to do is to decide which gatherings to host in your home this year.

This might be the year to surprise your family with An Easter Brunch. Color some eggs the night before and come Easter morning the children can have a jolly Easter Egg Hunt while you prepare the Poached Eggs with Smoked Salmon and Creamy Herb Sauce. Or, perhaps there is a mother-to-be in your extended family. Our very pretty Baby Shower Tea complete with delicious Tea Sandwiches in a Bread Basket would be a lovely way to entertain.

You will also find a nice surprise at the end of each seasonal collection of menus—a gift section filled with thoughtful food gifts to make and take along when visiting family and friends. What could be better than a summer cherry pie or an autumn pumpkin bread to thank your gracious hostess? A homemade gift is impossible to beat because it comes from the heart.

All of us here at *Gourmet* hope that you will enjoy the seasons and one another with *Holidays and Celebrations*.

GAIL ZWEIGENTHAL
Editor-In-Chief

Spring

TAKE ADVANTAGE OF THE HIGH SPIRITS OF THIS
lively season and give a party. Spring's holidays—
Easter and Passover—provide perfect opportunities
for entertaining, but your parties need not be limited to them. A
soft breezy evening is just right for a quiet anniversary dinner, and
a sunny afternoon, when fluffy clouds glide across a blue sky, is
ideal for a christening luncheon.

Spring is the time when we spy asparagus, rhubarb,
watercress, and juicy strawberries in the market. Brown paper
sacks brimming, we hasten home to prepare a simple meal of fresh
salmon and spring peas, shad roe, and young asparagus. Such
meals are only a prelude to the feasts we plan for Easter or
Passover. Later in the Spring may come a glorious luncheon
celebrating the season's bounty of garden vegetables or an intimate
dinner replete with fillet of sole and peppery watercress salad.

We have assembled five menus to celebrate Spring, each one
quite different from the next. You may have other ideas for which
our menus can be easily adapted. And why not? Each one bursts
with the fresh, tender flavors of this sweet season. The sprightly
Easter brunch, for example, could be served on any Spring
weekend. And, for a more formal occasion, the eggs in aspic,
crown roast of lamb, tender asparagus, and baby carrots constitute
an elegant menu that ought not to be saved *only* for Easter. Serve
this on a Saturday night when you entertain very special friends.

Throughout the book, as well as here, we have tried to point
out some of the more exotic ingredients in our menus. We also
suggest ways to organize your time so that your party will run
smoothly and you will be able to enjoy it; many of the dishes can

be prepared in advance and we urge you to make use of this convenience. The importance of careful advance planning cannot be overstated. Make comprehensive lists, remembering to include such items as new candles, cocktail napkins, and ice. Take inventory of your best china and crystal, if the occasion warrants them, making sure they are washed and shiny before you are ready to set them out.

Spring is one of the seasons we tend to be extravagant with flowers—they are so welcome after Winter's doldrums. Arrange bright yellow daffodils and graceful tulips on the table and elsewhere about the house. As tempting as it may be to place a large bouquet on the dining table, take care to keep the arrangement low so that your guests can see one another across the table. A pretty bowl of fruit makes an attractive centerpiece, too, if you decide to keep the flowers on the sideboard or in the living room.

Whatever the occasion, let the natural happiness of the season infuse your mood and your home as you welcome your guests. Spring is a time for rejoicing, a time of new beginnings and revitalized energy. With our menus on hand, you will be sure to give parties that reflect this joyous time of year.

AN EASTER BRUNCH

**POACHED EGGS WITH SMOKED
SALMON AND CREAMY HERB SAUCE**

CARAWAY RYE TOAST

**SPRING SALAD OF ENDIVE, WATERCRESS,
AND SNOW PEAS**

**ORANGE SHERBET WITH
BITTER CHOCOLATE SAUCE**

SERVES EIGHT

By this time of year, sunshine fills each day with renewed strength and cheerfulness. What better way to welcome a bright Easter morning than with a splendid brunch of seasonal Spring foods? Our menu allows you ample time to hide colorful hard-cooked eggs for an egg hunt designed to keep the children in the party happy and excited.

As the symbols of Spring's rebirth, eggs are charming on the brunch table as well as hidden outdoors among the crocuses. We have a recipe calling for eggs that are poached so that they retain their familiar oval shape when they are served with smoked salmon. Be sure to use the freshest eggs you can find, since these hold their shape the best. Many markets and specialty stores sell organic or "country" eggs, which tend to be fresher than others. And do not hesitate to follow our instructions for poaching them ahead of time. While we are talking about freshness, use *fresh* herbs for the cream sauce, which, by the way, can be made 2 hours ahead and kept warm. Bake the loaf of caraway rye bread the day before the brunch. Just before serving, nestle the eggs and salmon on toasted slices of bread. Blanch and refresh the snow peas when you wash the greens; allow them all to dry completely before mixing and dressing the salad. Nothing spoils a delicate salad faster than damp greens. Oil-based dressings will not adhere to wet greens. Keep washed and dried greens crisp by wrapping them in cloth kitchen towels and storing them in the refrigerator. Plastic bags do not permit the greens to breathe.

Scoops of orange sherbet served with a deliciously bitter chocolate sauce and strips of candied orange peel complete the meal. The sherbet can be made a day or two before the meal and kept frozen until served. The candied peel keeps well in the refrigerator for a day. However, if finding the time to make the sherbet escapes you, the simple and quick chocolate sauce also tastes good on ice cream or pound cake.

POACHED EGGS WITH SMOKED SALMON AND CREAMY HERB SAUCE

2 tablespoons white vinegar
8 very fresh large eggs
1 cup minced scallion
⅔ cup dry white wine
1½ cups chicken stock (page 198)
½ cup heavy cream
1 tablespoon arrowroot
⅔ cup sour cream
cayenne to taste
salt to taste
3 tablespoons minced fresh chives, *or*
    dill, *or* basil
caraway rye bread (recipe follows), toasted
1 pound smoked salmon, sliced thin

FILL A WIDE 3-INCH-DEEP SKILLET THREE-FOURTHS full with water. Add the vinegar and bring to a rolling boil over high heat. Reduce the heat to a bare simmer. Break and drop in the eggs, 1 at a time. Or break the eggs, 1 at a time, into a saucer and slide them into the pan. As each egg is dropped in, push the white back immediately toward the yolk with a large slotted spoon, moving the egg gently.

Simmer for 4 minutes or until the yolks are set and transfer with the slotted spoon to a pan of cold water. Let stand until needed. Drain the eggs carefully in the slotted spoon, blot carefully with paper towels, and trim. If poached correctly, the yolk will be covered completely by the white and the egg will have returned to its original oval shape.

In a saucepan bring the scallion and wine to a boil over moderately high heat and boil until reduced to ½ cup. Add the stock and boil the mixture until reduced to 1 cup. Bring the mixture to a simmer. In a bowl combine the cream and arrowroot and add it to the mixture. Cook for 1 minute, or until thickened slightly. Add the sour cream, cayenne, and salt and simmer, stirring, for 3 minutes. Strain the sauce into another pan and keep warm.

Reheat the poached eggs in a saucepan of simmering water to cover for 30 seconds, or until heated through. Drain on paper towels. Bring the sauce to a simmer and stir in the herbs.

On heated serving plates top the toast with salmon, a poached egg, and sauce. Serves 8.

CARAWAY RYE BREAD

2½ teaspoons active dry yeast
½ cup warm water
1½ cups warm milk
3 tablespoons molasses
2 tablespoons unsalted butter, melted
1 tablespoon salt
1 tablespoon caraway seeds plus
    additional for garnish
2½ cups rye flour
3 to 3½ cups all-purpose flour
1 large egg, beaten lightly

IN A SMALL BOWL PROOF THE YEAST IN THE WARM water until foamy. In a large bowl combine the milk, molasses, butter, salt, and caraway seeds and add the yeast mixture. Stir in the flours and combine until a dough is formed.

Knead on a lightly floured surface for 8 to 10 minutes. Transfer to a buttered bowl and turn to coat with the butter. Let rise in a warm place, covered with plastic wrap and a dish towel, for 1½ to 2 hours, or until double in bulk.

Punch down the dough and form into a loaf. Fit the loaf into a loaf pan, 9 by 5 by 3 inches, and brush with the egg. Sprinkle with the additional caraway seeds. Let rise in a warm place, covered loosely with a dish towel, for 30 minutes, or until the top is 1 inch above the rim.

Preheat the oven to 400° F.

Bake the loaf in the middle of the oven for 30 to 35 minutes, or until it is browned and the bottom sounds hollow when tapped. Turn out onto a rack to cool. Makes 1 loaf.

**WAGNER VINEYARDS FINGER LAKES
JOHANNISBERG RIESLING '89**

SPRING SALAD OF ENDIVE, WATERCRESS, AND SNOW PEAS

3 tablespoons fresh lemon juice
1 tablespoon red-wine vinegar
1 teaspoon grated lemon zest
salt and freshly ground pepper to taste
⅓ cup extra-virgin olive oil
¼ cup minced fresh basil, *or* chives, *or* parsley
1 large red bell pepper, roasted (page 199) and sliced
¼ pound mushrooms, sliced
½ cup minced scallion
¼ pound snow peas
1 head romaine, torn into bite-size pieces
3 Belgian endive, sliced diagonally
2 bunches of watercress, stems removed
1 cucumber, peeled and sliced

 IN A BOWL COMBINE THE LEMON JUICE, VINEGAR, lemon rind, salt, and pepper and add the oil, whisking. Stir in the herbs, red pepper, mushrooms, and scallion. Marinate, covered, for 30 minutes.

In a saucepan of boiling salted water blanch the snow peas for 30 seconds, or until crisp-tender, and drain. Refresh under cold water and pat dry.

In a bowl combine the romaine, endive, watercress, snow peas, and cucumber. Add the dressing and toss to combine. Serves 8.

ORANGE SHERBET WITH BITTER CHOCOLATE SAUCE

2 ounces sugar cubes (about thirty cubes)
2½ pounds navel oranges
1 tablespoon fresh lemon juice
zest from 3 additional navel oranges, cut into julienne strips
⅔ cup granulated sugar
2 tablespoons water
bitter chocolate sauce (recipe follows)

○ RUB THE SUGAR CUBES OVER THE SURFACE OF ALL BUT 2 of the oranges until each cube is slightly orange colored. Using the fine side of a grater, grate the

zest from the remaining 2 oranges, being careful not to grate the pith. Squeeze the oranges to yield 2 cups juice.

In a saucepan heat 1 cup of the orange juice with the sugar cubes over moderately low heat, stirring, until the sugar is dissolved. Transfer to a bowl and stir in the remaining 1 cup orange juice, grated zest, and lemon juice. Chill, covered loosely, until cold. Freeze in an ice-cream freezer according to the manufacturer's instructions.

In a saucepan cover the julienne orange zest with cold water. Bring to a boil, boil for 1 minute, and drain. Repeat the procedure 2 more times.

In a heavy saucepan heat the julienne zest with the granulated sugar and water over moderately low heat, stirring and washing down any sugar crystals clinging to the sides with a brush dipped in cold water, until the sugar is dissolved. Simmer, undisturbed, for 10 to 15 minutes, or until the zest is translucent. There should be syrup left in the pan. Transfer the zest and syrup to a small bowl and let it cool.

Spoon some of the sauce onto dessert plates and top with a scoop of sherbet. Garnish with the candied peel. Serves 8.

BITTER CHOCOLATE SAUCE

6 ounces semisweet chocolate, chopped
3 ounces unsweetened chocolate, chopped
⅔ cup milk
1 tablespoon orange-flavored liqueur

○ IN A HEAVY SAUCEPAN MELT THE CHOCOLATES WITH the milk over moderately low heat, stirring, until smooth. Stir in the liqueur and let the sauce cool. Makes about 1½ cups.

Crown Roast of Lamb;
Saffron Rice Timbales;
Gingered Carrots

AN ELEGANT EASTER DINNER

CRAB IMPERIAL

CROWN ROAST OF LAMB

SAFFRON RICE TIMBALES

GINGERED CARROTS

**ASPARAGUS WITH SCALLION
AND PARSLEY**

**STRAWBERRY RHUBARB
MERINGUE PIE**

SERVES SIX

Springtime's gentle fragrances fill the house as you prepare to celebrate Easter with a magnificent menu. If luck is with you, the holiday will fall on the kind of warm weekend that holds the promise of bright flowers and soft blue skies—just the right variables for Spring lamb, tender asparagus, baby carrots, and saffron-scented rice. These marvelously seasonal dishes are welcomed by rich, delicious Crab Imperial, then bade farewell with a spectacular meringue-topped strawberry rhubarb pie.

Because both the starter and the dessert can, for the most part, be prepared well ahead of time, the meal quickly becomes manageable. Crab Imperial, an American classic dating back to the turn of the century, calls for blue crabs, which are harvested along the Atlantic Coast. The best, many claim, come from Chesapeake Bay. We don't argue. Their season stretches from March to November,

which makes them appropriate for an early Spring dinner. Turn the cooked crabs over and, with the tip of a small knife, lift up the pointed apron, or tail flap, then twist it off and discard. To get at the meat inside, turn the crab right side up, grasp the top shell at the back where the apron was removed, and pry up the top shell, being careful to keep the shell intact for stuffing. You may also discover green-tinged tomalley inside. Don't discard it. This is the liver and, as with lobster, it is considered very good eating and is, indeed, included in the stuffing. The stuffed and fried crabs reheat nicely in about 10 minutes in a 375° F. oven. If you have only one oven, heat the crabs after the lamb has cooked and while it is standing. If possible, reheat them in a second oven.

A crown roast of lamb is a glorious thing. Two racks, consisting of the curved rib sections, are set upright and tied to form a circle. Ask the butcher to do this for you and at the same time to crack the chine bone between each rib for easy carving. The meat from these small chops is delectable and tender—figure on at least two chops for each person. The roast requires less than an hour in the oven, followed by a decent standing time, which gives you the chance to whisk up an easy Port and cream sauce. Arrowroot gives the sauce sheen and a more delicate flavor than if flour were used to thicken it.

Saffron lightly flavors rice as it infuses it with a pretty yellow color. Although you can buy ground saffron, the fragile dried threads are preferred. They are the hand-gathered stamens from crocuses that grow primarily in Spain. An ounce of saffron contains more than 10,000 stamens, which explains its significant cost. Fortunately, a little goes far and once bought, saffron keeps for a long time in a tightly capped jar. The timbales are easily formed with the cooked rice, which is baked in the oven with the lamb. Butter the molds ahead of time so they are ready to fill with the warm, moist rice.

Asparagus, simply cooked and garnished with scallions, lemon zest, and a sprinkling of parsley, pairs with tender young carrots, which are enlivened with the fresh taste of ginger and the sparkle of orange juice. Both are cooked on top of the stove in minutes and demand only a fraction of your attention. Of course, it is a good idea to trim the vegetables well ahead of time.

Our meal ends with a pie crowned with a cloud of meringue that hovers over a filling bursting with two of Spring's most abundant treasures: rhubarb and strawberries. By all means, bake the *pâte brisée* crust the morning of the party, or the day before, and also prepare the tart-sweet filling. You will have to whip the meringue while your guests linger over the main course, but with the ingredients already measured, this should not take long. The oven, which was heated to 350° F. for the lamb, will come back to temperature quickly, too. It is a help if you have two ovens and can heat the broiler of one while the pie bakes for a scant 10 minutes in the other. Then, pop the hot pie under the broiler for a few minutes while you finish grinding the coffee beans or arranging the liqueur glasses for after-dinner relaxation.

CRAB IMPERIAL

12 small *or* 6 large live blue crabs
vegetable shortening for deep frying
½ pound lump crab meat, picked over
⅓ cup mayonnaise
1 large egg, beaten lightly
3 tablespoons minced pimiento
2 tablespoons soda cracker crumbs
2 tablespoons minced fresh
    parsley leaves
2 teaspoons Worcestershire sauce
½ teaspoon dry mustard, or to taste
⅛ teaspoon cayenne, or to taste
3 dashes of Tabasco, or to taste
salt and freshly ground pepper to taste
6 thin lemon wedges for garnish

IN A LARGE KETTLE CONTAINING 2 INCHES BOILING water cook the crabs, covered, over high heat for 10 minutes, or until the shells have turned red. Drain in a large colander and rinse under cold water. Let cool until they can be handled.

Remove and reserve the claws. Shell the crabs, reserving the backs, the meat, and tomalley. Wash and scrub the backs and let dry.

In a deep fryer heat 2½ inches of the vegetable shortening to 375° F.

Preheat the oven to 200° F.

In a bowl blend the reserved crab meat and tomalley and remaining ingredients until just combined and mound in the shells. Fry the shells filling side up in batches in the deep fryer for 1 minute, or until golden. Transfer the crabs with a slotted spoon to paper towels to drain. Keep warm on a baking sheet in the oven.

The crabs can be made 6 hours ahead and kept refrigerated, covered. Reheat, uncovered, on a baking sheet in a preheated 375° F. oven for 10 minutes, or until heated through. Garnish with the reserved claws and lemon wedges. Serves 6 as a first course.

CROWN ROAST OF LAMB

16-chop crown roast of lamb, trimmings
   reserved for the stock
3 garlic cloves, minced
½ teaspoon dried thyme, crumbled
½ teaspoon dried rosemary, crumbled
1 teaspoon salt
freshly ground pepper to taste
2 tablespoons arrowroot
¼ cup heavy cream
2 tablespoons Tawny Port
2½ cups brown stock (page 197),
   substituting the reserved lamb
   trimmings for the veal shanks, *or*
   canned beef broth
watercress leaves for garnish

PREHEAT THE OVEN TO 425° F.

Rub the lamb well with the garlic, herbs, salt, and pepper. Fit a ball of foil snugly in the center to maintain the shape of the crown while roasting and cover the bone ends with foil.

Put the lamb in an oiled pan just large enough to hold it and roast it in the middle of the oven for 20 minutes. Reduce the heat to 350° F. and roast for 20 minutes more for rare meat. Let stand, covered loosely, for 15 minutes.

In a bowl combine the arrowroot, cream, and Port until smooth. In a saucepan bring the stock to a boil over moderately high heat. Stir the arrowroot mixture and add in a stream, whisking until thickened slightly. Add salt and pepper to taste and transfer to a sauceboat.

Remove the foil from the lamb and transfer to a platter. Garnish with the watercress and paper frills, if desired. Serves 6.

SAFFRON RICE TIMBALES

1 teaspoon cuminseed
1 cinnamon stick
5 whole cloves
⅛ teaspoon cardamom seeds
   (about 2 pods)
1 bay leaf
¾ stick (6 tablespoons) unsalted butter
2 cups minced onion
2½ cups long-grain rice
½ teaspoon saffron threads
3 cups hot water
1 teaspoon salt

IN A FLAMEPROOF CASSEROLE COOK THE SPICES AND bay leaf in the butter over moderate heat, swirling the casserole, for 2 minutes. Add the onion and cook, stirring occasionally, until softened. Add the rice and cook over low heat, stirring, until it is transparent.

Preheat the oven to 350° F.

In a bowl let the saffron steep in the hot water for 5 minutes. Add the saffron water and salt to the casserole and bring the rice mixture to a boil, stirring. Bake the casserole, covered with a buttered round of wax paper and the lid, in the middle of the oven for 20 minutes, or until the liquid is absorbed and the rice is just tender.

Let stand for 10 minutes and discard the bay leaf, cloves, and cinnamon stick. Fill 6 buttered ½-cup timbale molds with some of the rice, pressing it into the molds gently. Invert the molds onto the platter with the lamb and serve the remaining rice separately. Serves 6.

GINGERED CARROTS

1½ pounds baby carrots, trimmed
⅓ cup fresh orange juice
¼ cup honey
2 tablespoons unsalted butter
1 tablespoon grated orange zest
1 teaspoon ground ginger
salt to taste
2 tablespoons minced crystallized ginger

IN A SAUCEPAN COMBINE ALL THE INGREDIENTS EXCEPT the crystallized ginger and add enough cold water to just cover the carrots. Bring to a boil and simmer, covered, for 6 to 8 minutes, or until the carrots are just tender.

Add the crystallized ginger and cook, uncovered, over moderately high heat until the liquid is reduced to ¼ cup. Cook, shaking the pan, until the liquid is almost completely reduced and the carrots are glazed. Arrange decoratively on the platter with the lamb. Serves 6.

ASPARAGUS WITH SCALLION AND PARSLEY

1½ pounds asparagus, peeled
2 tablespoons unsalted butter, melted
4 scallions, sliced thin
3 tablespoons minced fresh
    parsley leaves
1 tablespoon grated lemon zest

TRIM THE ASPARAGUS STALKS TO THE SAME LENGTH and tie with string in batches of 10 to 12. In a kettle cook in boiling salted water to cover for 8 to 10 minutes, or until tender. Transfer by the strings to a colander and drain tips up.

Remove the strings and arrange the asparagus in a heated serving dish. Brush with the butter and sprinkle with the scallions, parsley, and lemon zest. Serves 6.

Asparagus with Scallion and Parsley

STRAWBERRY RHUBARB MERINGUE PIE

pâte brisée (page 196)
egg wash made by beating lightly 1 large
    egg white
1½ pounds fresh rhubarb, cut into
    1-inch pieces
1¾ cups granulated sugar
1 teaspoon cinnamon
pinch of ground cloves
1 pint strawberries, sliced
2 to 3 tablespoons cornstarch, depending
    upon the juiciness of the fruit
3 tablespoons Chambord
    (black raspberry liqueur)
4 large egg whites
pinch of cream of tartar
pinch of salt
½ teaspoon vanilla
¼ cup confectioners' sugar, or to taste

Roll out the dough ⅛ inch thick on a floured surface and fit into a 9-inch pie plate. Crimp the edge decoratively and prick the bottom with a fork. Chill for 30 minutes.

Preheat the oven to 425° F.

Line the shell with wax paper and fill the paper with raw rice. Bake in the lower third of the oven for 15 minutes. Remove the rice and paper carefully and brush the shell with the egg wash. Bake the shell for 15 minutes more, or until golden. Let it cool on a rack. *The shell can be made 1 day ahead and stored, covered loosely, in a cool, dry place.*

In a large bowl let the rhubarb macerate with ¾ cup of the granulated sugar for 1 hour. In a saucepan combine the rhubarb mixture with the cinnamon and cloves and bring to a boil. Simmer, stirring occasionally, until the rhubarb is almost tender. Add the strawberries and simmer, stirring, until the rhubarb is tender.

In a small bowl combine the cornstarch and Chambord and add to the rhubarb mixture, stirring. Cook over moderately low heat until thickened. Transfer the filling to a bowl and let it cool. Chill, covered, overnight.

Preheat the oven to 350° F.

In a bowl with an electric mixer beat the egg whites until foamy. Add the cream of tartar and salt and beat until the whites hold soft peaks. Beat in the remaining 1 cup granulated sugar, a little at a time, and beat until the whites hold stiff peaks. Beat in the vanilla and transfer one-third of the meringue to a pastry bag fitted with a decorative tip.

Spoon the filling into the shell and spread the remaining meringue over it, smoothing the top. With the tip of a small knife, score the top, forming a latticework pattern. With the pastry bag, pipe meringue over the top of the pie, following the lattice design.

Sift the confectioners' sugar over the pie and bake it on a baking sheet in the middle of the oven for 10 minutes. Put the pie under a preheated broiler about 4 inches from the heat until golden. Makes one 9-inch pie.

CHÂTEAU LÉOVILLE-BARTON '76
(with first course)

CHÂTEAU GRAND-PUY-LACOSTE '66
(with main course)

PASSOVER SEDER

HAROSETH

CHOPPED CHICKEN LIVER

CHICKEN SOUP WITH MATZO BALLS

HERBED ROAST CHICKEN

MINTED SPINACH SOUFFLÉ

**BAKED TOMATOES WITH
PARSLEY BASIL STUFFING**

SWEET-AND-SOUR BEET SALAD

**PASSOVER SPONGECAKE WITH
CITRUS GLAZE**

DRIED FRUIT COMPOTE

SERVES SIX

The week of Passover is a time for families and friends to gather for joyful singing and lots of good eating. It is also a time for ritual and careful observance of tradition. Passover, which marks the deliverance of the ancient Jews from bondage in Egypt, celebrates all that is warm and reassuring about family life. The ceremony surrounding the seder, the holiday meal, is practiced in households across the country and around the world, varying here and there but essentially repeating and reinforcing the heritage that has been passed from father to son, from mother to daughter . . . from century to century.

The seder table, set with sparkling china, flatware, and wineglasses (including a large goblet for Elijah, who may visit any Jewish household during Passover), holds a plate of the foods that symbolize the Passover story. At the ceremony before the dinner, the head of the household holds up each item and, with the appropriate blessing or prayer, describes its significance. A roasted egg (the ancient symbol of life) and lamb bone represent ritual sacrifices; bitter herbs, often fresh horseradish, stand for the bitterness of slavery; *haroseth*, an apple and chopped nut combination, symbolizes the mortar made by the Hebrew slaves and its sweetness also reminds us of the sweetness of freedom; parsley or another green speaks of the renewal of Spring; salt water, in which the parsley is dipped, represents the Red Sea parting for the fleeing Jews and the tears of the slaves; and unleavened bread, usually a stack of wrapped matzo, echoes the condition of the bread the Hebrews took with them in their haste to leave Egypt.

During the ceremony, which involves a number of participatory responses, everyone drinks two glasses of wine. The hostess scurries back and forth to the kitchen, checking on the meal, and the children wonder where the "hidden" matzo might be. Our menu reflects a typical seder meal, beginning with *haroseth* and ending with a Passover spongecake, made without chemical leaveners or wheat flour. Chopped chicken liver, flecked with egg and fried onion, is traditional Sabbath fare, and as such is often served on Passover with the gefilte fish. The chopped livers are followed by chicken soup with matzo balls. The soup is dressed up a little on Passover with balls of matzo held together with egg yolks, beaten egg whites, and chicken fat. The liver and matzo balls can be made ahead of time, which should make preparing the meal easier.

The main course of this seder is a simple roast chicken nicely seasoned with shallots and herbs that are gently eased under the loosened skin just before the bird is set in the oven. Since the beet salad can be prepared the day before, and the tomatoes up to two hours before baking, the spinach soufflé is of the most concern. Ideally, it should be cooked in a separate oven from the chicken, as its temperature requirements are slightly different. The tomatoes can be slid into the same oven as the soufflé about 10 minutes later, but be prepared to move quickly, since the oven really ought not to be opened while the soufflé—any soufflé, for that matter—is rising.

Herbed Roast Chicken,
Baked Tomatoes with
Parsley Basil Stuffing

HAROSETH
(APPLE AND NUT SPREAD)

1½ cups peeled and coarsely chopped
    Granny Smith apple
½ cup coarsely chopped nuts
1 teaspoon grated lemon zest
¼ to ½ teaspoon cinnamon, or to taste
1 to 2 tablespoons sweet red wine
2 teaspoons honey

☺ IN A BOWL COMBINE ALL THE INGREDIENTS, USING AS much wine as necessary to make the mixture of spreading consistency. Makes 2 cups.

CHOPPED CHICKEN LIVER

1 pound chicken livers, trimmed
3 tablespoons chicken fat
1 large onion, minced
salt and freshly ground pepper to taste
2 large hard-cooked eggs, quartered
freshly grated nutmeg to taste
chopped toasted nuts for garnish

☺ + IN A BOWL OF SALTED WATER LET THE CHICKEN livers soak for 20 minutes. Drain and pat dry.

Preheat the broiler.

Broil the livers on a rack in a broiler pan about 4 inches from the heat, turning once, for 7 to 8 minutes, or until browned.

In a skillet heat the fat over moderate heat until hot. Add the onion and salt and pepper and cook, stirring occasionally, until golden. In a food processor process the livers, onion, and eggs until combined well and add the nutmeg and salt and pepper to taste. Transfer to a serving bowl and garnish with the nuts. Chill, covered, until ready to serve. Makes about 2 cups.

CHICKEN SOUP
WITH MATZO BALLS

3 large eggs, separated
1 teaspoon salt, or to taste
freshly ground pepper to taste
2 tablespoons minced fresh parsley
    leaves
2 tablespoons chicken fat
⅓ cup seltzer
¾ cup matzo meal
8 cups chicken stock (page 198) *or*
    canned chicken broth
cooked carrot slices and minced fresh
    parsley leaves for garnish, if desired

☺ IN A BOWL WHISK THE EGG YOLKS, SALT, PEPPER, parsley, fat, and seltzer until combined well. In another bowl beat the egg whites until they hold stiff peaks and fold into the yolk mixture. Fold in the matzo meal, a little at a time, and blend until the mixture holds its shape but is still light. Chill, covered, for at least 2 hours.

With dampened fingertips, gently form the mixture into 12 matzo balls. (Do not roll the balls between your hands or they will lose their lightness.) Arrange on a plate and chill, covered loosely, until ready to cook.

In a large saucepan bring the stock to a boil. Add the matzo balls and simmer gently, covered, for 40 minutes, or until tender when pierced with a wooden toothpick.

The matzo balls can be cooked 1 day ahead and kept refrigerated, covered. Reheat in the stock. Garnish the soup with the carrot slices and parsley. Serves 6.

HERBED ROAST CHICKEN

6- to 6½-pound roasting chicken
salt and freshly ground pepper to taste
½ cup minced shallot
3 tablespoons vegetable oil
2 tablespoons minced fresh tarragon
  leaves, *or* 1 teaspoon dried
¼ cup snipped fresh chives, *or* ¼ cup
  minced fresh parsley leaves
1½ teaspoons grated lemon zest
½ carrot, sliced
½ celery stalk, sliced
1 onion, sliced
2 garlic cloves, sliced
1 bay leaf
1 teaspoon dried thyme, crumbled

PREHEAT THE OVEN TO 450° F.

Season the chicken with salt and pepper. Loosen the breast skin by slipping the fingers between the skin and the flesh, being careful not to pierce the skin.

In a small skillet cook the shallot in 2 tablespoons of the oil over moderate heat, stirring, until softened. Stir in the fresh herbs, lemon zest, and salt and pepper to taste. Pat the mixture under the breast skin, smoothing to cover the breast meat. Combine the remaining ingredients (except the remaining oil), fill the body cavity with the mixture, and truss the chicken.

Put the chicken on a rack in a roasting pan and brush with the remaining 1 tablespoon oil. Sprinkle the chicken with salt and pepper and bake in the middle of the oven for 30 minutes. Reduce the heat to 350° F. and bake, basting frequently, for 1½ to 2 hours more, or until the juices run clear when the fleshy part of a thigh is pricked with a skewer. Let the chicken stand, covered loosely, for 15 minutes before carving. Serves 6.

MINTED SPINACH SOUFFLÉ

½ cup minced onion
2 tablespoons vegetable oil
1 cup cooked chopped spinach
1 cup chicken stock (page 198) *or* canned
  chicken broth
4 teaspoons potato starch
4 large egg yolks
2 tablespoons minced fresh mint leaves,
  or to taste
salt and freshly ground pepper to taste
4 large egg whites

PREHEAT THE OVEN TO 400° F.

In a saucepan cook the onion in the oil over moderate heat, stirring, until softened. Add the spinach and cook, stirring, for 2 minutes. In a small bowl combine the stock and starch. Add the stock mixture to the saucepan and cook, stirring, until thickened. Transfer to a bowl and let cool for 5 minutes. Stir in the egg yolks, 1 at a time, and season with the mint and the salt and pepper.

In a large bowl beat the egg whites until they hold stiff peaks and fold into the spinach mixture. Spoon into an oiled 1½-quart soufflé dish and put in the middle of the oven. Immediately reduce the heat to 375° F. and bake for 30 to 35 minutes, or until puffed and golden. Serves 6.

HAGAFEN CELLARS JOHANNISBERG
RIESLING NAPA VALLEY '88

BAKED TOMATOES WITH PARSLEY BASIL STUFFING

6 ripe but firm tomatoes, cored and
   halved
¼ cup minced shallot
¼ cup olive oil
2 garlic cloves, minced
¼ cup minced fresh parsley leaves
½ teaspoon dried thyme, crumbled
3 tablespoons minced fresh basil leaves
salt and freshly ground pepper to taste
½ cup toasted and chopped skinned
   hazelnuts *or* blanched almonds

PREHEAT THE OVEN TO 375° F.

Gently squeeze the seeds and juice from the tomato halves and arrange the halves in an oiled gratin dish. In a bowl combine the remaining ingredients except the nuts. Divide among the tomato halves and sprinkle with the nuts. *The tomatoes can be made 2 hours ahead up to this point and kept refrigerated, covered.*

Bake the tomatoes, uncovered, in the middle of the oven for 20 minutes, or until sizzling and lightly golden. Serves 6.

SWEET-AND-SOUR BEET SALAD

2 pounds beets (5 to 6 large), trimmed,
   leaving 2 inches of stem attached
1 bay leaf
4 whole cloves
salt and freshly ground pepper to taste
1 large shallot, minced
1 tablespoon sugar
2 to 3 tablespoons white vinegar
3 tablespoons vegetable oil
2 tablespoons minced fresh dill
1 to 2 teaspoons grated fresh
   horseradish, if desired
endive leaves for garnish

IN A SAUCEPAN COMBINE THE BEETS WITH ENOUGH water to cover them by 2 inches and add the bay leaf, cloves, and salt and pepper. Bring to a boil and simmer, covered, for 35 to 40 minutes, or until tender. Drain and let cool.

Peel and slice the beets and in a bowl combine with the shallot. In a small bowl whisk the remaining ingredients and add to the beets. Toss well and chill, covered, for 2 hours or overnight. Serve with the endive. Serves 6.

Passover Spongecake with Citrus Glaze

PASSOVER SPONGECAKE WITH CITRUS GLAZE

10 large eggs, separated
1¼ cups sugar
¼ cup fresh orange juice
2 tablespoons fresh lemon juice
1 tablespoon grated orange zest
1½ teaspoons grated lemon zest
⅓ cup potato starch
⅓ cup matzo cake meal
1 teaspoon cinnamon
¼ teaspoon salt
⅓ cup finely ground blanched almonds
citrus glaze (recipe follows)
⅓ cup sliced blanched almonds, toasted

☙ IN A BOWL BEAT THE EGG YOLKS WITH AN ELECTRIC mixer until smooth. Gradually add 1 cup of the sugar and beat until the mixture ribbons when the beater is lifted. Beat in the juices and zests. Into another bowl sift the starch, matzo cake meal, cinnamon, and salt. Gradually add the starch mixture to the yolk mixture and beat until combined well. Stir in the ground almonds.

Preheat the oven to 325° F.

In a very large bowl beat the egg whites with a pinch of salt until they hold soft peaks. Beat in the remaining ¼ cup sugar, a little at a time, and beat the mixture until it holds stiff peaks. Stir one-fourth of the whites into the yolk mixture and fold in the remaining whites gently but thoroughly.

Pour into an ungreased 10-inch tube pan and smooth the top. Bake for 1½ hours, or until a cake tester inserted halfway between the center and edge comes out clean. Remove the pan from the oven and suspend it upside down on the neck of a bottle. Let it cool completely.

Run a thin knife around the inside of the pan and invert the cake onto a rack. Brush the glaze over the cake and garnish with the sliced almonds. *The cake can be made 1 day ahead and kept in an airtight cake container.* Makes one 10-inch cake.

CITRUS GLAZE

⅔ cup sugar
⅓ cup water
1 tablespoon grated orange zest
2 teaspoons grated lemon zest
1 tablespoon fresh orange juice
1 tablespoon fresh lemon juice

☙ IN A SMALL HEAVY SAUCEPAN BRING THE SUGAR AND water to a boil over moderately high heat, stirring, and cook until translucent. Add the zests and simmer for 3 to 5 minutes, or until the syrup forms a thread when pressed between 2 fingers. Stir in the juices and let the glaze cool for 5 minutes.

DRIED FRUIT COMPOTE

1½ pounds mixed dried fruits such as apricots, apples, pears, prunes, and raisins
1½ cups dry white wine
1½ cups water
4 whole cloves
¾ cup fresh orange juice
2 tablespoons fresh lemon juice
3 tablespoons honey
1 tablespoon grated orange zest
1 tablespoon grated lemon zest
½ teaspoon cinnamon
¼ teaspoon ground ginger

☙ IN A STAINLESS STEEL OR ENAMELED SAUCEPAN combine the fruits, wine, and water and bring to a boil. Simmer for 15 to 20 minutes, or until the fruit is tender. Transfer the fruit with a slotted spoon to a serving bowl.

Add the remaining ingredients to the cooking liquid and boil the mixture over moderately high heat until reduced to 1 cup. Let it cool and strain over the fruit. *The compote can be made 1 day ahead and kept refrigerated, covered.* Serve cold or at room temperature. Serves 6.

AN ANNIVERSARY DINNER

**CHILLED JERUSALEM ARTICHOKE
AND RUGOLA SOUP**

SOLE AND SHRIMP EN PAPILLOTE

RICE PILAF

**WATERCRESS, PEAR, AND GRAPE SALAD
WITH CHRYSANTHEMUM PETALS**

CHOCOLATE AND KAHLÚA MOUSSE

SERVES TWO

We have planned a spectacular dinner to help you celebrate a very special anniversary. The food is as elegant as you could hope for, but, with advance preparation, requires a spare 20 minutes or so of your time in the kitchen before the first course. There is a chilled soup that must be made at least two hours ahead of time, and preferably sooner than that. Ladle it into your best soup bowls after you slip the parchment packets into the oven, and enjoy it while the fish cooks.

Jerusalem artichokes, the base of the soup, are knobby, woody-looking things that have nothing whatsoever to do with globe artichokes. They are the tubers of a species of sunflower and in some markets are called sunchokes. Their mild flavor

melds nicely with bitter *rugola* and tart white wine. A bit of heavy cream refines and smooths the soup as no other ingredient can.

Few presentations make the impression of foods cooked in parchment. When the lightly browned paper packets are slit open at the table, the hot cooking aromas pour forth, exciting the appetite. For this dish, tomatoes and onion are cooked very slowly until they form a thick sauce. You may prepare the vegetables up to this point an hour or so before dining and leave them in the pan until it is time to spoon them over the sole. As they heat in the parchment, they infuse the fish and shrimp with a hint of sweetness. We instruct you to cut the parchment into hearts. This may seem like a purely sentimental gesture, but in fact the shape is easy to manipulate and the obvious point at the bottom of the heart neatly folds up and tucks into the packet to secure it.

Pretty as a picture, the watercress and pear salad is garnished with green grapes and chrysanthemum petals. Many specialty food shops carry unsprayed flowers suitable for eating, as do some reliable florists. If you cannot locate one, make the salad anyway. The satiny rich and creamy dressing blends with the peppery cress and sweet fruit to give it marvelous flavor.

Chocolate and Kahlúa is a marriage that was meant to be, and making the mousse is as easy as dancing at a wedding. The long-stemmed glasses make this simple finale an elegant one. And it is sinfully good.

CHILLED JERUSALEM ARTICHOKE AND RUGOLA SOUP

½ pound Jerusalem artichokes
   (sunchokes)
2¼ cups chicken stock (page 198) *or*
   canned chicken broth
¼ cup dry white wine
½ cup firmly packed *rugola* leaves
½ cup heavy cream
salt and white pepper to taste

◒ PEEL THE JERUSALEM ARTICHOKES AND CHOP COARSE. In a stainless steel or enameled saucepan bring the stock, artichokes, and wine to a boil over moderate heat and simmer, covered partially, for 20 minutes, or until the artichokes are tender.

In a food processor or blender purée the mixture in batches with the *rugola* and add the cream in a stream. Add the salt and white pepper and transfer to a bowl. Chill, covered, for at least 2 hours. Serves 2.

SOLE AND SHRIMP EN PAPILLOTE

1 small onion, minced
2 tablespoons olive oil
1½ pounds plum tomatoes, peeled,
   seeded, and chopped
1 garlic clove, minced
¼ teaspoon dried rosemary, crumbled
¼ teaspoon dried thyme, crumbled
1 bay leaf
salt and freshly ground pepper to taste
2 tablespoons minced fresh basil *or*
   parsley leaves
2 sole fillets, 4 ounces each
6 ounces large shrimp, shelled and
   deveined
fresh lemon juice to taste

◒ PREHEAT THE OVEN TO 375° F.

In a stainless steel or enameled saucepan cook the onion in the oil over moderate heat until softened. Add the tomatoes, garlic, dried herbs, salt, and pepper and simmer, covered, stirring occasionally, for 25 to 30 minutes, or until almost all the liquid is evaporated. Discard the bay leaf and stir in the basil.

Cut 2 heart shapes, each 14 inches long in the center, from parchment paper and butter one side of each heart, leaving a 1½-inch border. Spread half the tomato sauce lengthwise along the center of the buttered side of each heart. Top with a fillet, folded in half crosswise, skinned side out. Arrange the shrimp around the fillets and sprinkle with the lemon juice, and salt and pepper to taste.

Fold each heart in half lengthwise and, beginning with the top edge of each heart, fold and crimp the sides together to seal the packets. Transfer carefully to a baking sheet and turn the points under to keep the packets closed. Bake in the middle of the oven for 15 to 20 minutes, or until the paper has turned beige.

Transfer to serving plates and cut a cross in the top of each packet. Fold back the edges. Serves 2.

RICE PILAF

½ cup minced onion
2 tablespoons unsalted butter
1 cup long-grain rice
1½ cups chicken stock (page 198) *or*
    canned chicken broth
½ bay leaf
salt and freshly ground pepper to taste

PREHEAT THE OVEN TO 350° F.
    In a flameproof casserole cook the onion in the butter over low heat, stirring, for 5 minutes, or until softened. Add the rice and stir to coat well. Add the remaining ingredients and bring to a boil, stirring. Bake, covered with a buttered round of wax paper and the lid, in the middle of the oven for 20 minutes, or until the liquid is absorbed and the rice is just tender. Serves 2.

WATERCRESS, PEAR, AND GRAPE SALAD WITH CHRYSANTHEMUM PETALS

1 large bunch of watercress, rinsed well
    and tough stems removed
1 Comice pear, peeled, cored, and
    sliced thin
¼ pound green seedless grapes, halved
petals from 1 unsprayed chrysanthemum
¼ cup cream French dressing
    (recipe follows)

ARRANGE THE WATERCRESS IN THE BOTTOM OF A salad bowl and arrange the pear around the edge. Put the grapes in the center and sprinkle with the chrysanthemum petals. Serve with the dressing. Serves 2.

CREAM FRENCH DRESSING

5 tablespoons heavy cream
2 tablespoons fresh lemon juice
¼ teaspoon salt
freshly ground pepper to taste
1 tablespoon olive oil

IN A BOWL WHISK THE CREAM, LEMON JUICE, SALT, AND pepper for 12 seconds. Add the oil, drop by drop, and whisk until the dressing is combined well. Makes about ½ cup.

POUILLY-FUMÉ '88

CHOCOLATE AND KAHLÚA MOUSSE

3 tablespoons sugar
1 tablespoon cornstarch
1 large egg
½ cup water
2 ounces unsweetened chocolate
  chopped fine
1 tablespoon Kahlúa
½ cup well-chilled heavy cream

◎ IN A SMALL SAUCEPAN WHISK TOGETHER THE sugar and the cornstarch and whisk in the egg and the water, whisking until the mixture is smooth. Bring the mixture to a boil over moderate heat, whisking, and simmer it, whisking vigorously, for 1 minute. Remove the pan from the heat, add the chocolate and the Kahlúa, and stir the mixture until the chocolate is melted. Transfer the mixture to a metal bowl set in a bowl of ice and cold water and with a hand-held mixer beat it until it is cold and lightened slightly. In a bowl beat the cream until it just holds stiff peaks, fold it into the chocolate mixture gently but thoroughly, and spoon the mousse into 2 long-stemmed glasses. Chill the mousse until ready to serve. Serves 2.

Watercress, Pear, and Grape Salad with Chrysanthemum Petals

A CHRISTENING LUNCHEON

SHRIMP AND SCALLOPS WITH FRESH AND SUN-DRIED TOMATO SAUCE

VEAL AND OYSTER MUSHROOM FRICASSEE

SEMOLINA PARTY RIBBONS

GREEN BEAN, BELL PEPPER, AND ICICLE RADISH SALAD

LEMON CAKE WITH LEMON MERINGUE FROSTING

SERVES TWENTY

A pretty luncheon is a lovely way to welcome the newest member of any family. The tiny guest of honor, draped in a flowing white dress and snugly bonneted, may choose a nap after the rigors of the ceremony, but the proud parents, grandparents, and assorted relations and friends will want to gather and celebrate the pure joy of the occasion.

Our menu, which could be served any day of the year, calls forth the light colors and gentle flavors of Spring. We suggest you begin preparing it several days before the party, particularly if you plan to make the pasta. As with making your own bread, making your own pasta is genuinely rewarding. Still, if time is short, you might opt to buy fresh fettuccine instead. Our pasta recipe calls for semolina flour—not to be confused with the cereal semolina—easily found in Italian markets, specialty food shops, and many supermarkets. It is made from hard durum flour and produces a satisfyingly sturdy pasta that stands up very well indeed to a fricassee as full-bodied as ours, made with veal and oyster mushrooms.

Oyster mushrooms, both dried and fresh, are widely available. The British call them "shellfish of the woods" because their drooping caps somewhat resemble oyster shells. Although plentiful in the wild, they are commonly cultivated and can be found quite easily—in a market, rather than under a tree. Their flesh is meaty and mildly flavored. Dried oyster mushrooms plump up nicely in warm water, providing the stew with a hint of earthiness not so apparent in the fresh ones.

The fricassee is accompanied by a vegetable salad of green beans, bell peppers, and icicle radishes. Not to be confused with the much larger *daikon,* icicle radishes are pure white, long, and slender and are frequently sold with the tops

*Lemon Cake with
Lemon Meringue Frosting*

trimmed. Their flavor is similar to that of the red globe radish, and some are more peppery than others. It's a good idea to trim the vegetables early on the morning of the party so they will be ready when it is time to toss the salad.

The lemon cake is a light, frothy confection, filled with a thickened lemon cream similar in taste and texture to lemon curd, and frosted with a billowy white frosting. The cake can be made a day ahead of time, as can the filling, but we recommend frosting it on the day of the party to ensure the best texture for the meringue.

to a simmer over moderate heat, stirring, and remove from the heat. (The seafood should be opaque and springy to the touch.) Let the mixture cool. Strain the cooking broth and reserve 5 cups for the sauce. Keep the seafood in the remaining broth until ready to use. *The seafood can be made 1 day ahead up to this point and kept refrigerated, covered.*

Preheat the oven to 350° F.

In a large baking dish bake the seafood and its broth in the middle of the oven, covered, stirring occasionally, for 7 to 10 minutes, or until just heated through. Spoon the sauce onto heated serving plates and top with the drained seafood. Garnish with the basil. Serves 20.

FRESH AND SUN-DRIED TOMATO SAUCE

1 large onion, minced
3 tablespoons olive oil
3 pounds plum tomatoes, peeled, seeded, and chopped
3 ounces sun-dried tomatoes (not packed in oil)
3 garlic cloves, minced
cheesecloth bag containing ½ teaspoon dried thyme, 6 parsley sprigs, and 1 bay leaf
5 cups shellfish broth from preceding recipe
salt and freshly ground pepper to taste

◯ IN A SAUCEPAN COOK THE ONION IN THE OIL OVER moderate heat until softened. Add the fresh and dried tomatoes, garlic, and cheesecloth bag and bring to a boil. Simmer, covered, stirring occasionally, for 30 minutes, or until almost all of the liquid is evaporated. Discard the cheesecloth bag. In a food processor or blender purée in batches. *The sauce can be made 1 day ahead up to this point and kept refrigerated, covered.*

In a saucepan combine the purée with 4 cups of the shellfish broth and bring to a simmer. Simmer, stirring occasionally, for 10 minutes, adding more of the remaining 1 cup broth if too thick. Season with salt and pepper and serve warm. Makes about 7 cups.

SHRIMP AND SCALLOPS WITH FRESH AND SUN-DRIED TOMATO SAUCE

6 cups water
1 cup dry white wine
2 pounds large shrimp, shelled, deveined, and shells reserved
1 onion, minced
1 large celery stalk, sliced
1 small carrot, sliced
cheesecloth bag containing 12 parsley sprigs, 12 peppercorns, 12 coriander seeds, ½ teaspoon dried thyme, and 1 bay leaf
2 pounds sea scallops, halved if large
salt to taste
fresh and sun-dried tomato sauce (recipe follows)
24 large basil leaves, cut into thin strips, for garnish

◯ IN A LARGE STOCKPOT COMBINE THE WATER, WINE, reserved shrimp shells, vegetables, and cheesecloth bag. Bring to a boil and simmer for 20 minutes. Let cool and strain the stock into a saucepan.

Add the shrimp, scallops, and salt to the stock with enough water to just cover them. Bring

VEAL AND OYSTER
MUSHROOM FRICASSEE

2 ounces dried oyster mushrooms
    (available at specialty food shops)
4 cups hot water
6½ to 7 pounds boneless veal shoulder,
    cut into 2-inch pieces
salt and freshly ground pepper to taste
6 to 8 tablespoons olive oil
4 celery stalks, sliced
white part of 3 leeks, washed well
    and sliced
3 carrots, sliced
3 garlic cloves, chopped
1 cup dry white wine
1 large onion stuck with 2 cloves
cheesecloth bag containing 12 parsley
    sprigs, 1½ teaspoons dried thyme,
    2 bay leaves, and 1 teaspoon
    dried rosemary
3 strips of lemon zest, each 3 inches long
8 to 10 cups chicken stock (page 198) *or*
    canned chicken broth
2 pounds fresh oyster *or* white
    mushrooms, sliced
juice of 1 lemon
½ cup all-purpose flour
¾ stick (6 tablespoons) unsalted butter
1 cup heavy cream, or to taste
¼ cup minced fresh tarragon, *or* chervil
    leaves, *or* snipped fresh chives
semolina party ribbons (recipe follows)
    as an accompaniment

⊙ IN A SMALL BOWL LET THE DRIED MUSHROOMS SOAK IN the hot water for 20 minutes, or until softened. Drain, reserving the liquid. Strain the soaking liquid and slice the mushrooms.

Pat the veal dry and sprinkle with the salt and pepper. In a large casserole cook the veal in batches in the oil over moderate heat until no longer pink. Do not brown it. Transfer to a plate.

Add the celery, leek, carrots, and salt and pepper to taste to the casserole and cook, stirring, until the vegetables are softened. Add the garlic and cook, stirring, for 1 minute. Add the veal, wine, onion, cheesecloth bag, lemon zest, strained

mushroom soaking liquid, and enough stock to cover the veal and bring to a boil. Simmer, covered partially, skimming the froth and stirring occasionally, for 1½ hours, or until the veal is tender.

Transfer the veal to a large casserole and strain the cooking liquid into a large bowl. There should be about 10 cups liquid.

In a large saucepan combine the fresh mushrooms with water to cover and add some of the lemon juice and salt and pepper to taste. Bring to a boil and simmer for 3 to 5 minutes, or until cooked but still firm. Drain.

In a heavy saucepan cook the flour in the butter over low heat, stirring, for 3 minutes. Add the strained cooking liquid and simmer, whisking occasionally, for 20 minutes. Strain over the veal and add the dried and fresh mushrooms and salt and pepper to taste. *The dish can be made 1 day ahead up to this point. Let it cool and keep refrigerated, covered.*

Cook the fricassee over moderate heat until heated through and stir in the cream. Bring to a boil and simmer, stirring occasionally, for 10 minutes. Add salt, pepper, and lemon juice to taste. Garnish with the tarragon and serve over the semolina ribbons. Serves 20.

SEMOLINA PARTY RIBBONS

2½ pounds semolina pasta dough
    (page 38), cut into fettuccine
    (procedure on page 38), *or* commercial
    fresh or dried fettuccine
1 cup chicken stock (page 198) *or* canned
    chicken broth
¾ stick (6 tablespoons) unsalted butter,
    melted

⊙ IN 2 LARGE KETTLES OF BOILING SALTED WATER COOK the fettuccine, stirring, for 3 to 5 minutes for fresh pasta or according to the package instructions for dried pasta, or until al dente. Drain and transfer to a large bowl. Add the stock and butter and toss well. Serves 20.

SEMOLINA PASTA DOUGH

1¾ cups semolina flour (available at
    health food stores)
½ teaspoon salt
2 large eggs
1 tablespoon olive oil
3 tablespoons water

☉+ IN A FOOD PROCESSOR BLEND THE FLOUR AND SALT
for 30 seconds. In a small bowl whisk the eggs, oil,
and water and add to the flour mixture. Blend until
the dough just begins to form a ball, adding more
water, drop by drop, if too dry. Process for 15 seconds more to knead it. Remove from the processor
and let it rest, covered with an inverted bowl, at
room temperature for 1 hour. Makes about 1
pound. (Make 3 batches for the semolina party ribbons, page 37.)

TO ROLL AND CUT FETTUCCINE

☉ SET THE SMOOTH ROLLERS OF A PASTA MACHINE AT
the highest number. (The rollers will be wide
apart.) Divide each pound of dough into 4 pieces
and flatten 1 piece into a rectangle. Cover the re-
mainder with an inverted bowl.

Dust the rectangle with flour and feed it
through the rollers. Fold in half and feed through
10 more times, folding in half each time and dusting with flour if necessary to prevent sticking.

Turn the dial down 1 notch and feed the
dough through the rollers without folding. Continue feeding through without folding, turning the
dial 1 notch lower each time, until the lowest notch
is reached. The dough should be a smooth, long
sheet about 5 inches wide and ¹⁄₁₆ inch thick.

To cut into fettuccine: Use the blade of the
pasta machine that cuts ¼-inch wide strips. Feed
one end of a pasta sheet through the blades, holding the other end straight up from the machine.

Catch the strips from underneath before the sheet
goes completely through the rollers.

Put the cut strips across floured jelly-roll
pans or let them hang over the tops of straight-
backed chairs. Let dry for 5 minutes. Roll out and
cut the remaining dough in the same manner.

*The fettuccine can be made 2 days ahead,
sprinkled with cornmeal, and kept refrigerated in
plastic bags.*

GREEN BEAN, BELL PEPPER, AND
ICICLE RADISH SALAD

2 pounds green beans, trimmed
2 pounds red, yellow, and green bell
    peppers, sliced thin
2 pounds icicle radishes, peeled and
    quartered lengthwise
¼ cup fresh lemon juice
3 tablespoons red-wine vinegar
1 tablespoon Dijon-style mustard, or
    to taste
salt and freshly ground pepper to taste
½ cup olive oil
½ cup walnut oil (available at specialty
    food shops and some supermarkets), or
    to taste
¼ cup snipped fresh chives
1½ cups walnut pieces, toasted

☉+ IN A LARGE SAUCEPAN OF BOILING SALTED WATER
cook the beans for 7 minutes, or until tender. Drain
and refresh under cold water.

In a bowl combine all the vegetables and
chill, covered, overnight, or until ready to serve.

In a bowl whisk together the lemon juice,
vinegar, mustard and salt and pepper to taste. Add
the oils in a stream and whisk until emulsified.
Toss the vegetables with the dressing and sprinkle
with the chives and walnuts. Serves 20.

LEMON CAKE WITH LEMON MERINGUE FROSTING

2 cups cake flour (not self-rising)
2 teaspoons baking powder
½ teaspoon salt
1½ sticks (¾ cup) unsalted butter, cut into bits and softened
1½ cups sugar
3 large eggs, beaten lightly
1 tablespoon grated lemon zest
1 teaspoon lemon extract
1 cup milk

FOR THE FILLING:
4 large egg yolks
½ cup sugar
¼ cup fresh lemon juice
1 tablespoon grated lemon zest
½ stick (¼ cup) unsalted butter

FOR THE FROSTING:
⅓ cup water
1 cup sugar
4 large egg whites
⅛ teaspoon cream of tartar
pinch of salt
1 tablespoon grated lemon zest
1 teaspoon lemon extract

PREHEAT THE OVEN TO 350° F.

Into a bowl sift together the flour, baking powder, and salt and set aside. In a large bowl cream the butter with an electric mixer. Add the sugar, a little at a time, and beat until light and fluffy. With the motor running, add the eggs, a little at a time, and beat until combined well. Beat in the lemon zest and lemon extract.

Sift in one fourth of the flour mixture and stir gently. Add ⅓ cup of the milk and blend carefully. Continue to add the flour mixture alternately with the milk, ending with a batch of flour mixture. Divide between 2 buttered and floured 9-inch round cake pans and bake in the middle of the oven for 30 to 35 minutes, or until a cake tester inserted in the centers comes out clean. Let stand for 5 minutes and turn out onto racks to cool. *The layers can be made 1 day ahead and kept in a cool place, wrapped in plastic wrap.*

Make the filling: In the top of a double boiler set over simmering water combine all the ingredients and cook the mixture, stirring, for 10 minutes, or until thick. Do not boil. Transfer the filling to a bowl and let it cool. Chill, covered with plastic wrap, for at least 1 hour. *The filling can be made 1 day ahead and kept refrigerated, covered.*

Make the frosting: In a small heavy saucepan bring the water and sugar to a boil over moderate heat, stirring and washing down any sugar crystals with a brush dipped in cold water until the sugar is dissolved. Boil, undisturbed, until the syrup reaches the hard-ball stage, or a candy thermometer registers 248° F.

In the bowl of an electric mixer beat the egg whites with the cream of tartar and salt until they hold stiff peaks. With the motor running, add the hot syrup in a stream and beat the mixture until cool. Beat in the lemon zest and lemon extract.

Set 1 of the cake layers on a serving plate and spread it with the filling. Top with the second layer and spread the frosting on the top and sides of the cake. *The cake can be made 1 day ahead and kept refrigerated in an airtight cake container.* Makes one 9-inch cake.

**WEHLENER SONNENUHR RIESLING
KABINETT '87**

Hamantaschen,
Chocolate-Dipped
Fruit Balls

Spring Gifts

J ust in time, Spring bursts forth every year. The dreary mud and dull thud of March raindrops seem endless until one day the skies clear, a robin hops onto the fence post, and green shoots are clearly visible among the brown grasses. From that day, you know that the miracle of Spring will happen again. It is a season for quiet rejoicing, hard work, and lots of spontaneous humming. It is also a time to visit friends and relatives you may have neglected during a self-imposed Winter hibernation. How better to refresh these relationships than with gifts of food from the kitchen? Whether you bring a plate full of Purim cookies, a loaf of Easter bread, or a jar of homemade jelly from the larder, your gift will be as welcome as the first crocus peeking out from under the leaves.

The following cookie recipes celebrate Purim, the joyous Jewish holiday that commemorates Queen Esther's overthrow of Haman, an evil court minister who plotted to kill all Jews when a favorite Jewish minister of the king refused to bow before him. The queen revealed that she herself was a Jew and the king ordered Haman's death. Some say the traditional *hamantaschen,* tri-cornered cookies, represent Haman's ears (like a donkey's); others say they represent his purse or hat. These cookies, as well as the Chocolate-Dipped Fruit Balls, make excellent *shalach-monos,* gifts of baked delicacies sent to family and friends.

HAMANTASCHEN
(FILLED TRI-CORNERED COOKIES)

⅔ cup unsalted butter, softened
½ cup sugar
1 large egg
3 tablespoons milk *or* water
1 teaspoon grated lemon zest
½ teaspoon vanilla
2¾ cups all-purpose flour
prune *or* apricot filling (recipe follows)

IN A BOWL WITH AN ELECTRIC MIXER CREAM THE BUTTER with the sugar until it is light and fluffy, add the egg, milk, zest, and vanilla and beat until the mixture is smooth. Stir in the flour, blending the mixture until a ball of dough is formed. Chill the dough, wrapped in plastic wrap, for 2 hours, or until firm. Roll out one fourth of the dough ⅛ inch thick on a lightly floured surface, keeping the remaining dough wrapped and chilled. Cut out rounds with a 2-inch cutter and with a spatula transfer them to a baking sheet. Put rounded ½ teaspoons of the filling in the center of each round and fold up the edges to form triangular cookies, pinching the corners together but leaving the filling exposed. Bake the cookies in a preheated 375° F. oven for 10 to 15 minutes, or until the corners are golden, transfer them to a rack, and let them cool. Make *hamantaschen* with the remaining dough and filling in the same manner. The cookies keep, stored in an airtight container, for up to 5 days. Makes about 48 cookies.

PRUNE OR APRICOT FILLING

1 pound pitted sour prunes (available at some specialty foods shops), *or* pitted sweet prunes, *or* dried apricots
2 teaspoons fresh lemon juice, or to taste
1 teaspoon grated lemon zest
1 teaspoon cinnamon
½ cup sugar
½ cup walnuts, chopped fine

◷ IN A SAUCEPAN COMBINE THE PRUNES OR THE APRICOTS with enough water to cover them by 1 inch, bring the water to a boil, and simmer the fruit for 5 minutes, or until it is plump. Drain the fruit well and let it cool. In a food processor purée the cooked fruit, lemon juice, zest, and cinnamon until the mixture is just smooth. Transfer the mixture to a small bowl and stir in the sugar and the walnuts.
The prune filling may be made up to 3 days in advance and kept covered and chilled, and the apricot filling may be made up to 2 hours in advance and kept covered. Makes about 2 cups.

CHOCOLATE-DIPPED FRUIT BALLS

2 pounds (about 5 cups) dried fruit such as raisins, figs, apricots, *or* pitted prunes or dates
1 cup walnuts
1 to 2 tablespoons fruit juice *or* fruit-flavored liqueur
confectioners' sugar for dredging
4 ounces semisweet chocolate, chopped

IN A FOOD PROCESSOR CHOP FINE THE DRIED FRUIT AND the walnuts and mix in enough of the juice to hold the mixture together. Shape the mixture into 1-inch balls, roll the balls lightly in the sugar, and let them stand at room temperature, uncovered, for 24 hours. In the top of a double boiler set over barely simmering water melt the chocolate, stirring occasionally, until it is smooth and remove it from the heat. Coat half of each ball with the chocolate, letting the excess drip off and wiping the underside of the ball gently against the side of the double boiler. Chill the balls on a baking sheet lined with a piece of parchment paper until the chocolate has hardened. The confections keep, chilled, in an airtight container for up to 2 weeks. Makes about 50 to 60 confections.

GREEK EASTER BREAD

Brightly colored eggs nestle in this braided loaf. The eggs, hard-cooked and dyed, are not meant to be eaten, but the tangy bread, flavored with orange juice and sprinkled with sesame seeds, certainly is. Set the loaf in a pretty basket lined with a colorful cloth napkin and then give it to a friend as an adult version of the Easter basket.

FOR THE EASTER EGGS:
2 cups water
½ cup white vinegar
3 tablespoons red food coloring
1 drop blue food coloring
4 large eggs, rinsed well

1 cup milk
¾ stick (6 tablespoons) unsalted butter, cut into bits
2 packages active dry yeast (1½ tablespoons)
¼ cup plus 1 teaspoon sugar
2 large eggs, beaten
¼ cup fresh orange juice
1 tablespoon grated orange zest
½ teaspoon salt
4½ to 5 cups all-purpose flour
egg wash made by beating 1 egg with 1 tablespoon milk
1 tablespoon sesame seeds

MAKE THE EASTER EGGS: IN A STAINLESS STEEL OR enameled saucepan combine all the ingredients. Add enough water, if necessary, to cover the eggs. Bring to a simmer over moderate heat and simmer for 12 minutes. Transfer the eggs with a slotted spoon to a rack to cool.

In a saucepan heat the milk and butter over low heat, stirring, until the butter is melted. Let the mixture cool to lukewarm.

In a large bowl proof the yeast in ½ cup of the milk mixture with 1 teaspoon of the sugar for 15 minutes, or until foamy. Add the remaining milk mixture and ¼ cup sugar, the eggs, orange juice, orange zest, and salt and combine well. Stir in 4½ cups of the flour, or enough to form a soft but not sticky dough.

Knead the dough on a lightly floured surface, incorporating more flour if too sticky, for 8 to 10 minutes, or until smooth. Form into a ball, put in a buttered bowl, and turn to coat with the butter. Let it rise, covered loosely, for 1½ hours, or until double in bulk.

Punch down the dough and divide into thirds. On a floured surface form each piece into a 20-inch rope. Braid the ropes and transfer them to a buttered baking sheet, forming the braid into a round and pinching the ends together. Nestle the Easter eggs among the braids and let the bread rise, covered loosely, for 45 minutes, or until almost double in bulk.

Preheat the oven to 375° F.

Brush the loaf with some of the egg wash and bake in the middle of the oven for 25 minutes. Brush with more egg wash and sprinkle with the sesame seeds. Bake the bread for 10 minutes more, or until the loaf sounds hollow when the bottom is tapped. Let it cool on a rack. (The Easter eggs are not meant to be eaten after they are baked.)

The bread can be made 1 day ahead and kept in a cool, dry place, wrapped tightly in plastic wrap. Makes 1 loaf.

HOT CROSS BUNS

For many, hot cross buns represent springtime and all its beginnings. We suggest taking the simple yeast rolls with sugary glaze, traditional fare at Easter, with you if you are invited out for Easter breakfast. Or tote them along for late-afternoon tea.

> **2½ packages active dry yeast
>   (about 2 tablespoons)**
> **¾ cup lukewarm milk plus 2 to
>   3 teaspoons more for the icing**
> **¼ cup firmly packed light brown sugar**
> **2 large eggs, beaten lightly**
> **¾ stick (6 tablespoons) unsalted butter,
>   softened**
> **¾ teaspoon salt**
> **1 teaspoon cinnamon**
> **½ teaspoon freshly grated nutmeg**
> **¼ teaspoon ground cloves**
> **¼ teaspoon ground allspice**
> **4 to 4½ cups all-purpose flour**
> **½ cup currants *or* raisins**
> **egg wash made by beating 1 egg with
>   2 teaspoons water and pinch of salt**
> **⅓ cup confectioners' sugar**

IN A LARGE BOWL PROOF THE YEAST IN ¾ CUP OF THE milk with 1 teaspoon of the brown sugar for 15 minutes, or until foamy. Stir in the remaining sugar, eggs, butter, salt, and spices. Add enough of the flour, 1 cup at a time, to make a soft and slightly sticky dough.

Knead the dough on a lightly floured surface for 8 to 10 minutes, or until smooth and elastic. Put the dough in a large buttered bowl and turn to coat with the butter. Let it rise, covered with plastic wrap and a dish towel, for 1 to 1½ hours, or until double in bulk.

Punch down the dough and flatten into a rectangle 21 inches long and about ½ inch thick. Sprinkle with the currants and roll up into a 21-inch log. Cut the log into 16 pieces and stretch both sides of the dough over the filling to enclose it completely. Seal the seam. Arrange seam side down on lightly buttered and floured baking sheets. Let rise, covered loosely, until almost double in bulk.

Preheat the oven to 425° F.

Brush the buns with the egg wash and with a sharp knife or razor cut a cross in the top of each. Bake in the middle of the oven for 15 minutes, or until they sound hollow when the bottoms are tapped. Transfer to racks to cool.

In a small bowl beat the confectioners' sugar with enough of the remaining milk to form a thick icing. Drizzle into the crosses on the buns. Makes 16 buns.

HERBED VEGETABLE PÂTÉ

Although it does not keep for more than a day or two in the refrigerator, this pâté is just right for a Spring party. It must be made ahead of time but requires no cooking. Its smooth consistency makes it ideal for spreading on crackers or small chunks of French bread. Bring it with you when you are asked to contribute to a party, or as a wonderful addition to a picnic in the park.

> **2 cups pot cheese *or* large-curd cottage
>   cheese**
> **6 ounces radishes, trimmed and chopped**
> **2 small red bell peppers, chopped**
> **1 cucumber, peeled, seeded, and chopped**
> **1 bunch of watercress, rinsed well and
>   stems removed**
> **1 tablespoon Worcestershire sauce**
> **1½ to 2 teaspoons salt, or to taste**
> **1 teaspoon dried summer savory,
>   crumbled**
> **¾ teaspoon dried basil, crumbled**
> **¾ teaspoon dried marjoram, crumbled**
> **freshly ground pepper to taste**
> **pumpernickel or whole-wheat bread as
>   an accompaniment**

PURÉE THE CHEESE THROUGH THE FINE DISK OF A FOOD mill into a bowl or force it through a sieve into a bowl. In a food processor or blender blend the cheese with the remaining ingredients until the mixture is smooth.

Line a 1-quart loaf pan with a triple thickness of rinsed and squeezed cheesecloth, leaving enough overhang to fold over the top. Spoon the mixture into the pan and rap sharply on the counter to expel any bubbles. Smooth the top with a spatula.

Fold the overhanging cheesecloth over the pâté and cover the top of the loaf pan with a double layer of foil. Weight the pâté with a 2-pound weight and chill for at least 6 hours. *The pâté can be made ahead up to this point and kept refrigerated, covered and weighted, overnight.*

Remove the weight and foil and unfold the cheesecloth. Invert a platter over the pan and invert the pâté onto it. Discard the cheesecloth and blot up any liquid. Slice the pâté and serve it with the bread. Serves 10 to 12 as an hors d'oeuvre.

MUSHROOM, SPINACH, AND WALNUT PÂTÉ

1½ to 2 cups walnuts
about 1½ pounds spinach, trimmed,
    washed, and patted dry
1 pound mushrooms, trimmed
1 onion, minced
½ stick (¼ cup) unsalted butter
1 garlic clove, minced
3 tablespoons medium-dry Sherry
2 teaspoons salt
1 teaspoon dried chervil, crumbled
¾ teaspoon dried rosemary, crumbled
freshly ground pepper to taste
1 cup pot cheese *or* large-curd cottage
    cheese
2 eggs, lightly beaten
⅓ cup parsley, minced
¼ teaspoon freshly grated nutmeg

PREHEAT THE OVEN TO 375° F.

In a food processor fitted with the steel blade grind enough walnuts to measure 1⅓ cups and transfer them to a large bowl. In the food pro-

cessor mince enough spinach to measure 2 cups and transfer it to the bowl.

In the food processor mince the mushrooms. In a heavy skillet cook the onion in the butter over moderate heat for 3 to 5 minutes, or until it is softened, add the mushrooms and the garlic, and cook the mixture, stirring occasionally, for 5 minutes. Add the Sherry, salt, chervil, rosemary, and pepper and cook the mixture over low heat, stirring occasionally, for 7 to 10 minutes, or until the liquid is evaporated. Transfer the mixture to the bowl containing the walnuts and spinach, stir the mixture, and let it cool.

Purée the pot cheese through the fine disk of a food mill into the bowl or force it through a sieve into the bowl. Add the eggs, parsley, and nutmeg and combine the mixture well.

Line a buttered 1-quart loaf pan with parchment paper, leaving enough overhang to fold over the top, and butter the paper. Spoon the mixture into the pan, rap the pan sharply on the counter to expel any bubbles, and smooth the top with a spatula. Fold the overhanging paper over the pâté and cover the pan with a double layer of foil. Put the loaf pan in a baking pan, add enough hot water to the baking pan to reach halfway up the sides of the loaf pan, and bake the pâté in the oven for 1 hour and 30 minutes. Transfer the loaf pan to a rack and let it stand for 30 minutes.

Weight the pâté with a 2-pound weight for 1 hour. Remove the weight and foil, invert a platter over the pan, and invert the pâté onto the platter. Remove the paper, slice the pâté, and serve it at room temperature. Seves 8 to 10 as a first course or 20 as an hors d'oeuvre.

BLOOD ORANGE CORDIAL

Our dictionary defines a cordial as an "aromatized and sweetened spirit; a liqueur." What could be more aromatic than a blending of the heady flavors of Cognac, oranges, and cinnamon? We choose to elaborate on the definition by suggesting that you serve cordials when you want to extend the utmost hospitality—to be, in effect, most cordial. Our brew takes 2 months to blend and stand, so plan ahead and make a batch when you first see blood oranges in the market.

> **3 to 4 blood oranges (available at specialty produce markets)**
> **½ cup sugar**
> **2 cups Cognac *or* other brandy**
> **3-inch cinnamon stick, broken into pieces**

☕+ WITH A VEGETABLE PEELER, REMOVE THE ZEST IN strips from 2 of the oranges and reserve it. Squeeze enough juice to yield 1 cup. In a saucepan simmer the juice and sugar, stirring, until the sugar is dissolved. Let the mixture cool.

Stir in the Cognac, reserved zest, and cinnamon stick and transfer the mixture to a sterilized jar (page 199). Seal tightly with the lid and store in a cool, dry place, shaking occasionally, for 1 month. Strain the cordial through a fine sieve into a decorative bottle and let it stand, covered, for 1 more month before serving. Makes about 2 cups.

PIQUANT MINT JELLY

> **1 cup firmly packed fresh mint leaves**
> **1 cup cider vinegar**
> **1 cup water**
> **2½ cups sugar**
> **2 drops green food coloring, if desired**
> **6 tablespoons liquid pectin**

☕+ IN A FOOD PROCESSOR FITTED WITH THE PLASTIC blade crush the mint with the vinegar. Transfer to a stainless steel or enameled saucepan and add the water. Bring the mixture to a boil over moderate heat and boil for 1 minute. Let it cool.

Strain through a sieve into a saucepan, pressing hard on the solids. Stir in the sugar and food coloring. Bring the mixture to a boil over moderate heat, stirring, and stir in the pectin. Boil for 1 minute. Remove the pan from the heat and skim the froth.

Spoon the jelly into sterilized ½-pint Mason-type jars (page 199) and seal with paraffin (page 199). Makes about 1 pint.

CHOCOLATE ALMOND BARK

> **1 cup sugar**
> **3 ounces unsweetened chocolate, chopped**
> **1 teaspoon vanilla**
> **1 cup slivered and toasted blanched almonds**

☕+ IN A HEAVY 14-INCH SKILLET COOK THE SUGAR OVER moderately low heat, stirring and breaking up any lumps as they form, until melted, about 15 to 20 minutes. Remove from the heat. Add the chocolate and vanilla and stir until the chocolate is melted. Stir in the almonds.

Pour immediately onto a buttered baking sheet and with a buttered spatula spread ¼ inch thick. Let cool and break into pieces. *The candy can be made 1 week ahead and stored in an airtight container lined with wax paper; separate the layers with wax paper.* Makes about ¾ pound.

PEANUT BRITTLE

Everybody loves peanut brittle. It is not as pretty as some candies, but its crunchy goodness quickly makes up for this fact. Be sure the tin you use for brittle is airtight—otherwise the moisture attracted by the sugar will render the brittle soft. Break it into small, manageable shards and hide a cache of it in your favorite grown-up's Easter basket.

> **1 cup sugar**
> **½ cup water**
> **⅓ cup light corn syrup**
> **pinch of cream of tartar**
> **1 cup raw peanuts (available at natural food stores)**
> **1½ teaspoons unsalted butter, softened**
> **¼ teaspoon vanilla**
> **almond oil *or* peanut oil**

IN A HEAVY SAUCEPAN COOK THE SUGAR, WATER, CORN syrup, and cream of tartar over low heat, stirring, for 2 minutes. Rotate the skillet, washing down any sugar crystals clinging to the sides with a brush dipped in cold water. Cook over moderately high heat, rotating the skillet, until a candy thermometer registers 230° F.

Add the peanuts and cook, swirling the pan, until golden. Remove from the heat and add the butter and vanilla. Transfer immediately to a marble or metal surface oiled with the almond oil and spread thin. Let the brittle cool for 1 hour and break into pieces.

The brittle can be made 1 week ahead and stored in a cool place in an airtight container lined with wax paper; separate the layers with wax paper. Makes about 1½ pounds.

PRALINES

Different from French *praline*, which is hardened carmelized sugar mixed with nuts often ground to a powder, these very American candies originated in New Orleans. The soft, tender rounds are made with cream and native pecans and make an appreciated gift, especially for those with a sweet tooth.

> **2 cups firmly packed light brown sugar**
> **1 cup granulated sugar**
> **1 cup heavy cream**
> **½ teaspoon salt**
> **¼ teaspoon cream of tartar**
> **½ stick (¼ cup) unsalted butter, cut into bits**
> **1½ teaspoons vanilla**
> **2½ cups pecan halves**

☺+ IN A HEAVY 2-QUART SAUCEPAN COOK THE SUGARS, cream, salt, and cream of tartar over moderate heat, stirring and washing down any sugar crystals clinging to the sides of the pan with a brush dipped in cold water, until the sugar is dissolved. Boil over moderately high heat, undisturbed, until a candy thermometer registers 238° F.

Remove the saucepan from the heat and let the mixture cool until the thermometer registers 220° F. Stir in the butter and vanilla and beat until creamy. Stir in the pecans. Drop by tablespoons 2 inches apart onto oiled baking sheets and let the pralines cool.

The pralines can be made 2 weeks ahead and stored, wrapped individually in wax paper, in an airtight container in a cool, dry place. Makes about 36.

Summer

S UMMER HAS ARRIVED IN ALL ITS GLORY. THE GARDEN, filled with vegetables, is starting to show real progress, and the Summer perennials are beginning to bloom. Long, hot days and dusky evenings call out for casual entertaining, and so most of our Summer menus are designed for outdoor parties, cookouts, and picnics. Whether we spread a blanket beneath a tree in the park, tote a hamper to the beach, or set the table on the deck, our parties are in step with the weather.

Caught up with the sheer fun of the season, we have devised menus for the important holidays—Memorial Day, the Fourth of July, and Labor Day—as well as for events such as a small at-home wedding and a graduation day buffet. We take the Summer host and hostess through the all-too-brief warm months with menus that rely on the glorious bounty of the season while reflecting America's love for eclectic combinations of food. There really is no excuse during this time of year not to buy fresh seasonal produce, and we offer numerous recipes that allow you to do so. Look for the ripest, plumpest, and juiciest fruits and vegetables you can find. Avoid bruised specimens or ones that have been imported. These are fine in the cold months when little else is available, but now is the time to support the local farmers and buy the best-tasting produce around. Freshly picked bright red tomatoes, golden yellow corn on the cob, tender peas found in vibrant green pods, plump juicy strawberries . . . our recipes are filled with them.

As with all our menus, we have singled out dishes that either require advance preparation or *can* be made ahead to save you time at the party. We also explain ingredients and procedures that may be unfamiliar to you. When it comes to our wedding luncheon, we take you through the advance preparation step by step with a day-by-day schedule suggesting precisely what to do and when to do it. Copy our countdown and keep it taped to the refrigerator door for easy reference. It will assure the success so important for a party as special as this one.

All parties are special, of course. The Memorial Day Picnic is meant to be a carefree event offering coleslaw and pasta salad, both deliciously different from what you might ordinarily expect. The Fourth of July cookout is a smaller, more structured affair with a menu that includes grilled swordfish and sugar snap peas. If you are celebrating this holiday with a larger group, you'll be interested in our buffet menu, which includes steamed clams and orange-flavored chicken breasts with bacon. A smaller graduation buffet offers roasted Rock Cornish game hens. And, finally, we celebrate the close of Summer with roast striped bass for Labor Day.

Take a few minutes to leaf through the following pages to get ideas for the sort of Summer party you might want to give. A formal party, a boisterous cookout, a splendid buffet, or a small, intimate dinner for a few close friends, they are all here. As the sun sets and shadows lengthen, sit back and enjoy yourself with your guests. After all, these are the days we wait for all year long.

Red Cabbage Coleslaw,
Sesame Chicken Wings

MENU

A MEMORIAL DAY PICNIC

QUESADILLAS

BEER RIBS

MINIATURE TOURTIÈRES

SESAME CHICKEN WINGS

**FRANKFURTERS IN
CARAWAY MUSTARD PASTRY**

EAST INDIAN LAMB KEBABS

**PENNE AND VEGETABLE SALAD
WITH INDONESIAN PEANUT SAUCE**

RED CABBAGE COLESLAW

PEACH CRISP

SERVES TWELVE

Not according to the calendar—or to a querulous schoolchild with several more weeks until vacation—but for many of us, perhaps, Memorial Day *is* the beginning of Summer. And what is more worthy of celebration than that? Round up a dozen friends and stage a backyard party where the food is as intriguing as it is simple to prepare. Plan on using large plates and oversized napkins (pretty tea towels work well), and give the mugs a good frosting in the freezer before setting them out for a variety of thirst-quenching beers.

The pleasure of this party is that nearly everything can be made ahead of time. Devised of finger foods and salads, the menu is a glorious jumble of cuisines and flavors capped off with an all-American peach crisp that is as easy to make (dare we say it?) as pie.

The tiny ribs, the *tourtières* (pork-filled turnovers), and the chicken wings can all be cooked the day before the party and reheated in minutes in the same oven. And, if it's easier, you can take care of the reheating an hour or so before serving, since all three dishes are delicious served at room temperature. When the guests begin to arrive, sprinkle the topping for the *quesadillas* (which you have put together an hour or so earlier) on the toasted tortilla wedges and bake them to serve hot.

The frankfurters, our own special rendition of "pigs in a blanket," can be assembled and frozen a few days ahead of time and then cooked in a moderately hot oven before serving. Just be sure to let them thaw first, overnight in the refrigerator or for a couple of hours at room temperature. These can be served at room temperature or, better yet, slightly warm. If the weather is cooperative, light the charcoal grill to cook the lamb kebabs. Few things evoke the good feeling of summer as quickly as those first fledgling coals. Soak the bamboo skewers for a few hours beforehand, and while you might be tempted to let the guests thread their own with the marinated lamb and cherry tomatoes, it's probably easier and not as messy if you do it in the kitchen ahead of time.

Both the pasta salad, which is deceptively spicy if the full measure of pepper flakes is used, and the coleslaw are no-fuss affairs. To keep the crunch in the cabbage, we suggest mixing up the slaw no more than three hours before serving.

Peach crisp is a snap to make. If the rest of the food has not done so already, its bright, sweet, fruity taste will assure your guests that Summer has officially arrived. The greengrocer's nectarines may look riper and better than the peaches at this early point in the season, so do not hesitate to substitute them. The flavor will be as good. You should bake the crisp on the day it will be served, but be sure to give it time to cool. An hour or so is fine.

QUESADILLAS
(TORTILLA WEDGES WITH MONTEREY JACK AND JALAPEÑOS)

8 flour tortillas, each 7 inches in diameter
½ stick (¼ cup) unsalted butter, softened
¾ pound Monterey Jack, grated
8 scallions, minced
½ cup drained and minced bottled pimiento
4 bottled pickled *jalapeño* peppers, minced (wear rubber gloves)
2 tablespoons minced fresh coriander leaves, if desired
1 teaspoon ground cumin

PREHEAT THE OVEN TO 400° F.

Spread the tortillas on 1 side with the butter and put them buttered side up on ungreased baking sheets. Toast them in the middle of the oven for 5 minutes, or until barely golden. *The tortillas can be toasted 2 hours ahead and kept covered.*

In a bowl toss together the remaining ingredients and sprinkle on the tortillas. Bake in the middle of the oven for 5 to 8 minutes, or until the cheese is bubbly. Serve the tortillas cut into wedges. Makes about 48 hors d'oeuvres.

BEER RIBS

⅓ cup dark beer
⅓ cup soy sauce
⅓ cup Dijon-style mustard
¼ cup firmly packed dark brown sugar
1 onion, minced
1 teaspoon Worcestershire sauce
4 pounds lean pork spareribs, trimmed of excess fat and halved crosswise by a butcher

IN A LARGE BOWL COMBINE WELL ALL THE INGREDIENTS except the spareribs. In a kettle cover the spareribs with salted water. Bring them to a boil and simmer, skimming the froth, for 20 minutes. Drain and rinse briefly under cold water.

Cut the ribs into 1-rib sections and add to the bowl of marinade, stirring to coat well. Let the ribs marinate, covered, at room temperature, stirring occasionally, for 2 hours. Alternatively, chill them covered, overnight.

Preheat the oven to 350° F.

Arrange the ribs meaty side up in one layer in lightly oiled baking pans and brush with some marinade. Bake them in the middle of the oven, turning and basting occasionally, for 1 hour, or until tender and glazed.

The ribs can be baked 1 day ahead and kept refrigerated, covered. Reheat in baking pans in a preheated 350° F. oven for 10 to 15 minutes, or until heated through. Serve warm or at room temperature. Serves 12.

MINIATURE TOURTIÈRES
(FRENCH-CANADIAN PORK TURNOVERS)

FOR THE DOUGH:
2 sticks (1 cup) unsalted butter, well softened
8 ounces cream cheese, well softened
2½ cups all-purpose flour
1 teaspoon salt

FOR THE FILLING:
1 pound ground pork, crumbled
1 onion, minced
1 bay leaf
¼ teaspoon dried savory, crumbled
⅛ teaspoon dried thyme, crumbled
¼ teaspoon ground cloves
¼ teaspoon dry mustard
salt and freshly ground pepper to taste
½ cup hot water
1 boiling potato, boiled, peeled, and mashed
egg wash made by beating 1 egg with 1 teaspoon water

MAKE THE DOUGH: IN A BOWL CREAM THE BUTTER AND cream cheese. Sift in the flour, ¼ cup at a time, with the salt, stirring, and combine well. Form the dough into a ball, dust with flour, and flatten slightly. Chill, wrapped in wax paper, for at least 3 hours or overnight.

Make the filling: In a large heavy skillet combine the pork, onion, herbs and spices, and water and bring to a boil, stirring. Simmer the mixture, stirring, for 20 minutes, or until most of the liquid is evaporated. Discard the bay leaf. Transfer the mixture to a bowl and add the potato. Combine well and let the filling cool.

Preheat the oven to 400° F.

Halve the dough and on a floured surface roll out one half ⅛ inch thick, keeping the remaining dough chilled. With a 4-inch cutter cut out rounds. Brush the rounds with some of the egg wash and put 1 tablespoon of the filling in the center of each. Fold in half, sealing the edges with the tines of a fork, and put on ungreased baking sheets. Reroll the scraps and make more turnovers in the same manner. Repeat with the remaining dough and filling.

Brush the turnovers with the remaining egg wash and cut 3 steam vents in each turnover. Bake them in the middle of the oven for 20 minutes, or until golden.

The turnovers can be made 1 day ahead and kept refrigerated, covered. Reheat, uncovered, on baking sheets in a preheated 350° F. oven for 10 minutes or until heated through. Serve warm or at room temperature. Makes 30 hors d'oeuvres.

SESAME CHICKEN WINGS

⅓ cup soy sauce
2 tablespoons honey
2 tablespoons cider vinegar
1 tablespoon minced gingerroot
1 tablespoon Oriental sesame oil
2 garlic cloves, minced
¼ teaspoon cayenne, or to taste
3 pounds chicken wings, wing tips cut off
3 tablespoons sesame seeds

✸+ IN A LARGE BOWL COMBINE ALL THE INGREDIENTS except the chicken wings and sesame seeds. Add the wings, stirring to coat well, and let them mari-nate, covered, at room temperature, stirring occasionally, for 2 hours. Alternatively, chill them, covered, overnight.

Preheat the oven to 425° F.

Stir the mixture and put the wings on racks in baking pans. Sprinkle with the sesame seeds and bake in the middle of the oven for 30 minutes, or until golden and tender. If desired, put the wings under a preheated broiler about 4 inches from the heat for 1 to 2 minutes to crisp the skin.

The wings can be made 1 day ahead and kept refrigerated, covered. Reheat, uncovered, in baking pans in a preheated 350° F. oven for 10 to 15 minutes, or until heated through. Serve warm or at room temperature. Makes about 20 hors d'oeuvres.

Miniature Tourtières; Quesadillas;
Frankfurters in Caraway Mustard Pastry;
Beer Ribs

FRANKFURTERS IN CARAWAY MUSTARD PASTRY

FOR THE DOUGH:
- **1⅓ cups all-purpose flour**
- **½ teaspoon salt**
- **1 stick unsalted butter, cut into bits**
- **1 large egg, beaten lightly**
- **1 tablespoon sour cream**

- **2 tablespoons Dijon-style mustard**
- **8 kosher beef frankfurters**
- **egg wash made by beating 1 egg with 1 teaspoon water**
- **2 teaspoons caraway seeds**

MAKE THE DOUGH: INTO A BOWL SIFT THE FLOUR AND salt and blend in the butter until the mixture resembles coarse meal. In another bowl beat the egg and sour cream and add to the flour mixture. Stir the mixture with a fork until it forms a dough. Form into a ball, dust with flour, and flatten slightly. Chill, wrapped in wax paper, for at least 1 hour.

Roll the dough into a rectangle ⅛ inch thick on a floured surface and trim into a strip with a width equal to the length of 1 frankfurter. Spread the dough with a thin layer of mustard and arrange 1 frankfurter along a short side. Roll the dough around the frankfurter to just enclose it, leaving a ½-inch overlap at the seam. Cut off the dough-enclosed frankfurter. Seal the seam and cut the frankfurter crosswise into thirds. Arrange the pieces seam side down on an ungreased baking sheet. Roll up the remaining frankfurters and cut them into pieces in the same manner. *The frankfurters can be made 2 days ahead up to this point and kept frozen, covered tightly with plastic wrap and foil. Let them thaw, covered loosely, in the refrigerator before baking.*

Preheat the oven to 375° F.

Brush the frankfurters with the egg wash and sprinkle with the caraway seeds. Bake in the middle of the oven for 20 minutes, or until golden and flaky. Serve warm or at room temperature. Makes 24 hors d'oeuvres.

EAST INDIAN LAMB KEBABS

⅓ cup fresh lemon juice
⅓ cup vegetable oil plus additional for
  brushing
2 garlic cloves, chopped
1½ to 2 teaspoons ground cumin,
  or to taste
1 teaspoon paprika
1 teaspoon cayenne
½ teaspoon salt
3 pounds boneless lamb shoulder, cut
  into ¾-inch pieces
26 bamboo skewers, each 8 inches long,
  soaked in water for 2 hours
3 green bell peppers, cut into ¾-inch
  pieces
26 cherry tomatoes
yogurt sauce (recipe follows) as an
  accompaniment

+ In a blender or food processor blend the lemon juice, oil, garlic, and seasonings until smooth. In a bowl combine the mixture with the lamb, stirring to coat well, and let it marinate, covered and chilled, overnight.

On each skewer thread 3 pieces of lamb alternately with 2 pieces of green pepper and 1 cherry tomato. Brush the kebabs lightly with oil. *The kebabs can be made 3 hours ahead up to this point and kept refrigerated, covered.*

Prepare a charcoal grill; alternatively, preheat the broiler.

Grill the kebabs, turning and brushing lightly with oil, for 10 to 15 minutes, or until the lamb is browned and firm to the touch. Or broil the kebabs on the rack of a broiler pan about 2 inches from the heat, turning and brushing lightly with oil, for 10 to 15 minutes. Serve the kebabs warm or at room temperature with the sauce. Makes 26 hors d'oeuvres.

YOGURT SAUCE

1¾ cups plain yogurt
2 tablespoons fresh lemon juice
½ cup fresh coriander leaves, chopped
salt to taste

In a bowl whisk together all the ingredients and chill the sauce, covered, for 1 hour. *The sauce can be made ahead and kept refrigerated, covered, overnight.* Makes about 2 cups.

PENNE AND VEGETABLE SALAD WITH INDONESIAN PEANUT SAUCE

FOR THE SAUCE:
  1 cup water
  ¾ cup creamy peanut butter
  3 tablespoons soy sauce
  2 tablespoons fresh lemon juice
  1 teaspoon red pepper flakes, or to taste
  ¼ teaspoon ground cumin
  ⅛ teaspoon turmeric

  ½ pound green beans, cut diagonally into
    ½-inch pieces
  1 pound penne, cooked al dente
  2 carrots, halved lengthwise and sliced
    thin diagonally
  1 large seedless cucumber, quartered
    lengthwise, seeded, and sliced thin
    diagonally
  8 scallions, cut diagonally into ¼-inch
    pieces
  ⅓ cup roasted peanuts, chopped

Make the sauce: In a blender or food processor blend all the ingredients until smooth.

In a saucepan of boiling salted water blanch the beans for 1 minute. Drain and refresh under cold water. Drain well and add to the penne with the carrots, cucumber, and scallions. *The salad can be combined 2 hours ahead up to this point and tossed with two thirds of the sauce.*

Just before serving, add the remaining sauce and sprinkle with the peanuts. Serves 12.

RED CABBAGE COLESLAW

1 large head of red cabbage, shredded
1 pound large carrots, grated coarse
4 celery stalks, cut into 1½-inch
   julienne strips
1 bunch of scallions, cut into 1½-inch
   julienne strips
⅓ cup fresh lemon juice
¼ cup cider vinegar
1½ tablespoons Dijon-style mustard, or
   to taste
1 cup vegetable oil
1 tablespoon celery seeds
salt and freshly ground pepper to taste

In a large bowl toss the vegetables. In a blender or food processor blend the lemon juice, vinegar, and mustard. With the motor running, add the oil in a stream and blend until just emulsified. Add the celery seeds and salt and pepper to taste. Pour over the vegetables and toss well. Chill, covered. *The coleslaw can be made 3 hours ahead and chilled, covered.* Serves 12.

ANCHOR STEAM BEER

SAMUEL SMITH'S TADCASTER ALE

GRANT'S IMPERIAL STOUT

FIRESTONE NON-ALCOHOLIC
MALT BEVERAGE

PEACH CRISP

FOR THE FILLING:
  6 pounds peaches, peeled and sliced
  ⅓ cup firmly packed light brown sugar
  ½ stick (¼ cup) unsalted butter,
    cut into bits
  3 tablespoons fresh lemon juice
  2 tablespoons flour
  ½ teaspoon ground ginger
  ½ teaspoon freshly grated nutmeg

FOR THE TOPPING:
  1½ cups all-purpose flour
  1½ cups granulated sugar
  1½ cups chopped pecans, *or* walnuts, *or*
    hazelnuts
  1½ sticks (¾ cup) unsalted butter,
    chilled and cut into bits
  1 teaspoon cinnamon
  ¼ teaspoon salt

vanilla ice cream as an accompaniment,
  if desired

Preheat the oven to 375° F.

Make the filling: In a bowl toss the peaches with the remaining ingredients and divide between 2 buttered 11- by 8-inch baking pans.

Make the topping: In a bowl combine all the ingredients until the mixture resembles coarse meal and sprinkle over the filling.

Bake in the middle of the oven for 50 minutes to 1 hour, or until bubbling and golden. Serve warm or at room temperature with the ice cream. Serves 12.

MENU

A SMALL WEDDING LUNCHEON

**POACHED WHOLE SALMON IN ASPIC
WITH DILLED CUCUMBER SAUCE**

STEAMED MUSSELS IN ASPIC

TARAMA-FILLED EGGS

**TURKEY BALLOTTINE
WITH MADEIRA SAUCE**

**BAKED CHERRY TOMATOES
WITH CHIVES**

DUCHESSE POTATOES

**WHITE WEDDING CAKE
WITH STRAWBERRY CREAM FILLING**

SERVES FOURTEEN

We cannot think of a more thoughtful gift for a bride and groom than preparing their wedding luncheon. Truly a labor of love, it also demands precise planning and careful attention to detail. On this very special day, everything must be perfect. Our menu, which includes a stunning array of sophisticated foods, is designed to ensure the conscientious cook glorious success.

This is a luncheon for a small, intimate wedding, when, most probably, the guests will gather in a private home and sit down to the meal after a short cocktail hour. The menu concludes with a traditional wedding cake—a rather small one easily baked and decorated in a home kitchen. Since the génoise cake layers freeze well, we suggest you bake them a week or two beforehand. With this in mind, we suggest the following schedule:

• Bake the génoise cake layers. When they are completely cool, wrap them in plastic wrap and then foil and freeze them.

3 DAYS BEFORE THE WEDDING

Take the cake layers from the freezer and let them thaw overnight in the refrigerator.

• Clean out and rearrange the refrigerator to make ample room for the food that will have to be stored in it. If you have only one refrigerator, consider renting or borrowing space in another.

• Make a shopping list and do the shopping.

• Make the *court bouillon* for the salmon and mussels and refrigerate it.

2 DAYS BEFORE THE WEDDING

• Take the cake layers from the refrigerator and let them finish thawing on the counter. Make the buttercream. Whip the cream. Using a long, serrated knife, slice the layers in half horizontally. This will be easiest to do when the cakes are completely thawed but still cold. Set the layers on cardboard rounds and fill and frost both tiers. Cover and refrigerate. The rounds are available at bakeries, baking supply stores, and some cookware shops. You can also make them yourself.

• Poach the salmon and let it cool in the *court bouillon*. Drain, cover with plastic wrap, and chill.

• Bone the turkey breast (unless the butcher has done it for you; remind him to save the fillets). Make the stuffing.

• Clarify the poaching liquid, but do not add gelatin. Cover and chill.

1 DAY BEFORE THE WEDDING

• Skin the salmon, add the gelatin to the clarified stock, and chill until ready for the first coating. Brush the salmon with its first coat of aspic and decorate with carrots, scallions, and olives. Chill the salmon. Continue to coat salmon as directed.

• Assemble the ballottine and roast it, rolled and wrapped in cheesecloth. When cool, refrigerate.

• Prepare the Madeira sauce but do not thicken. Cool and chill.

• Make the cucumber sauce, cover, and chill.

• Steam the mussels and let them cool. Brush with aspic and chill.

• Hard-cook the eggs.

• Make the potatoes, pipe them onto a baking sheet, drizzle them with melted butter, cover, and refrigerate.

• Wash and trim the cherry tomatoes.

THE MORNING OF THE WEDDING

• Make the *tarama*-filled eggs, cover, and refrigerate. Take the eggs from the refrigerator about 45 minutes before serving and garnish with caviar.

• An hour before lunch, put the turkey in the oven and let it heat for 1 hour. Baste often.

• Heat the Madeira sauce and thicken it with the arrowroot.

• Take the potatoes from the refrigerator and let them come to room temperature.

• Take the cake tiers from the refrigerator. Leave the tiers on their cardboard rounds. Set the larger tier on the serving plate. Set the 7-inch cake tier on the 10-inch tier. Mark the center of the larger tier so as to be sure to place the smaller tier in the right place. Decorate the cake with fresh flowers, marzipan flowers, or fresh strawberries. (Arrange any fresh fruit at the last minute to avoid berry juice bleeding onto buttercream.) Leave the cake in a safe, cool place (not in the refrigerator).

• Serve the salmon, its sauce, and the mussels chilled. Serve the eggs at the same time.

• Cook the cherry tomatoes.

• Preheat the broiler.

• Put the potatoes in the oven to heat.

• Slice and arrange the turkey.

• Brown the potatoes under the broiler.

POACHED WHOLE SALMON
IN ASPIC

6½- to 7-pound salmon, cleaned with
head and tail intact
8 cups *court bouillon* (page 64)
1 cup finely chopped carrot
1 cup well-washed and finely chopped
green of leek
½ cup finely chopped celery
2 tomatoes, chopped
6 large egg whites, beaten lightly
shells of 6 large eggs, crushed
3 tablespoons Sercial Madeira
1 tablespoon salt
cheesecloth bag containing 12 parsley
sprigs, ½ teaspoon dried thyme, and
½ bay leaf
4 tablespoons unflavored gelatin
blanched carrot and scallion strips and
black olives for garnish
dilled cucumber sauce (page 64) as an
accompaniment

MEASURE THE SALMON AT ITS THICKEST POINT TO determine cooking time. Rinse the salmon and center it on a triple thickness of cheesecloth, leaving a 6-inch border at either end. Fold the cheesecloth over the fish to enclose it. Twist the ends gently and tie with string. Put the salmon on the rack of a fish poacher and tie the cheesecloth ends to the rack to secure the fish.

Put the rack in the poacher and add the *court bouillon* and enough water to cover the fish by 1 inch. Bring to a simmer and poach at a bare simmer for 10 minutes per inch of thickness, or until firm. Let the fish cool in the *court bouillon*.

Transfer the fish on the rack to a work surface with the fish head to your left. Untie the ends of the cheesecloth. Transfer the fish to the work surface, lifting by the cheesecloth at each end, and unfold the cheesecloth. Strain 8 cups of the *court bouillon* into a saucepan and reserve it.

With a sharp knife, remove the skin on the top of the fish, leaving the head and tail sections intact. Scrape away the top layer of flesh carefully, especially down the center, to remove the fatty brown

tissue. Using the cheesecloth for leverage, roll the fish over gently. Remove the skin and fatty brown tissue from the underside and with pliers or tweezers pull out the bones along the back. Roll the fish over gently and transfer with spatulas to a large rack set over a jelly-roll pan. Sprinkle with some of the reserved *court bouillon*. Chill, covered loosely.

To the remaining strained *court bouillon*, add the vegetables, egg whites, egg shells, Madeira, salt, and cheesecloth bag and bring the mixture to a boil, whisking. Simmer the mixture, undisturbed, for 30 minutes. Ladle it through a colander lined with a double thickness of rinsed and squeezed cheesecloth into a large bowl.

In a small bowl sprinkle the gelatin over 1 cup of the strained stock and let it soften for 10 minutes. Set the bowl in a bowl of hot water and stir the stock until the gelatin is dissolved. Stir into the remaining stock and let it cool.

Transfer 3 cups of the liquid aspic to a bowl and set the bowl in a bowl of cracked ice. Stir the aspic with a ladle until thickened to the consistency of raw egg white.

Coat the fish with a layer of thickened aspic and chill until set. Dip the carrot and scallion strips in the aspic and arrange them decoratively with the olives on the fish. Chill until set.

Transfer 3 more cups of liquid aspic to the bowl and thicken it in the same manner. Coat the fish with another layer of aspic and chill it until set. Transfer the remaining aspic to a bowl and reserve it, covered and chilled, for coating the steamed mussels in aspic.

The salmon can be made ahead and kept refrigerated, covered loosely with plastic wrap, overnight. Serve with the dilled cucumber sauce. Serves 14 to 16 as a first course.

COURT BOUILLON

8 cups water
2 cups dry white wine
2 cups chopped onion
1 cup chopped celery
1 cup well-washed and chopped leek
½ cup chopped carrot
½ cup chopped fresh parsley leaves
1 tablespoon salt
cheesecloth bag containing 1 teaspoon
    peppercorns, 1 teaspoon dried thyme,
    and 1 bay leaf

+ IN A STAINLESS STEEL OR ENAMELED KETTLE combine all the ingredients and bring to a boil. Simmer for 30 minutes and let it cool. Strain. Makes about 8 cups.

Poached Whole Salmon in Aspic;
Tarama-Filled Eggs; Steamed
Mussels in Aspic

DILLED CUCUMBER SAUCE

2 pounds cucumbers, peeled, seeded,
    and grated
1 tablespoon salt
2 cups sour cream *or* drained plain yogurt
½ cup minced scallion
½ cup heavy cream
2 to 3 tablespoons fresh lemon juice
2 to 3 tablespoons white-wine vinegar
1 cup snipped fresh dill
white pepper to taste

+ IN A COLANDER TOSS THE CUCUMBER WITH THE SALT and let it drain for 30 minutes. Squeeze dry by handfuls in a dish towel. In a food processor purée the cucumber, sour cream, scallion, cream, lemon juice, and vinegar and transfer to a ceramic or glass bowl. Stir in the dill, white pepper, and salt to taste. Chill, covered, for at least 2 hours.

The sauce can be made ahead and kept refrigerated, covered, overnight. Makes about 4 cups.

STEAMED MUSSELS IN ASPIC

24 mussels, cleaned (procedure on page 199)
1 small onion, minced
½ cup dry white wine
cheesecloth bag containing 12 parsley sprigs, ½ teaspoon dried thyme, and ½ bay leaf
2 cups chilled aspic from poached whole salmon in aspic (page 63)

+ IN A KETTLE COMBINE THE MUSSELS, ONION, WINE, and cheesecloth bag and steam, covered, over high heat, shaking the kettle once or twice, for 5 to 6 minutes, or until the shells have opened. (Discard unopened shells.) Let them cool in the liquid.

Drain the mussels and discard the black rims. Arrange the mussels in the shells on a rack set over a jelly-roll pan. Set the bowl of aspic in a pan of hot water and stir until melted. Transfer to a bowl of cracked ice and with a ladle stir until it is the consistency of raw egg white.

Coat each mussel with a layer of aspic and brush the outside of the shells with the remaining aspic. Chill until set.

The mussels can be made ahead and kept refrigerated, covered loosely with plastic wrap, overnight. Makes 24 mussels.

TARAMA-FILLED EGGS
(EGGS WITH CARP ROE FILLING)

8 hard-cooked large eggs
½ stick (¼ cup) unsalted butter, softened
1 tablespoon *tarama* (carp roe, available at specialty food shops and some supermarkets), or to taste
3 tablespoons mayonnaise
2 teaspoons fresh lemon juice, or to taste
1 teaspoon Dijon-style mustard
cayenne to taste
salt and white pepper to taste
salmon caviar for garnish

+ HALVE THE EGGS LENGTHWISE AND REMOVE THE yolks. Arrange the whites on a plate lined with paper towels and chill, covered loosely. In a food processor blend the yolks with the remaining ingredients, except the caviar, transfer them to a bowl, and chill, covered, for at least 1 hour. *The filling can be made ahead and kept refrigerated, covered, overnight.*

Let the filling soften at room temperature for 15 minutes and transfer it to a pastry bag fitted with a decorative tip. Pipe into the whites and garnish with the caviar. Makes 16 filled halves.

TURKEY BALLOTTINE WITH MADEIRA SAUCE

FOR THE STUFFING:
1 pound finely ground veal
¼ pound ground fresh pork fat
3 large eggs
1 cup heavy cream
½ cup minced fresh parsley leaves
¼ teaspoon freshly grated nutmeg, or to taste
salt and freshly ground pepper to taste

6½-pound turkey breast, boned (procedure on page 67)
½ teaspoon dried thyme, crumbled
salt and freshly ground pepper to taste
½ pound sliced baked ham
reserved fillets from boning the breast, halved lengthwise
2 tablespoons unsalted butter
2 tablespoons olive oil
6 cups brown stock (page 197) *or* canned beef broth
cheesecloth bag containing 12 parsley sprigs, 1 teaspoon dried thyme, and 1 bay leaf
2 tablespoons arrowroot
2 tablespoons Sercial Madeira
¼ cup heavy cream

MAKE THE STUFFING: IN A FOOD PROCESSOR BLEND THE veal and fat. With the motor running, add the eggs, 1 at a time, and combine well. With the motor still running, add the heavy cream in a stream. Transfer

Turkey Ballottine,
Duchesse Potatoes

the mixture to a large bowl and add the remaining ingredients. Chill, covered, for at least 30 minutes.

On a double thickness of cheesecloth arrange the turkey breast skin side down with a long side facing you. Sprinkle it with the thyme and salt and pepper to taste. Smooth half the stuffing over the turkey breast, leaving a 1-inch border. Cover the stuffing with a layer of the ham, using slightly more than half. Smooth the remaining stuffing over the ham and arrange the remaining ham slices, with the short ends facing you, on the turkey breast.

Center the turkey fillets lengthwise on the ham and fold the ham over them. Beginning with the long side of the breast nearest you, roll it carefully away from you into a cylinder. Fold the cheesecloth over to enclose it and twist the ends, maintaining the cylinder shape. Tie the ends securely with string.

Preheat the oven to 350° F.

In a roasting pan heat the butter and oil over moderate heat until hot and in it brown the turkey, patted dry. Add the stock and cheesecloth bag and bring the mixture to a boil. Braise the ballottine, covered tightly with foil, in the middle of the oven, basting occasionally, for 1½ hours, or until the juices run clear when the breast is pricked with a skewer.

The ballottine can be made 1 day ahead up to this point and kept refrigerated, covered, in the cooking liquid. To reheat, bring to a boil over moderately high heat, baste, and heat, covered, in a preheated 350° F. oven, basting frequently, for 1 hour.

Transfer the ballottine to a rack to cool. Unwrap it. Skim the braising liquid and strain it into a saucepan. In a small bowl combine the arrowroot, Madeira, and cream.

Bring the strained liquid to a boil and stir in the arrowroot mixture. Cook the mixture over moderately high heat until it is thickened slightly. Keep the sauce warm, covered with a buttered round of wax paper.

Transfer the ballottine to a carving board and slice half of it into ½-inch slices. Transfer the slices and remaining ballottine to a platter and serve warm with the sauce. Serves 14.

TO BONE A TURKEY BREAST

◖ WITH A SHARP KNIFE AND YOUR FINGERS, CUT and pull the wishbone from the turkey breast. Turn skin side down and, starting at the severed backbone and working toward the ridge of the breastbone, cut the breast meat of half the breast away from the carcass, keeping the knife angled against the bones and pulling the meat away as it is cut.

Turn so the other side of the backbone is facing you and cut away the meat in the same manner. With the knife angled against the breastbone, sever the meat completely and discard the carcass.

Lay the breast skin side down. Remove the fillets, trim off any tendons and sinews, and reserve. Cut the breast to a uniform 1-inch thickness by slicing horizontally into the thicker sections. Use some of the trimmings to patch any areas where there is little or no meat.

Cover the breast with moistened wax paper and with a mallet or the flat side of a cleaver pound to flatten slightly.

BAKED CHERRY TOMATOES WITH CHIVES

3 pints cherry tomatoes
3 tablespoons unsalted butter, melted
salt and freshly ground pepper to taste
¼ cup snipped fresh chives

◖ PREHEAT THE OVEN TO 350° F.

Arrange the tomatoes in a well-buttered gratin dish and toss with the butter, salt, and pepper. Bake in the middle of the oven for 20 to 25 minutes, or until hot but not blistered. Toss the tomatoes with the chives. Serves 14.

DUCHESSE POTATOES

5 pounds russet or other baking potatoes
¾ stick (6 tablespoons) unsalted butter,
  softened
4 large whole eggs
2 large egg yolks
1 cup half-and-half
freshly grated nutmeg to taste
salt and white pepper to taste
melted unsalted butter for drizzling

PREHEAT THE OVEN TO 400° F.

Bake the potatoes in the oven for 1 hour, or until tender. Halve them lengthwise and scrape the pulp into a bowl. Press the pulp through a ricer into a large bowl.

Reduce the heat to 350° F.

With an electric mixer beat in the softened butter, 1 tablespoon at a time, the eggs and yolks, 1 at a time, and the half-and-half. Beat until smooth and add the nutmeg, salt, and white pepper. Transfer the mixture to a pastry bag fitted with a large decorative tip. On a buttered baking sheet pipe into 14 large rosettes and drizzle them with the melted butter. *The rosettes can be made 1 day ahead and kept refrigerated, covered loosely.*

Bake the rosettes in the middle of the oven for 10 to 15 minutes if the potatoes are at room temperature or for 25 to 30 minutes if chilled, or until heated through. Put them under the broiler about 6 inches from the heat until the tops are golden. Serve on the platter with the ballottine. Serves 14.

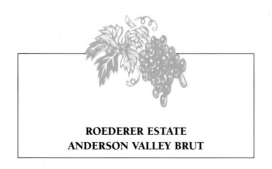

ROEDERER ESTATE
ANDERSON VALLEY BRUT

WHITE WEDDING CAKE WITH STRAWBERRY CREAM FILLING

FOR THE GÉNOISE:
  9 large eggs
  1½ cups granulated sugar
  1½ cups all-purpose flour
  1 teaspoon salt
  2¼ teaspoons vanilla
  9 tablespoons clarified butter
    (procedure follows)

  1½ pints strawberries, sliced
  ½ cup plus 2 tablespoons granulated
    sugar
  ½ cup water
  1 to 2 tablespoons vanilla *or* kirsch,
    or to taste
  1½ cups well-chilled heavy cream
  2 tablespoons confectioners' sugar,
    or to taste
  vanilla buttercream (recipe follows)

PREHEAT THE OVEN TO 350° F.

Butter a round 10-inch cake pan and a round 7-inch cake pan, both pans 2 inches deep. Line the bottoms with wax paper and butter the paper. Dust the pans with flour and knock out the excess.

Make the *génoise:* In a metal bowl whisk the eggs and sugar. Set the bowl in a pan of simmering water and stir until warm and the sugar is dissolved. Remove the bowl from the pan and beat with an electric mixer at moderate speed for 10 to 15 minutes, or until cooled and triple in volume.

While the eggs are being beaten, sift together the flour and salt onto a sheet of wax paper. In a bowl combine the vanilla and clarified butter. Sift and fold the flour mixture in batches into the egg mixture until just combined. Stir one-fourth of this mixture into the butter mixture and then fold the butter mixture quickly into the batter.

Pour the batter into the pans, smoothing the tops, and bake in the middle of the oven for 20 to 25 minutes, or until golden and a tester inserted in the centers comes out clean. Let the layers cool in the pans on a rack for 5 minutes. Invert the layers onto the racks, remove the paper carefully, and let them cool completely.

The layers can be made 1 day ahead and kept at room temperature, wrapped in plastic wrap. Or they can be frozen for up to 1 week, wrapped in plastic wrap. Let them thaw in the refrigerator.

In a bowl let the sliced strawberries macerate in 2 tablespoons of the granulated sugar for 30 minutes.

In a small heavy saucepan bring the water and remaining ½ cup granulated sugar to a boil and simmer until the syrup is clear. Let it cool. Drain the juices from the strawberries and add the juices with the vanilla to the syrup. Have ready 2 cardboard rounds (available at specialty food shops), one 9 inches in diameter and one 6 inches in diameter.

In a chilled bowl beat the cream with the confectioners' sugar until it holds soft peaks. Fold in the strawberries.

Put 1 teaspoon of the buttercream in the center of the 9-inch cardboard round and top it with the 10-inch cake layer. Halve the layer horizontally with a serrated knife and brush the cut sides of both halves with some of the syrup. Spread the bottom half with two-thirds of the whipped cream filling. Top it with the remaining half, cut side down, and sprinkle the layer with some more of the syrup.

Prepare the 7-inch cake layer separately in the same manner, using the 6-inch cardboard round and the remaining whipped cream filling. Spread the top and sides of both layers with the remaining buttercream and chill separately for at least 2 hours, or until firm. *The cake layers can be made 1 day ahead up to this point and kept refrigerated in separate airtight cake containers.*

Arrange the 10-inch layer on a platter. Position the 7-inch layer with the cardboard base on top and place fresh flowers decoratively around the base or cascading down the sides.

TO CLARIFY BUTTER

unsalted butter, cut into 1-inch pieces

 IN A HEAVY SAUCEPAN MELT THE BUTTER OVER LOW heat. Remove the saucepan from the heat and let it stand for 3 minutes. Skim the froth and discard it. Strain the butter through a sieve lined with a double thickness of rinsed and squeezed cheesecloth into a bowl, leaving the milky solids in the bottom of the pan.

Pour the clarified butter into a jar or crock and store, covered, in the refrigerator. The butter keeps indefinitely, covered and chilled. When clarified, butter loses about one fourth of its original volume.

VANILLA BUTTERCREAM

1½ cups sugar
½ cup water
7 large egg whites
pinch of salt
⅛ teaspoon cream of tartar
5 sticks (2½ cups) unsalted butter, softened
2 to 3 tablespoons vanilla *or* kirsch, or to taste

+ IN A SMALL, HEAVY SAUCEPAN BRING THE SUGAR AND water to a boil and boil over moderate heat, stirring and washing down any sugar crystals clinging to the sides with a brush dipped in cold water until the syrup reaches the hard-ball stage, or a candy thermometer registers 248° F.

In a large bowl beat the egg whites and salt with an electric mixer until frothy. Add the cream of tartar and beat until the whites hold stiff peaks. With the mixer running, add the hot syrup in a stream and beat the mixture until completely cool. Beat in the butter, a little at a time, and add the vanilla. Chill, covered, until firm but still soft enough to spread.

Strawberry Kiwi Bowl,
Palmiers

MENU

**CHILLED PEA
AND WATERCRESS SOUP**

**TARRAGON-ROASTED
ROCK CORNISH GAME HENS**

LEMON ASPARAGUS

GLAZED BABY CARROTS

NEW POTATOES WITH SHALLOT

**COMPOSED SALAD
WITH CHIVE DRESSING**

CHEESES AND FRENCH BREAD

STRAWBERRY KIWI BOWL

PALMIERS

SERVES SIX

After the hats have been tossed high into the Summer sky, the diplomas proudly displayed, and enough photos snapped to satisfy Grandma, you will want to return home and fête the proud graduate with a Kir Royale toast and a simple yet dignified meal that befits his or her new status in life. We have assembled a menu that celebrates the familiar, yet somehow always new, flavors of the garden, just as graduation day symbolizes the division between the recognized and the still-to-come.

As all good students learn early in their academic careers, it is a good idea to be prepared. The pea and watercress soup is one that begs for early attention, as early as a day before serving. Try for fresh peas if at all possible. Tiny green peas are a glory of the season and ought not to be missed.

The Rock Cornish game hens are easily prepared several hours ahead of time, up to trussing and arranging in the baking dish. Keep them in the refrigerator until roasting time and then drizzle the melted butter over them just before their quick 45-minute stint in the oven.

As helpful as it is to be prepared, there's nary a student who has not left many a task until the last minute. We have done the same with our vegetables. All three are quickly and simply cooked—no fancy seasonings or sauces to disguise the honest young flavors.

Our dessert follows the theme of the familiar and the new. We offer a fruit bowl of strawberries, everyone's June favorite, and kiwi, a somewhat newer addition to the American fruit table. Because kiwis are now grown in California, the domestic crop dovetails nicely with the imported one (mostly from New Zealand) so that these fruits are available all year long. For the best flavor, buy them when they are still firm and let them ripen on the kitchen counter for several days. When they are slightly soft, similar to a ready-to-eat plum or an almost-ready peach, peel and cut them.

The fruit is accompanied by sugary *palmiers*, little pennant-shaped cookies of buttery goodness. These are made with a quick version of classic puff pastry, a dough you can make up to a month before the party and freeze. Traditional puff pastry takes hours to make, requiring 6 rollings and foldings, called turns, with several hours of chilling between them. Our pastry may not puff to the same flaky heights, but for these purposes it is absolutely delicious and appropriate. Consider it as a crash course in puff pastry; someday when you have time, go back and try the "real" thing.

KIR ROYALES
(for the toast)

MOULIN-À-VENT '89
(for the buffet)

KIR ROYALE

3 ice cubes
2 tablespoons crème de cassis
chilled Champagne
twist of lemon peel for garnish

 IN A CHILLED CHAMPAGNE GLASS OR GOBLET COMBINE the ice cubes and crème de cassis. Fill the glass with Champagne and garnish with the lemon twist. Makes 1 drink.

CHILLED PEA AND WATERCRESS SOUP

1 cup sliced scallion
2 tablespoons unsalted butter
3 cups hot chicken broth
2½ cups fresh peas (about
    2½ pounds unshelled)
1 teaspoon dried chervil, crumbled
1 teaspoon salt
½ teaspoon sugar
white pepper to taste
1 bunch of watercress, rinsed well, tough
    stems removed, and chopped coarse
½ cup heavy cream

+ IN A LARGE SAUCEPAN COOK THE SCALLION IN THE butter over moderate heat for 3 minutes, or until softened. Add the broth, peas, and seasonings and simmer, covered, for 20 minutes, or until the peas are very tender. Reserve 2 tablespoons of the peas for garnish.

Add the watercress and simmer the mixture for 5 minutes. In a food processor blend the mixture in batches for 10 seconds and purée it through a food mill or coarse sieve into a bowl. Let it cool.

Stir in the cream and chill the soup, covered, for at least 2 hours. Garnish with the reserved peas. Serves 6.

TARRAGON-ROASTED ROCK CORNISH GAME HENS

**6 Rock Cornish game hens, each
  1 pound
1 stick (½ cup) unsalted butter, softened
¼ cup minced shallot
¼ cup minced fresh parsley leaves
2 tablespoons fresh lemon juice
1 tablespoon dried tarragon, crumbled
1 teaspoon salt
½ teaspoon freshly ground pepper**

PREHEAT THE OVEN TO 400° F.

Loosen the skin of the Rock Cornish game hens by slipping the fingers between the skin and flesh, beginning at the top of the breast, working down as far as possible on the legs, and leaving the wings intact.

In a bowl cream ¾ stick of the butter with the remaining ingredients and divide the mixture among the hens, inserting it evenly under the skin and patting the skin to smooth the butter into a uniform layer. Truss the hens and arrange them on their sides in a well-buttered roasting pan. Melt the remaining 2 tablespoons butter and brush it over the hens.

Roast the hens in the middle of the oven for 10 minutes. Baste and turn them to the other side. Roast for 10 minutes more and baste again. Reduce the heat to 350° F. and turn the hens breast side up. Roast, basting twice, for 25 minutes more, or until the juices run clear when the fleshy part of a thigh is pricked with a skewer. Remove the trussing strings and arrange the hens on a heated serving platter. Serves 6.

LEMON ASPARAGUS

**2 pounds asparagus, peeled
2 tablespoons unsalted butter
3 tablespoons fresh lemon juice
salt and freshly ground pepper to taste**

TRIM THE ASPARAGUS STALKS TO THE SAME LENGTH and tie them with string in bunches of 10 to 12. In a kettle cook them in boiling salted water to cover for 8 to 10 minutes, or until tender but not limp. Transfer them by the string to a colander and drain tips up. Remove the strings.

In a large skillet melt the butter with the lemon juice and salt and pepper over moderate heat and add the asparagus. Turn to coat well. Serves 6.

GLAZED BABY CARROTS

**1½ pounds baby carrots, trimmed and
  peeled
2 tablespoons unsalted butter
1 tablespoon sugar
freshly grated nutmeg to taste
salt and freshly ground pepper to taste**

IN A KETTLE COOK THE CARROTS IN BOILING SALTED water to cover for 10 minutes, or until tender. Drain. In a skillet melt the butter over moderately high heat and stir in the sugar, nutmeg, and salt and pepper. Add the carrots and cook over moderate heat, shaking the pan, for 5 minutes, or until they are shiny. Serves 6.

NEW POTATOES WITH SHALLOT

2 pounds very small new potatoes
⅓ cup minced shallot
1 tablespoon unsalted butter, melted
salt and freshly ground pepper to taste

⊙ WITH A LEMON ZESTER PEEL THIN STRIPS OF SKIN around the length and around the width of each potato. In a kettle cook them in boiling salted water to cover for 20 minutes, or until tender. Drain.

In a large skillet cook the shallot in the butter over moderate heat until softened. Add the potatoes and salt and pepper and toss well. Serves 6.

COMPOSED SALAD WITH CHIVE DRESSING

3 oranges, peeled and cut into
¼-inch slices
1½ cups thinly sliced radish
1¼ cups chive dressing (recipe follows)
4 Belgian endives, trimmed and
separated into leaves
3 heads Bibb lettuce, separated into
leaves
3 California avocados, peeled, pitted, and
cut into ½-inch cubes

⊙ ARRANGE THE ORANGE SLICES IN 1 CORNER OF A LARGE serving plate. In a bowl toss the radish with ¼ cup of the dressing and arrange opposite the oranges. Toss the endive with ¼ cup of the dressing and arrange between the oranges and radish on 1 side of the plate. Toss the lettuce with ½ cup of the dressing and arrange opposite the endive. Toss the avocados with the remaining ¼ cup dressing and mound in the center. Serves 6.

Cheeses; French Bread; Composed Salad with Chive Dressing

CHIVE DRESSING

3 tablespoons fresh lemon juice
3 tablespoons white-wine vinegar
1 teaspoon Dijon-style mustard
salt and white pepper to taste
¾ to 1 cup extra-virgin olive oil,
    or to taste
2 tablespoons snipped fresh chives

IN A BOWL COMBINE THE LEMON JUICE, VINEGAR, mustard, salt, and white pepper and add the oil in a stream, whisking. Whisk until emulsified and stir in the chives. Makes 1½ cups.

STRAWBERRY KIWI BOWL

4 cups strawberries
8 kiwis, peeled and cut into ¼-inch slices

+ IN A LARGE SERVING BOWL COMBINE THE FRUITS, toss gently, and chill, covered, for 1 hour. Serves 6.

PALMIERS

sugar for sprinkling
quick puff paste (recipe follows)

SPRINKLE THE WORK SURFACE GENEROUSLY WITH sugar. Roll the dough into a strip 5½ inches wide and ¼ inch thick. Fold over the long sides to meet in the center and sprinkle with sugar. Fold in half lengthwise to form a long 4-layered band about 1½ inches wide. Chill the dough, wrapped in plastic wrap, for 20 minutes.

Preheat the oven to 425° F.

Cut the dough crosswise into strips ½ inch wide. Put cut side down about 2½ inches apart on an ungreased baking sheet and spread open the bottom ½ inch of each strip to form an inverted V. Bake in the middle of the oven for 10 minutes, or until the bottoms are caramelized. Turn, sprinkle with sugar, and bake for 10 minutes more. Transfer the palmiers with a spatula to racks to cool. Makes about 20 palmiers.

QUICK PUFF PASTE

2 cups all-purpose flour
½ teaspoon salt
2 sticks (1 cup) unsalted butter, chilled
    and cut into bits
½ cup ice water

SIFT TOGETHER THE FLOUR AND SALT. IN A FOOD processor blend the flour mixture and butter for 5 seconds. Sprinkle with the water and process with on/off pulses until it resembles very coarse meal and the butter is the size of lima beans. Transfer the dough to a sheet of plastic wrap and form into a ball. Chill it for 1 hour.

On a floured surface roll the dough into a 12- by 6-inch rectangle, dusting with flour if necessary to prevent sticking. Fold the top third over the center and the bottom third over the top to form a 6- by 4-inch rectangle. Press down the top edge with the rolling pin so it adheres and turn seam side down. Brush off any excess flour.

With an open side facing you, roll out the dough again into a 12- by 6-inch rectangle and fold in thirds as before. This completes 2 "turns." Make 2 more turns, always starting with the seam side down and an open end facing you. Chill the dough, wrapped in plastic wrap, for at least 30 minutes or for up to 3 days.

The dough can be made 1 month ahead and frozen, wrapped in plastic wrap and foil. Makes 1¼ pounds.

COOKING OUT ON THE FOURTH

**CHILLED CORN CHOWDER
WITH CORIANDER**

**HICKORY-GRILLED
GINGERED SWORDFISH**

**TWO-RICE SALAD WITH
TOASTED PECANS**

**SAUTÉED CHERRY TOMATOES AND
SUGAR SNAP PEAS**

**NECTARINES POACHED IN
WHITE ZINFANDEL**

SERVES SIX

Just about the time the sun begins to wane, you should think about lighting the charcoal fire. Toss a few handfuls of hickory chips into a bucket of water and let them soak as the coals turn from inky black to ashy gray. Later, when the fire is hot and ready for the fish, scatter the wet chips over the coals; their aromatic smoke will swirl around the fish, infusing it with an indescribably delicate flavor that renders it a fitting centerpiece for a Summer cookout.

This is a simple, intentionally light meal, easily assembled between kitchen and patio. It offers a few close friends the opportunity to celebrate a midsummer holiday with a casual supper that takes advantage of Summer's bright, bold flavors and places little or no reliance on the more expected "Summer" foods, such as mayonnaise-dressed potato salads and cream-based soups.

If possible, use fresh corn for the chowder—a zesty chilled soup that marries cumin with coriander and is thickened with a last-minute addition of yogurt. Make the corn soup the day before the party, or in the cool of the morning when you assemble the rice salad and poach the nectarines for dessert.

Follow the soup with swordfish steaks marinated in a gingery brew. Be careful not to over-marinate the fish—preferably for only 2 or 3 hours—

otherwise, when cooked, it may be spongy. Cook the fish over the hot, smoky fire, turning it only once and testing for doneness by poking the flesh with your fingertip after 6 or 7 minutes; it should feel firm. Lift the steaks from the grill at this point and serve them at once. While the fish grills, quickly sauté the tomatoes and sweet sugar snap peas in gently sputtering butter until just heated through but still crisp.

End the meal with sliced poached nectarines bathed in a simple sugar syrup fortified with lemon juice, sweet wine, and a hint of vanilla. By now the shadows will have darkened and somewhere, over the ridge or down the road, perhaps, the sky will fill with a blazing display of sparkling fireworks. Ahh, Summer.

CHILLED CORN CHOWDER WITH CORIANDER

1 cup minced onion
½ cup finely chopped red bell pepper
⅓ cup diced celery
salt and freshly ground pepper to taste
2 tablespoons vegetable oil
3 cups cooked fresh corn (about 5 to 6
    ears), or 1½ packages frozen corn, each
    10 ounces, thawed
2 garlic cloves, minced
2 tablespoons flour
1½ teaspoons ground toasted cuminseed
    (page 199)
1 bay leaf
4 cups chicken stock (page 198) or
    canned chicken broth
cayenne to taste
1 cup plain yogurt
3 tablespoons minced fresh coriander
    leaves

+ IN A SAUCEPAN COOK THE ONION, RED PEPPER, celery, and salt and pepper in the oil over moderate heat, stirring, until the onion is softened. Add the corn and garlic and cook the mixture, stirring, for 2

minutes. Add the flour, cuminseed, and bay leaf and continue to cook, stirring, for 1 minute.

Add the stock and bring the mixture to a boil, stirring. Add the cayenne and salt and pepper to taste and simmer the soup, covered, for 25 minutes. Let it cool and chill the soup, covered, for at least 2 hours. *The soup can be made ahead up to this point and kept refrigerated, covered, overnight.*

Remove the bay leaf and skim any fat from the surface. Stir in the yogurt, coriander, and salt to taste. Serves 6.

MICROWAVE DIRECTIONS

INGREDIENT CHANGES:

Use 3 cups fresh or thawed frozen corn; use 2 cans (about 14 ounces each) chicken broth; use ⅛ teaspoon cayenne.

DIRECTIONS:

Combine the onion, red pepper, celery, and garlic in a microwave-safe 3½-quart casserole; stir in the oil. Cover and microwave the mixture at high power (100%) for 3 minutes. Stir in the cuminseed and bay leaf. Microwave, uncovered, at high power (100%) for 5 minutes. Whisk in the flour until smooth. Add 1 can of the chicken broth; whisk again. Stir in the corn and cayenne. Cover and microwave at high power (100%) for 10 minutes until boiling. Remove the casserole from the oven; whisk in the yogurt and the remaining 1 can chicken broth. Season to taste with salt and pepper. Cover and chill as directed. Stir in the fresh coriander leaves before serving.

HICKORY-GRILLED
GINGERED SWORDFISH

1 tablespoon minced gingerroot
2 garlic cloves, minced
3 tablespoons fresh lemon juice
2 tablespoons vegetable oil
1 bay leaf, crumbled
salt and freshly ground pepper to taste
6 swordfish steaks, each about 6 ounces
and 1 inch thick
4 cups hickory chips, soaked in water for
20 minutes

+ IN A BOWL COMBINE THE GINGERROOT, GARLIC, lemon juice, oil, bay leaf, and salt and pepper. Arrange the swordfish steaks in a shallow glass baking dish and spoon the marinade over them. Let the fish marinate, covered and chilled, turning once, for 1 hour. *The swordfish can be prepared 3 hours ahead up to this point and kept refrigerated, covered.*

Prepare a charcoal grill and add the chips when the coals are ready.

Grill the steaks 4 inches above the coals for 3 to 4 minutes on each side, or until firm to the touch. Serves 6.

TWO-RICE SALAD WITH
TOASTED PECANS

1 cup wild rice, rinsed well
1 cup brown rice, rinsed well
4 tablespoons vegetable oil
6 ounces mushrooms, sliced
1 garlic clove, minced
½ cup minced scallion
¼ cup minced fresh parsley leaves
2 tablespoons walnut oil (available at
specialty food shops)
2 tablespoons fresh lemon juice
2 tablespoons red-wine vinegar
salt and freshly ground pepper to taste
⅓ cup pecan halves, toasted and broken
into large pieces

INTO A KETTLE OF BOILING SALTED WATER SPRINKLE THE wild rice, stirring, and boil for 15 minutes. Sprinkle in the brown rice, stirring, and boil for 15 minutes. Drain the rice mixture in a large colander and rinse under cold water. Set the colander over a pan of boiling water and steam the rice, covered with a dish towel and the lid, for 15 to 20 minutes, or until it is fluffy and dry. Transfer to a large bowl.

In a skillet heat 1 tablespoon of the vegetable oil over moderately high heat until hot. Add the mushrooms and cook, stirring, until the liquid is evaporated. Add the garlic and cook, stirring, for 1 minute. In a large bowl combine the rice, mushroom mixture, scallion, and parsley. *The salad can be made 6 hours ahead up to this point and kept refrigerated, covered.*

In a small bowl whisk the remaining 3 tablespoons vegetable oil, walnut oil, lemon juice, vinegar, and salt and pepper. Add the dressing and pecans to the salad and toss well. Serves 6.

MICROWAVE DIRECTIONS

INGREDIENT CHANGES:
Use 5½ cups hot (tap) water; add 1 teaspoon salt.

DIRECTIONS:
Stir together the mushrooms, garlic, and 1 tablespoon vegetable oil in a microwave-safe 3-quart casserole. Microwave, uncovered, at high power (100%) for 3 minutes. Transfer the mixture to a small bowl; reserve. Pour the 5½ cups water into same casserole; stir in the 1 teaspoon salt. Cover with the lid and microwave at high power (100%) for 5 to 6 minutes, until boiling. Stir in the wild rice. Cover and microwave at medium power (50%) for 10 minutes. Stir in the brown rice. Cover and microwave at medium power (50%) for 30 minutes. Let the rice stand, covered, 10 minutes. Stir in the mushroom mixture, scallion, and parsley. Make the dressing and dress the salad as directed.

SAUTÉED CHERRY TOMATOES
AND SUGAR SNAP PEAS

**1 pound sugar snap peas *or* snow peas,
 strings removed**
2 tablespoons unsalted butter
2 shallots, minced
1 pint cherry tomatoes
salt and freshly ground pepper to taste
**3 tablespoons snipped fresh chives, *or*
 minced fresh basil, *or* parsley leaves**

IN A SAUCEPAN OF BOILING SALTED WATER BLANCH THE
sugar snap peas for 30 seconds, or until crisp-
tender. Drain and refresh them under cold water.

In a skillet heat the butter over moderate
heat until hot but not smoking. Add the shallots
and cook, stirring, until softened. Add the peas, tomatoes, and salt and pepper and cook, stirring, until heated through. Stir in the chives. Serves 6.

NECTARINES POACHED
IN WHITE ZINFANDEL

½ cup sugar
½ cup water
1 strip of lemon rind, 2½ inches long
2 tablespoons fresh lemon juice
1 vanilla bean, split
2½ cups white Zinfandel
**6 ripe but firm nectarines (about
 2 pounds)**

+ IN A SAUCEPAN COOK THE SUGAR AND WATER OVER
moderate heat, stirring, until the sugar is dissolved.
Add the remaining ingredients and bring the mixture to a boil. Simmer, covered with a round of wax
paper and the lid, turning the nectarines once, for 6
to 8 minutes, or until just tender. Let the nectarines
cool in the liquid.

Remove the nectarines with a slotted spoon
to a bowl. Peel and slice them. Boil the poaching
liquid over moderately high heat until reduced to 2

cups and pour it over the nectarines. Chill, covered, for at least 2 hours.

*The dessert can be made ahead and kept re-
frigerated, covered, overnight.* Serves 6.

MICROWAVE DIRECTIONS

INGREDIENT CHANGES:
Omit the water; select 6 nectarines to weigh
2¼ pounds total.

DIRECTIONS:
Combine the sugar, lemon rind, lemon juice, vanilla bean, and Zinfandel in a microwave-safe 6-cup
measure. Cover with microwave-safe plastic wrap
vented at one edge and microwave at high power
(100%) for 5 minutes. Uncover and microwave 2
minutes longer. Prick the nectarines once with the
tines of fork; place them in a microwave-safe 8- or
9-inch square baking dish. Pour in the poaching
liquid. Cover with microwave-safe plastic wrap
vented at one edge and microwave at high power
(100%) for 5 minutes. Turn the nectarines over
and rearrange them. Cover again and microwave 4
to 6 minutes longer, until the nectarines are barely
tender. Let the nectarines cool in the liquid. Continue with the recipe as directed.

**CHARLES F. SHAW NAPA VALLEY
GAMAY BEAUJOLAIS '89**

Cornmeal Puffs; Smoked Salmon Cream;
Clams Steamed on the Grill

MENU

INDEPENDENCE DAY BUFFET

**SMOKED SALMON CREAM WITH
CORNMEAL PUFFS**

CLAMS STEAMED ON THE GRILL

**ORANGE-FLAVORED CHICKEN BREASTS
WITH BACON**

VEGETABLE BROCHETTES

CREAMED CORN AND LIMA BEANS

RADICCHIO AND LAMB'S-LETTUCE SALAD

RED, WHITE, AND BLUEBERRY MOLD

SERVES TWELVE

A small buffet supper, quietly refined but with a splash of Summer's informality, is a surefire way to entertain in warm weather. We have put together a party for twelve that takes full advantage of the season, combining the best that the markets, greengrocers, and home gardens have to offer. Along with the cornmeal puffs and salmon cream (the latter easily mixed in a food processor the day before the party; the former baked shortly before serving but ever so easy to mix) are steamed clams. No need to worry about steaming baskets and teetering pots of hot water. Simply wrap the clams and a few well-chosen herbs in foil and set the packets on the grill. A scant 10 minutes later, the clams are ready to eat. To save time, you can assemble the packets before-hand and stack them in the refrigerator.

While the grill is hot, lay skewers threaded with squash, onions, peppers, and mushrooms, all marinated for several hours, on the grill. These take about 20 minutes to cook and so must be timed to coincide with the chicken, which takes only minutes less.

Although the chicken, too, marinates for several hours, preparing it for grilling takes more tending than the vegetables. Likewise, the brown sauce can be made 1 month ahead but it takes time to cook, so allow time for this. The chicken can be cooked under a broiler if grilling space is at a premium or you may opt to use two grills. If grilling, it is a good idea to have extra coals on hand to supplement the fire and keep it hot. Place the extra coals around the rim of the hot fire, waiting to incorporate them for 10 or 15 minutes, until they have started to ash over and noxious gases have had time to burn off.

When your guests have had their fill of salmon and clams, set the grilled chicken and grilled brochettes on the table. Side by side with these are a dish of creamed corn and lima beans and a colorful tossed salad of tender greens.

For the dessert, we suggest taking out your ice cream freezer several days before the party to make two sherbets and an ice cream for our red, white, and blueberry mold. It's certainly worth the time and effort!

SMOKED SALMON CREAM

FOR THE POACHING LIQUID:
½ cup chopped onion
¼ cup chopped carrot
¼ cup chopped celery
2 tablespoons unsalted butter
cheesecloth bag containing 6 parsley sprigs, 6 peppercorns, ½ teaspoon dried thyme, and ½ bay leaf
½ cup dry white wine
3 cups water
salt to taste

1 pound fresh salmon fillets
½ pound smoked salmon, cut into 1-inch pieces
8 ounces cream cheese, softened and cut into bits
1 cup sour cream
1 onion, grated, if desired
freshly grated nutmeg to taste
salt and white pepper to taste
cornmeal puffs (recipe follows) as an accompaniment

MAKE THE POACHING LIQUID: IN A STAINLESS STEEL pan cook the vegetables in the butter over moderate heat, stirring, until softened. Add the remaining ingredients and simmer for 20 minutes. Let the mixture cool. Strain it into a bowl.

In a stainless steel or enameled saucepan arrange the fresh salmon and add enough of the poaching liquid to just cover it. Bring the liquid to a boil and poach the salmon at a bare simmer for 7 to 10 minutes, or until it just flakes when tested with a fork. Let it cool in the liquid. *The salmon can be prepared ahead up to this point and kept refrigerated, covered, overnight.*

Drain the salmon and remove the skin and any bones. Flake the fish. In a food processor blend it with the smoked salmon until combined. With the motor running, add the cream cheese, a little at a time, and sour cream and blend until smooth. Add the onion, nutmeg, and salt and white pepper to taste and blend until just combined. Transfer to a bowl and chill, covered.

The spread can be made ahead and kept refrigerated, covered, overnight. Let it stand at room temperature for 30 minutes before serving with the cornmeal puffs. Makes about 4 cups.

CORNMEAL PUFFS

1½ cups yellow cornmeal, preferably stone-ground
1 cup all-purpose flour
2 teaspoons baking powder
1½ teaspoons salt
¼ teaspoon cayenne
1 cup milk
2 large eggs, separated
¾ stick (6 tablespoons) unsalted butter, melted and cooled
pinch of cream of tartar

⊙ PREHEAT THE OVEN TO 425° F.

Into a bowl sift the cornmeal, flour, baking powder, salt, and cayenne. In another bowl combine the milk, egg yolks, and butter. Add the cornmeal mixture and stir until just combined.

Heat 36 greased gem tins (2 tablespoons each in size) in the oven for 3 minutes.

In a bowl beat the egg whites until foamy. Add the cream of tartar and a pinch of salt and beat until the whites hold stiff peaks. Fold into the batter. Spoon 1 heaping tablespoon into each gem tin. Bake in the middle of the oven for 12 to 15 minutes, or until golden. Invert the puffs onto racks and serve warm. Makes 36 puffs.

CLAMS STEAMED ON THE GRILL

72 small hard-shell clams, scrubbed
1½ cups minced scallion
1 stick plus 2 tablespoons (10
    tablespoons) unsalted butter, softened
⅓ cup minced fresh parsley leaves
4 garlic cloves, minced, or to taste
fresh lemon juice to taste
freshly ground pepper to taste

☾ PREPARE A CHARCOAL GRILL.

Arrange the clams in batches of 6 on pieces of heavy-duty foil large enough to enclose them tightly. Sprinkle with the scallion.

In a bowl combine the remaining ingredients and divide among the clams. Seal the foil packets tightly and steam them on the grill, shaking occasionally, for 7 to 10 minutes, or until the clams have just opened. Discard unopened clams. Serve immediately. Serves 12.

ORANGE-FLAVORED CHICKEN BREASTS WITH BACON

FOR THE MARINADE:
1 large onion, minced
⅓ cup fresh orange juice
grated zest of 1 orange
⅓ cup fresh lemon juice
4 tablespoons soy sauce
3 tablespoons white-wine vinegar
3 tablespoons honey
1½ tablespoons minced gingerroot
1½ tablespoons Dijon-style mustard
3 garlic cloves, minced
salt to taste

6 whole unskinned boneless chicken
    breasts, halved
3 cups brown sauce (page 197)
3 tablespoons cornstarch
3 tablespoons dry Sherry
1½ teaspoons Dijon-style mustard
1½ teaspoons brown sugar
salt and freshly ground pepper to taste

⅓ cup minced fresh coriander leaves
⅓ cup finely minced shallot
12 thick slices of bacon

MAKE THE MARINADE: IN A SHALLOW GLASS DISH JUST large enough to hold the chicken in one layer combine all the ingredients. Add the chicken and spoon the marinade over it. Let it marinate, covered, turning once, at room temperature for 2 hours. *The chicken can be prepared ahead up to this point and kept refrigerated, covered, overnight.*

Transfer the chicken to a plate. Transfer the marinade to a stainless steel pan and stir in the brown sauce. Bring to a boil and simmer, stirring occasionally, for 15 minutes. In a bowl combine the cornstarch and Sherry.

Return the sauce to a boil. Stir the cornstarch mixture and add it to the sauce in a stream, whisking. Whisk in the mustard, sugar, salt, and pepper and simmer for 1 minute, or until thickened slightly. Strain through a fine sieve into a small stainless steel pan and keep warm, covered with buttered wax paper.

Prepare a charcoal grill and lightly oil it.

In a small bowl combine the coriander and shallot. Pat the chicken dry and turn skin side down. Make a horizontal slit lengthwise along the thick side of each breast, beginning 1 inch from the top and ending 1 inch from the bottom, to form a pocket. Divide the coriander mixture among the pockets and add salt and pepper to taste. Pat the breasts back into shape. Wrap each breast with 1 slice of bacon and secure with wooden picks.

Grill the chicken, turning frequently, for 12 minutes, or until the bacon is crisp. Remove the bacon and reserve it. Grill the chicken skin side down until crisp, golden, and springy to the touch.

Or broil the chicken on a lightly oiled broiler pan about 4 inches from the heat for 5 to 7 minutes on each side, or until the bacon is crisp. Remove and reserve the bacon. Broil the chicken skin side up 3 to 5 minutes more, or until crisp, golden, and springy to the touch.

Transfer the bacon and chicken to a heated platter and nap with sauce. Serves 12.

Orange-Flavored Chicken Breasts
with Bacon, Vegetable Brochettes

VEGETABLE BROCHETTES

FOR THE MARINADE:
  1¼ cups olive oil
  ⅓ cup fresh lemon juice,
    or to taste
  3 tablespoons Sherry wine vinegar *or*
    red-wine vinegar
  3 tablespoons minced fresh basil leaves
    or 1 tablespoon dried, crumbled
  1½ tablespoons Dijon-style mustard
  1 bay leaf, crumbled
  2 teaspoons minced fresh thyme *or*
    ¾ teaspoon dried, crumbled
  2 teaspoons minced fresh marjoram *or*
    ¾ teaspoon dried, crumbled
  3 garlic cloves, minced, or to taste
  3 tablespoons minced fresh parsley
    leaves
  salt and freshly ground pepper
    to taste

  3 yellow squash
  3 zucchini
  24 small white onions, unpeeled
  3 large red bell peppers, each cut into
    12 pieces
  24 mushrooms
  12 wooden skewers, each 12 inches
    long, soaked in water for
    2 hours

MAKE THE MARINADE: IN A LARGE CERAMIC OR GLASS bowl combine all the ingredients.

In a saucepan of boiling salted water blanch the yellow squash for 5 minutes, drain, and refresh under cold water. Repeat the procedure with the zucchini, blanching for 7 minutes, and with the onions, blanching for 7 minutes.

Cut each yellow squash and zucchini into 8 slices. Peel the onions. Add these and all remaining vegetables to the marinade and toss well. Let the vegetables marinate, covered and chilled, for 2 hours. *The vegetables can be prepared ahead up to this point and kept refrigerated, covered, overnight.*

Prepare a charcoal grill.

Remove the vegetables from the marinade, reserving it, and thread them on the skewers. Grill the brochettes, turning and basting them with the marinade, for 15 to 20 minutes, or until tender. Serves 12.

CREAMED CORN AND LIMA BEANS

  3 cups fresh baby lima beans *or* two
    10-ounce packages frozen lima beans,
    thawed
  1½ cups finely minced onion
  ½ stick (¼ cup) unsalted butter
  6 cups cooked fresh corn (about 8 to
    10 ears) *or* three 10-ounce packages
    frozen corn, thawed
  3 cups milk
  ¾ cup heavy cream
  salt and fresh peppercorns to taste

IN A SAUCEPAN COOK THE LIMA BEANS IN BOILING salted water over moderate heat for 10 to 15 minutes, or until tender. Drain them.

In a saucepan cook the onion in the butter over moderate heat, stirring, until softened. Add the corn and 1½ cups of the milk and cook, stirring, for 5 minutes, or until the milk is absorbed. Add the fresh or frozen lima beans and remaining 1½ cups milk and cook, stirring, for 5 minutes, or until the milk is absorbed.

Stir in the cream and salt and cook, stirring, until thickened slightly. Grind the pepper liberally over the mixture. Serves 12.

RADICCHIO AND LAMB'S-LETTUCE SALAD

⅓ cup white-wine vinegar
¼ teaspoon salt
freshly ground pepper to taste
¾ cup olive oil
3 tablespoons heavy cream
⅓ cup crumbled Roquefort
few drops of fresh lemon juice
3 heads radicchio *or* other red-leaf
    lettuce, separated into leaves
8 small bunches of lamb's-lettuce *or*
    other soft-leaf lettuce, separated into
    leaves

IN A BOWL COMBINE THE VINEGAR, SALT, AND PEPPER and add the oil and cream in a stream, beating. Beat until emulsified. Stir in the Roquefort and lemon juice. In a large glass bowl arrange the lettuces and serve the salad with the dressing. Serves 12.

RED, WHITE, AND BLUEBERRY MOLD

4 cups raspberry sherbet*, slightly
    softened
4 cups coconut ice cream*, slightly
    softened
4 cups blueberry sherbet*, slightly
    softened
raspberry sauce* as an accompaniment

*recipe follows

OIL TWO LOAF PANS (EACH 1½ QUART) WITH FLAVORLESS vegetable oil and line them with parchment paper. Spoon 2 cups of the raspberry sherbet into each pan and smooth the tops with a spatula. Wipe the insides of the pans with a dish towel to prevent smudging. Freeze, covered tightly, for 1 hour, or until very firm.

Spoon 2 cups of the coconut ice cream into each pan and smooth the tops. Wipe the insides with a dish towel. Freeze, covered tightly, for 1 hour, or until very firm.

Spoon 2 cups of the blueberry sherbet into each pan and smooth the tops. Wipe the insides with a dish towel. Freeze, covered tightly, overnight. *The molds can be made 2 days ahead and kept frozen.*

Run a thin knife around the edge of each pan between the pan and the paper. Invert a chilled platter over each pan and invert the mold onto it. Discard the paper. Cut the molds crosswise into 1-inch slices and serve with the sauce. Serves 12.

RASPBERRY SHERBET

1⅓ cups sugar
1⅓ cups water
1-pound package frozen raspberries,
    thawed but not drained
2 tablespoons fresh lemon juice, or to
    taste

IN A SMALL SAUCEPAN BRING THE SUGAR AND WATER TO A boil over moderate heat, stirring, and cook, stirring, until the sugar is dissolved. Pour the syrup into a bowl. Chill for 1 hour, or until cold.

In a blender or food processor purée the raspberries and strain them through a fine sieve into the syrup. Add the lemon juice and combine well. Chill the mixture for at least 1 hour, or until cold. Freeze it in an ice-cream freezer according to the manufacturer's instructions. Makes about 4 cups.

COCONUT ICE CREAM

4 cups grated fresh coconut (page 199)
2 cups milk
1½ cups heavy cream
6 large egg yolks
1 cup sugar
1 teaspoon vanilla
**¼ teaspoon coconut extract, or to taste,
   if desired**

IN A HEAVY SAUCEPAN SCALD THE COCONUT, MILK, AND cream over moderate heat, but do not let it boil. Let the mixture cool for 30 minutes. Strain it through a fine sieve lined with a double thickness of rinsed and squeezed cheesecloth into a bowl, pressing hard on the solids. Bring the corners of the cheesecloth together, squeeze the remaining liquid into the bowl, and discard the solids.

In a large bowl beat the egg yolks and sugar until thick and lemon colored. Add the coconut liquid in a stream, stirring. Transfer the custard to a heavy saucepan and cook it over moderately low heat, stirring, until it coats the spoon. Transfer the custard to a bowl and stir in the vanilla and coconut extract. Let the custard cool, covered with a round of wax paper.

Chill the custard for 1 hour, or until cold, and freeze it in an ice-cream freezer according to the manufacturer's instructions. Makes about 4 cups.

BLUEBERRY SHERBET

1⅓ cups sugar
1⅓ cups water
**1-pound package frozen unsweetened
   blueberries, thawed but not drained**
**2 tablespoons fresh lemon juice, or to
   taste**

IN A SMALL SAUCEPAN BRING THE SUGAR AND WATER TO A boil over moderate heat, stirring, and cook, stir-

ring, until the sugar is dissolved. Pour the syrup into a bowl. Chill it for 1 hour, or until cold.

In a blender or food processor purée the blueberries and stir them into the syrup with the lemon juice. Chill the mixture for at least 1 hour, or until cold. Freeze it in an ice-cream freezer according to the manufacturer's instructions. Makes about 4 cups.

RASPBERRY SAUCE

**four 10-ounce packages frozen
   raspberries, thawed and drained**
**2 tablespoons fresh lemon juice, or to
   taste**
¼ cup fine granulated sugar, or to taste

IN A FOOD PROCESSOR OR BLENDER PURÉE THE raspberries with the lemon juice and strain the mixture through a fine sieve into a bowl, pressing hard on the solids. Stir in the sugar. Makes about 4 cups.

**TREFETHEN VINEYARDS
ESHCOL WHITE**

MENU

LABOR DAY DINNER

TOMATO SOUP WITH PISTOU

**ROAST STRIPED BASS WITH LEMON
AND PARSLEY**

LATE-SUMMER HARVEST CASSEROLE

MARINATED WHITE BEAN SALAD

COTTAGE CHEESE BREAD

DAMSON PLUM COBBLER

SERVES SIX

I t's hard to believe the Summer is nearly over. The nights are getting longer and the evening breezes carry a few leaves to the ground. August's tomatoes now belong to September: heavy, plump, red orbs with yellowing stem ends. Twisty vines are laden with squashes, and eggplant hang like dark, smooth, weighted eggs ready to be gathered. Outside the kitchen door, shiny-leaved herbs riot for space. A trip to the market easily becomes a major expedition—who, after all, can resist the lushness of stand after stand filled with fresh, ripe vegetables and fruits?

The weather is still warm and gentle and you may very well decide to set the table on the terrace or porch. The soup may be served warm or cold, depending on your inclination, and takes full advantage of the luscious tomatoes so readily available. Garnish the soup with *pistou*, a French ver-

sion of the basil, garlic, and olive oil mixture the Italians call *pesto*. The heady *pistou*, often made with tomatoes, too, is used here to season tomato soup just before serving it. Or make traditional *pesto* (page 95) with the fragrant basil crop to use in the soup.

Striped bass, a dense, fleshy white fish quite easily found in the markets, is endlessly versatile. When simply pan-cooked and then baked, as we suggest, it becomes the perfect foundation for a meal constructed of early Autumn's bounty and designed to be light and contemporary. A robust casserole made, it seems, with half the vegetables in the garden tastes marvelously full-bodied next to the mild fish, and because it can be served at room temperature, it is perfect for easy entertaining.

A white bean salad dressed with a mixture of vinegar, lemon juice, and mint gives the meal a lively sparkle. This should be made well ahead of time, as should the bread, a satisfyingly chewy rustic loaf with a discrete tang provided by cottage cheese and snipped chives.

The meal ends with a covered damson plum cobbler, the pastry crimped around the edges and vented to release steam during baking. Our friend Edna Lewis advises us that older varieties of damson plums—tiny, sharp-tasting fruit from old trees—make the best pies. Newer strains of the deep blue fruit are easier to find and taste wonderful, but do not have the same sour flavor. You may want to adjust the sugar depending on the sort of plum you buy. Both types are available only at Summer's end and, folded into a golden pastry case, sweetly end the meal . . . and the season.

⊙ IN A LARGE SAUCEPAN COOK THE ONION AND CELERY in the oil over moderate heat, stirring, until softened. Add the garlic and cook, stirring, for 1 minute. Add the tomatoes, stock, tomato paste, herbs, and salt and pepper and simmer, stirring occasionally, for 20 minutes. Discard the bay leaf.

Make the *pistou:* Crush the garlic with the salt until it forms a paste. In a food processor or blender purée the garlic paste, basil, and Parmesan. With the motor running, add the oil in a stream and blend until emulsified.

In the food processor or blender purée the soup in batches and return it to the saucepan. Serve the soup hot or cold with a dollop of the *pistou* swirled into each serving. Serves 6.

TOMATO SOUP WITH PISTOU
(TOMATO SOUP WITH BASIL GARLIC PASTE)

1 large onion, chopped, *or* the
   white part of 1 large leek, washed well
   and chopped
1 celery stalk, sliced
2 tablespoons olive oil
1 garlic clove, chopped
3 pounds tomatoes, peeled, seeded,
   and chopped
5 cups chicken stock (page 198) *or*
   canned chicken broth
1 tablespoon tomato paste
1 teaspoon minced fresh rosemary *or*
   ½ teaspoon dried, crumbled
1 teaspoon minced fresh thyme *or*
   ½ teaspoon dried, crumbled
1 bay leaf
salt and freshly ground pepper to taste

FOR THE PISTOU:
  2 garlic cloves
  ½ teaspoon salt, or to taste
  1 cup packed fresh basil leaves
  ½ cup freshly grated Parmesan
  ½ cup extra-virgin olive oil

ROAST STRIPED BASS WITH LEMON
AND PARSLEY

6 unskinned striped bass fillets, each
   6 ounces
salt and freshly ground pepper to taste
3 tablespoons dry vermouth
2 tablespoons unsalted butter, melted
2 tablespoons fresh lemon juice,
   or to taste
3 tablespoons minced fresh
   parsley leaves

⊙ PREHEAT THE OVEN TO 500° F.

Pat the fillets dry and season them with salt and pepper. In a gratin dish combine the vermouth and butter, add the fillets, and turn to coat well. Roast the fillets skin side down in the upper third of the oven for 6 to 8 minutes, or until they just flake. Transfer the fillets to a heated platter, sprinkle with the lemon juice, and garnish with the parsley. Serves 6.

LATE-SUMMER HARVEST CASEROLE

5 tablespoons olive oil
1-pound eggplant, cut into 1-inch pieces
salt and freshly ground pepper to taste
1 pound zucchini, cut into ¼-inch slices
1 small green bell pepper and 1 small red
   bell pepper, cut into 1-inch pieces
1 large onion, sliced
2 cups peeled, seeded, and chopped
   tomato (about 4 large tomatoes)
2 to 3 garlic cloves, minced, or to taste
2 tablespoons tomato paste
1 teaspoon minced fresh thyme *or*
   ½ teaspoon dried, crumbled
1 tablespoon minced fresh basil *or*
   ½ teaspoon dried, crumbled
1 teaspoon minced fresh rosemary *or*
   ½ teaspoon dried, crumbled
1 bay leaf
3 tablespoons minced fresh basil *or*
   parsley leaves for garnish

PREHEAT THE OVEN TO 350° F.

In a large nonstick skillet heat 2 tablespoons of the oil over moderately high heat until hot. Add the eggplant, and salt and pepper, and cook, stirring, until golden. Transfer to a flameproof casserole.

Add 1 tablespoon oil to the skillet and in it cook the zucchini with salt and pepper, stirring, until golden. Transfer to the casserole. Add 1 tablespoon oil to the skillet and in it cook the peppers with salt and pepper, stirring, until golden. Transfer to the casserole. Add the remaining 1 tablespoon oil to the skillet and in it cook the onion with salt and pepper, stirring, until golden. Transfer to the casserole.

Add the tomato and garlic to the skillet and cook, stirring, until almost all the liquid is evaporated. Transfer to the casserole. Add the tomato paste and herbs (excluding the garnish). Stir gently to combine and bring to a simmer, covered with a round of wax paper and the lid.

Bake in the oven for 30 minutes. Discard the bay leaf and garnish with the fresh basil. Serve hot or at room temperature. Serves 6.

MARINATED WHITE BEAN SALAD

1 pound dried small white beans, picked
   over and soaked in water overnight
1 white onion studded with 4 cloves
½ celery stalk including the leaves
1 bay leaf
½ teaspoon red pepper flakes
1 teaspoon salt

FOR THE DRESSING:

2 to 3 tablespoons red-wine vinegar,
   or to taste
¼ cup fresh lemon juice
1 tablespoon Dijon-style mustard
1 to 2 garlic cloves, minced, or to taste
salt and freshly ground pepper to taste
6 tablespoons olive oil
2 tablespoons water
3 tablespoons minced fresh mint, *or* dill,
   or tarragon leaves
3 tablespoons minced fresh
   parsley leaves
1 teaspoon grated lemon zest

1 small red onion, minced
1 cup small black olives, such as niçoise

IN A LARGE KETTLE COMBINE THE BEANS, WHITE ONION, celery, bay leaf, pepper flakes, and 1½ cups water and bring to a simmer. Cook, covered, for 15 minutes. Add the salt and cook for 10 to 15 minutes, or until the beans are tender. Drain and refresh the beans under cold water. Discard the onion, celery, and bay leaf.

Make the salad dressing: In a food processor or blender process all the ingredients until emulsified.

In a large bowl combine the beans and dressing and toss well. Let them stand, covered, for 2 hours. Garnish with the red onion and olives.

The salad can be made 1 day ahead and kept refrigerated. Serve the salad at room temperature. Serves 6.

COTTAGE CHEESE BREAD

1 tablespoon active dry yeast
½ cup lukewarm water
2½ cups all-purpose flour
1 cup creamed cottage cheese
1 large egg, beaten lightly
⅓ cup snipped fresh chives *or*
   2 tablespoons freeze-dried
1 tablespoon sugar
1 teaspoon salt
melted unsalted butter for brushing
   the loaf

IN A LARGE BOWL PROOF THE YEAST IN THE WATER FOR 15 minutes, or until foamy. Add 1 cup of the flour and the remaining ingredients except the butter and beat until well combined. Stir in the remaining 1½ cups flour, ½ cup at a time, and beat with a wooden spoon until well combined.

Transfer the dough to a buttered bowl and let it rise, covered loosely, in a warm place for 1½ hours, or until double in bulk. Stir down the dough and transfer it to a buttered loaf pan, 9 by 5 by 3 inches. Let it rise, covered loosely, for 30 minutes, or until nearly double in bulk.

Preheat the oven to 350° F.

Bake the loaf in the middle of the oven for 10 minutes. Brush the top with the melted butter and bake for 30 to 35 minutes more, or until it sounds hollow when the bottom is tapped. Let it cool in the pan on a rack for 5 minutes and turn out onto the rack to cool completely. *The bread can be made 1 day ahead and kept, wrapped in plastic wrap.* Makes 1 loaf.

DAMSON PLUM COBBLER

1 tablespoon cornstarch
2 tablespoons Tawny Port
2 pounds damson plums, quartered
⅔ cup sugar
½ teaspoon cinnamon
½ teaspoon grated lemon zest
3 tablespoons unsalted butter, cut
   into bits
½ recipe flaky pie pastry (page 196)
egg wash made by beating 1 egg with
   1 teaspoon water

IN A SMALL BOWL COMBINE THE CORNSTARCH AND PORT. In a saucepan cook the plums and sugar over moderate heat, stirring, until the sugar is dissolved. Bring the mixture to a boil and stir in the cornstarch mixture. Return the mixture to a boil, stirring, and stir in the cinnamon, lemon zest, and butter. Let the filling cool.

Preheat the oven to 375° F.

Spread the filling in a 9-inch pie plate. Roll out the dough ⅛ inch thick on a lightly floured surface. Drape the dough over the rolling pin and unroll it over the filling. Crimp the edge decoratively and brush the top with the egg wash. Cut slits in the dough for steam vents and bake in the middle of the oven for 45 minutes, or until golden. Makes one 9-inch cobbler.

**ST. CLEMENT NAPA VALLEY
CHARDONNAY '87**

Summer Gifts

From the earliest days of Spring and long into Fall, the garden, orchards, and woods yield all sorts of good things to eat at once or to store. Never is this more apparent than during the lush, green months of Summer, a time when you will be invited for casual meals served outdoors, weekend visits, and family get-togethers. As informal as Summer entertaining tends to be, you won't want to arrive empty-handed. Consider bringing along a freshly baked cherry or blackberry pie made with fruit you pick yourself or, more probably, buy at the local farmstand. Offer a gift of kitchen-made *pesto,* sweet bread-and-butter pickles, or flavorful peach or gingered lemon syrup to pour over homemade ice cream. Transport the pie in a simple basket, tie ribbons around the Mason jars holding the pickles or *pesto*, or include a small crockery condiment bowl as part of the gift. The smile of appreciation on the face of your host will be your reward.

Cherry Pie with Almond Lattice Topping

CHERRY PIE WITH ALMOND LATTICE TOPPING

pâte brisée (page 196)
**5 cups fresh sour cherries *or* two 1-pound
  cans sour cherries, drained
2 tablespoons quick-cooking tapioca
1 to 1½ teaspoons fresh lemon juice
½ teaspoon salt
1 cup sugar
¼ teaspoon almond extract
⅛ teaspoon ground cloves
2 tablespoons unsalted butter, softened
7 ounces (about ⅔ cup) almond paste
  (available at specialty food shops)
½ teaspoon grated lemon zest
2 large egg yolks
⅓ cup all-purpose flour
egg wash made by beating 1 egg yolk with
  1 teaspoon water**

ROLL OUT THE DOUGH ⅛ INCH THICK ON A LIGHTLY floured surface and fit it into a 9-inch pie plate. Crimp the edge and chill for 1 hour.

Working over a bowl, pit the fresh cherries. In the bowl combine the cherries well with the tapioca, lemon juice, salt, sugar, almond extract, and cloves. Let the mixture stand, stirring occasionally, for 15 minutes.

Preheat the oven to 425° F.

In a large bowl with an electric mixer cream the butter. Add the almond paste and lemon zest and beat until combined well. Add the egg yolks, 1 at a time, beating well after each addition. Beat in the flour and beat until combined well. Transfer the almond mixture to a pastry bag fitted with a ¼-inch plain tip.

Spoon the cherry filling into the shell, pressing down gently to level the top. Pipe the almond mixture over it in lattice strips about 1 inch apart. Brush the edge of the shell with the egg wash and bake in the lower third of the oven for 25 minutes. Reduce the heat to 350° F. and bake for 15 to 20 minutes more, or until golden and bubbling. Let the pie cool on a rack. Makes one 9-inch pie.

OLD-FASHIONED BLACKBERRY PIE

**1 recipe flaky pie pastry (page 196)
1¼ cups sugar, or to taste, plus
  additional for garnish
3 to 4 tablespoons all-purpose flour
pinch of salt
1 teaspoon grated lemon zest
4 cups fresh blackberries *or* raspberries
2 tablespoons unsalted butter**

HALVE THE DOUGH AND FORM EACH HALF INTO A BALL. Flatten the balls slightly and chill, wrapped in wax paper, for 45 minutes.

Preheat the oven to 425° F.

In a bowl combine the sugar, 3 tablespoons of the flour, salt, and zest. Add the blackberries and toss to coat well. Add up to 1 tablespoon additional flour if the berries are very juicy.

Roll out 1 ball of dough ⅛ inch thick on a floured surface and fit it into a 9-inch pie plate. Trim the dough flush with the edge. Spread the filling in the shell and dot with the butter.

Roll out the remaining ball of dough ⅛ inch thick on a floured surface and drape it over the filling. Trim the top crust, leaving a 1-inch overhang. Fold it under the bottom crust and crimp the edge decoratively. Sprinkle the top with sugar. Make slits in the top crust for steam vents and bake the pie in the lower third of the oven for 10 minutes.

Reduce the heat to 375° F. and bake for 40 to 50 minutes more, or until golden and bubbly. Let the pie cool on a rack. Serve warm or at room temperature. Makes one 9-inch pie.

RATATOUILLE PÂTÉ

¾-pound eggplant, peeled and cut into
½-inch cubes
5 teaspoons salt
1 pound zucchini, cut into ¼-inch slices
1¼ pounds onions, chopped
3 garlic cloves, minced
¼ cup olive oil
2 pounds tomatoes, peeled, seeded, and
cut into ¼-inch slices
1 green bell pepper, cut into ¼-inch
strips
dried marjoram to taste
paprika to taste
freshly ground pepper to taste
½ cup heavy cream
2 large eggs, beaten lightly
½ cup finely grated Gruyère
½ teaspoon dried orégano, crumbled
½ teaspoon dried basil, crumbled

FOR THE TOMATO COULIS:
¼ cup minced onion
¼ cup minced shallot
2 tablespoons unsalted butter
4 large tomatoes, peeled, seeded, and
chopped
½ teaspoon salt
¼ teaspoon freshly ground pepper
⅛ teaspoon sugar
cheesecloth bag containing 4 parsley
sprigs, 1 bay leaf, and pinch of dried
thyme

IN A COLANDER TOSS THE EGGPLANT WITH 1 TABLESPOON
of the salt and drain for 1 hour. Pat the eggplant
dry. In a colander toss the zucchini with 1 teaspoon
of the salt and drain for 30 minutes. Pat the zucchini dry. In a heavy skillet cook the onions and garlic
in the oil over low heat for 15 minutes, or until softened but not colored.

Preheat the oven to 325° F.

In a 1½-quart loaf pan layer half the onion
mixture, half the eggplant, half the tomato, half the
green pepper, and half the zucchini, sprinkling
each layer with marjoram, paprika, salt, and pepper to taste. Layer the remaining vegetables in the
same manner.

Bake, covered with foil and weighted with a
2-pound weight, in the middle of the oven for 30
minutes. Remove the weight and foil and transfer
the pâté to a rack to stand for 30 minutes.

In a bowl combine the remaining ingredients and the remaining 1 teaspoon salt and pour it
over the pâté, allowing it to seep into the layers.
Bake, covered with a double layer of foil, in the
oven for 35 to 45 minutes, or until a knife inserted
in the center comes out clean.

Make the tomato coulis: In a heavy skillet
sweat the onion and shallot in the butter, covered
with a buttered round of wax paper and the lid,
over moderately low heat until soft. Add the remaining ingredients and cook, covered, over low
heat for 10 minutes. Cook, uncovered, over moderately high heat, stirring, for 10 to 12 minutes
more, or until thick. Discard the cheesecloth bag
and strain into a bowl.

Transfer the pâté to a rack and remove the
foil. Let it stand for 15 minutes. Run a thin knife
around the inside of the pan and invert a platter
over it. Invert the pâté onto the platter and slice it
with a serrated knife. Serve with the coulis. Serves
8 to 10 as a first course or 12 as a side dish.

PESTO

Pesto is usually tossed with thin pasta, but don't
stop there. Spoon it over tomatoes, mix it into potato salad, or dollop it on baked potatoes. It is also
marvelous as an addition to vegetable soup and
white-fleshed fish.

4 cups coarsely chopped fresh basil
leaves
2 garlic cloves, crushed
1 cup pine nuts
½ cup olive oil
1 cup freshly grated Parmesan
salt to taste

IN A BLENDER IN BATCHES OR IN A FOOD PROCESSOR
purée all the ingredients and transfer to a bowl. Put
plastic wrap directly on the surface to prevent dis-
coloration. *The pesto can be made 2 weeks ahead and
kept refrigerated, covered.* Makes 2 cups.

MARINATED SUN-DRIED TOMATOES

There is good reason why these wrinkled red tomatoes have made such an impression on the American cooking scene. Mere shadows of their former juicy selves, they taste just as good, albeit different. Try them in salads of tossed summer greens; serve them with tangy goat cheese or with mild cow cheeses; or use them as a bright accompaniment to grilled meats.

> ⅔ cup olive oil plus additional for
> covering
> ¼ cup dry white wine
> cheesecloth bag containing
> 12 peppercorns, ½ teaspoon
> dried basil, ½ teaspoon dried orégano,
> and 1 bay leaf
> ½ teaspoon salt
> ¼ pound sun-dried tomatoes
> (not packed in oil)

IN A HEAVY SAUCEPAN COMBINE THE OIL, WHITE WINE, cheesecloth bag, and salt and bring to a boil over moderate heat. Stir in the tomatoes and simmer for 7 minutes, or until softened. Remove the pan from the heat and let it stand, covered, for 30 minutes. Remove the cheesecloth bag. Transfer the tomatoes to a decorative glass container and add oil to cover. *The tomatoes can be made ahead and kept in a cool, dry place for up to 3 days or in the refrigerator for up to 2 weeks.* Serve in salads or pasta sauces.

BREAD-AND-BUTTER PICKLES

The name suggests that these slivers of cucumbers and onions pickled in a slightly sweet brine are commonplace, meant for everyday consumption. There is also a theory that in other times they were a source for the "bread and butter" income many farmers depended on from small roadside stands. The pickles utilized the abundant cucumber crop and were ever so easy to make in the farmhouse kitchen. We think these pale green pickles are wonderful alongside meat at table, on sandwiches, eaten directly from the jar, and, not surprisingly, with thin slices of buttered bread.

> 1¼ pounds Kirby cucumbers, cut into
> ½-inch slices
> 1 onion, sliced very thin
> 2 tablespoons kosher salt
> 2 cups ice cubes
> 1 cup cider vinegar
> 1 cup sugar
> ¼ teaspoon turmeric
> 1 tablespoon mustard seeds
> ½ teaspoon celery seeds
> ¼ teaspoon cayenne, or to taste

+ IN A LARGE BOWL COMBINE THE CUCUMBERS AND onion, sprinkle with the salt, and toss well. Add the ice cubes and chill, covered, overnight.

Drain the mixture in a colander and rinse under cold water. In a saucepan bring the remaining ingredients to a boil, stirring. Add the cucumbers and onion and bring just to a simmer, stirring. Transfer to a bowl and cool. Chill the pickles, covered, for 24 hours.

The pickles can be made 1 week ahead and kept refrigerated, covered. Or, spoon the hot pickles into sterilized 1-pint Mason-type jars (page 199), filling the jars to within ½ inch of the top. Seal with the lids. Put the jars on a rack in a kettle and pour in enough hot water to cover them by 2 inches. Bring to a boil and boil, covered, for 10 minutes. Transfer the jars with tongs to a rack to cool. Store in a cool, dark, dry place. Makes about 4 pints.

SPICED WATERMELON RIND CHUTNEY

This would be a thoughtful gift for a transplanted Southerner or for anyone who enjoys eating mildly spicy chutney with ham, lamb, and other meats. When you make it, call the children in from the backyard to eat the sweet pink flesh of the watermelon. You could also scoop it into melon balls to use in a fruit salad, or mash it to make light and refreshing watermelon ice.

> 3- to 3½-pound piece of watermelon
> 2½ tablespoons salt
> 2 cups peeled and diced tart apple
> 2 cups white vinegar
> 1 cup chopped onion
> 1 cup firmly packed light brown sugar
> ¾ cup currants
> ¾ cup raisins
> ¾ cup drained and minced ginger
>   in syrup (available at specialty
>   food shops)
> ½ cup granulated sugar
> 1 lemon, sliced thin and seeded
> 3 garlic cloves, minced
> 1 tablespoon mustard seeds
> 1 teaspoon celery seeds
> 1 teaspoon cinnamon
> 1 teaspoon ground cloves
> 1 teaspoon ground allspice
> 1 teaspoon cayenne
> 1½ teaspoons cornstarch combined with
>   1 tablespoon water
> freshly ground pepper to taste

+ PEEL AND DISCARD THE GREEN SKIN FROM THE watermelon rind. Scoop out the flesh and reserve for another use. Cut the rind into 1-inch cubes. Put the rind in a kettle with 1 tablespoon of the salt and water to cover and bring to a boil over high heat. Boil the rind for 3 minutes, or until just tender, drain, and cool.

In a bowl combine the rind with the apple, vinegar, onion, and remaining 1½ tablespoons salt and let it stand, covered, for 3 hours.

In a large stainless steel saucepan combine the remaining ingredients except the cornstarch and pepper. Strain the liquid from the rind mixture into the saucepan and bring it to a boil over high heat. Cook, stirring, until the sugar is dissolved. Add the rind mixture and cook for 5 minutes. Stir in the cornstarch mixture and chill, covered, overnight.

Bring the mixture to a boil and add salt and pepper to taste. Transfer it to sterilized 1-pint Mason-type jars (page 199), filling the jars to within ½ inch of the top, and seal with the lids. Put the jars on a rack in a kettle and pour in enough hot water to cover them by 2 inches. Bring the water to a boil and boil, covered, for 10 minutes. Transfer the jars with tongs to a rack and cool. Store in a cool, dark, dry place.

Serve the chutney as a condiment with roasted or grilled meats or with curries. Makes about 5 pints.

SHERRY SHALLOT VINEGAR

When you plan to give flavored vinegar as a gift, use a funnel to pour it from the Mason jars into handsome glass bottles with good stoppers. Tie some colorful ribbons around the neck of the bottle and affix a personalized label.

> 1¼ cups white-wine vinegar
> ¾ cup dry Sherry
> 2½ cups peeled and halved shallots

+ IN A STERILIZED 1-QUART MASON-TYPE JAR (PAGE 199) combine all the ingredients and seal with the lid. Let the mixture stand at room temperature for at least 3 weeks. Strain the vinegar through a fine sieve into a sterilized 1-pint Mason-type jar and seal with the lid. (Reserve the shallots for another use such as salads.) Makes about 1 pint.

ROSEMARY VINEGAR

    4 cups white-wine vinegar
    2 large rosemary sprigs
    2 shallots, peeled and halved

+ IN A STAINLESS STEEL OR ENAMELED SAUCEPAN bring the vinegar to a simmer. Pour it into a sterilized 1-quart Mason-type jar (page 199) and add the rosemary and shallots. Seal the vinegar with the lid and store in a cool, dry place for at least 2 weeks. Before giving as a gift, strain the vinegar and add fresh rosemary sprigs. Makes about 1 quart.

ALL-PURPOSE BOURBON
MARINADE

Once you try it, this marinade may very well become the only one you ever make. Happily combining the tastes of the Orient with more than a splash of very American bourbon, the full-bodied brew tenderizes beef, chicken, duck, and ribs while infusing them with glorious flavor.

    ⅓ cup bourbon
    ¼ cup soy sauce
    ¼ cup firmly packed light brown sugar
    1 large onion, chopped
    3 tablespoons Dijon-style mustard
    1 teaspoon Worcestershire sauce

IN A CERAMIC OR GLASS DISH COMBINE ALL THE ingredients. Use the marinade to marinate pork, beef, or chicken in the refrigerator, covered, overnight and to baste meat or poultry as it is grilled. Makes about 1 cup.

JALAPEÑO JELLY

It is a lovely idea to include a jar of this sweet yet peppery jelly in a basket with an assortment of cheeses and crackers. It also tastes fine spread on fresh biscuits filled with slices of country ham.

    5 cups sugar
    ¾ cup cider vinegar
    ¾ cup herb-flavored white vinegar
    2 large green bell peppers, seeds and ribs
      discarded
    5 *jalapeño* peppers, ribs discarded
      (wear rubber gloves)
    6 ounces liquid pectin (¾ cup)
    green food coloring, if desired

IN A LARGE SAUCEPAN BRING THE SUGAR AND THE vinegars to a boil over moderately low heat, stirring. In a food processor chop the bell peppers and *jalapeños* (with some *jalapeño* seeds, depending upon the hotness desired). Stir the pepper mixture into the vinegar mixture and simmer, skimming the froth, for 10 minutes. Stir in the pectin and boil rapidly for 1 minute. Skim the froth and add 1 to 2 drops of the food coloring. Transfer the jelly to sterilized ½-pint Mason-type jars (procedure on page 199), wipe the rims with a damp cloth, and seal with the lids.

    Serve the jelly as a condiment with grilled or broiled meats or with cream cheese on crackers as a canapé. Makes 2½ pints.

PEACH SYRUP

Keep a jar of this syrup on hand to drizzle over ice cream. It also works well to moisten layers of gén-oise, which tends to be a dry-crumbed cake that benefits from a little liquid brushed between the layers before frosting. Or try mixing the syrup with seltzer water over ice for a pleasantly refreshing drink. Better yet, stir a spoonful or two into ice-cold vodka.

1½ pounds peaches, peeled and chopped
½ cup sugar
⅛ teaspoon ground allspice

◉ IN A STAINLESS STEEL OR ENAMELED SAUCEPAN bring all the ingredients to a boil over moderate heat, stirring and washing down any sugar crystals clinging to the sides with a brush dipped in cold water until the sugar is dissolved. Simmer the mixture, undisturbed, for 10 minutes. Let it cool to lukewarm and strain through a fine sieve into a glass container, pressing hard on the solids. *The syrup can be made ahead and kept refrigerated indefinitely, covered tightly.* Makes about 1½ cups.

GINGERED LEMON SYRUP

1 cup fresh lemon juice
¾ cup sugar
3 tablespoons peeled and minced
   gingerroot

◉ IN A STAINLESS STEEL OR ENAMELED SAUCEPAN BRING all the ingredients to a boil over moderate heat, stirring and washing down any sugar crystals clinging to the sides with a brush dipped in cold water until the sugar is dissolved. Simmer the mixture, undisturbed, for 10 minutes. Let it cool to lukewarm and strain through a fine sieve into a glass container, pressing hard on the solids. *The syrup can be made ahead and kept refrigerated indefinitely, covered tightly.* Makes about 1 cup.

BRANDIED CHERRIES

1 pound firm Bing cherries
1 cup sugar
¼ cup water
1½ cups brandy

◉+ RINSE THE CHERRIES AND TRIM THE STEMS TO 1 inch. With a needle prick each cherry in 5 or 6 places. In a saucepan combine the cherries with water to cover and bring to a boil over low heat. Simmer for 2 minutes. Transfer the cherries to a bowl of cold water and let them cool. Drain. Repeat the procedure 2 more times.

In another saucepan bring the sugar and water to a boil over low heat, washing down any sugar crystals clinging to the sides with a brush dipped in cold water until the sugar is dissolved. Simmer the syrup for 3 minutes and remove it from the heat. Add ½ cup brandy, 2 tablespoons at a time, stirring, and let it cool. Stir in the remaining 1 cup brandy.

Put the cherries, stem end up, in a sterilized 1-quart Mason-type jar (procedure on page 199) and pour the syrup over them. Add more brandy if necessary to cover completely. Seal the jar with the lid and store in a cool place for at least 1 month. Serve the cherries over ice cream, frozen yogurt, or pound cake. Makes 1 quart.

BLUEBERRY CORDIAL

1 cup sugar
3 cups blueberries, picked over
2 cups vodka

◉+ RINSE A HEATPROOF 2-QUART JAR WITH BOILING water and drain it. In it combine all the ingredients and seal tightly. Let the mixture stand in a cool, dark place, shaking occasionally, for 2 months.

Strain the cordial through a very fine sieve lined with a triple thickness of rinsed and squeezed cheesecloth into a bowl. Discard the blueberries. Serve as an after-dinner drink or with tonic over ice as a cocktail. Makes about 3 cups.

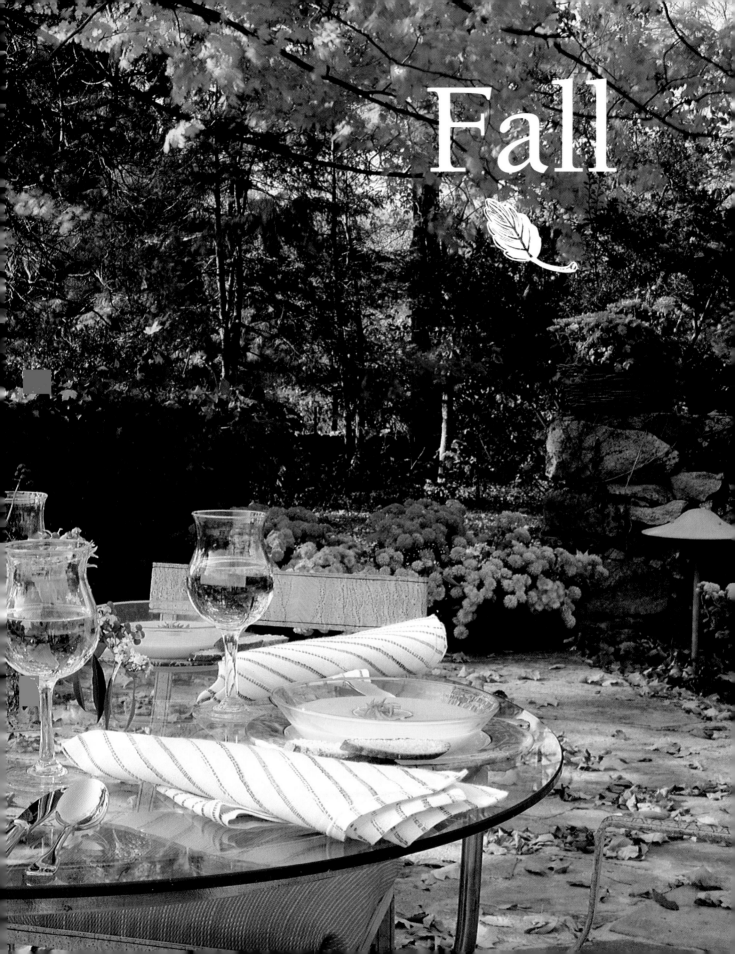

Fall

VACATION IS OVER, THE AIR IS COOLER, AND THE nights are longer. Autumn has arrived with its stunning display of color and still-warm sunshine. Suddenly it is necessary to open datebooks to keep track of busy schedules. Even as we plan committee meetings and attend to all the back-to-school frenzy, we find ourselves yearning to entertain. After all, the markets are filled with the fruits of the harvest, and the idea of setting a pretty table, drawing the curtains, and lighting the first fire of the season is irresistibly appealing.

We have come up with three very different menus custom-made for Thanksgiving — a day that marks the beginning of the Winter holidays while celebrating the best of the late-Fall foods. Our Victorian Thanksgiving boasts roast turkey with corn bread, ham, and apricot stuffing, while our Southern turkey day menu stuffs the bird with pecans and rice. Of course our vegetarian feast excludes the turkey, but be assured that you will find traditional fare here too: squash, sweet potatoes, Brussels sprouts, chestnuts, and cranberries. (While each menu offers an exciting innovation or two, *Gourmet* always pays allegiance to tradition.)

Weeks before Thanksgiving, you may find yourself planning a patio dinner featuring grilled duck for an Indian Summer weekend when it is still warm enough to set up tables outside. Or perhaps you will decide to give a rollicking birthday party for a good friend with south-of-the-border dishes. On a gentler theme, we have put together a traditional tea to honor a young mother-to-be, complete with dainty sandwiches and chocolate-covered cookies.

There are some things to remember when you plan a party, regardless of its size. Organization is the key. Make several lists

and give yourself a flexible timetable. Shop early, and try to buy everything you will need to avoid last-minute dashes. If you get to the market and *think* you probably have a fresh clove of garlic at home, do not take any chances. Buy more garlic. Plan your color scheme around your dishes, table linens, and seasonal flowers. If you have decided on paper products but cannot find the marigold yellow or forest green you envisioned, make an on-the-spot decision to buy another color rather than wasting precious time searching in several stores.

If you are entertaining a large number of people, consider renting glasses, flatware, china, and linens. Think about the flow of guests in your house, too. For a buffet, you might do best pushing the dining table against a wall (hook the chandelier up to avoid bumps). If you plan to have a bar, arrange it in a room separate from the food. This will eliminate crushes at the two most popular spots.

Fall is a time of rejuvenation, the season when our pulses quicken and the crackle of leaves underfoot reminds us that the lazy days of Summer are over. The darkening weekends provide wonderful opportunities to get together with people we may not have seen for several months. We hope that our menus will help you embrace the season and enjoy its harvest.

Fajitas with Peppers and Red Onions;
Flour Tortillas; Chunky Guacamole;
Fresh Tomato Salsa

MENU

A SOUTH-OF-THE-BORDER BIRTHDAY

CHILE CON QUESO

FAJITAS WITH PEPPERS AND RED ONIONS

FLOUR TORTILLAS

FRESH TOMATO SALSA

CHUNKY GUACAMOLE

CORN AND ROASTED RED PEPPER RELISH

**HOT MILK SPONGECAKE WITH
PENUCHE ICING**

FRESH FRUIT MOSAIC

SERVES SIXTEEN

Above all else, birthday parties should be fun and lively and in some small way take us back to the days when we eagerly anticipated the yearly event and the requisite party. If you plan the party around bright, sunny Mexican food, you will create a festive mood that will immediately and happily affect everyone who walks in the door.

Mexican food is either prepared very quickly and eaten right away or cooked for a long, long time. Our party fare falls in the first category. Yes, the corn relish and the fruit dessert can be prepared as far ahead of time as the day before and the *guacamole* and the *salsa* can be mixed several hours in advance. But the *chile con queso*—a mild, smooth cheese dip designed for coating crispy *tostadas*—must be made shortly before serving and kept warm in a chafing dish or fondue pot.

The main event—soft, warm *fajitas* filled with rare grilled steak smothered in peppers and onions and flavored with garlic, lime juice, and coriander—is assembled as it is eaten or, if not, just before serving. We recommend you make your own *tortillas* for the *fajitas*. Throughout Mexico, women can be seen cooking the flat hearth bread on sizzling hot braziers. They heat each one for mere seconds on a side before they artfully flip it off the griddle and drop the next one on. In northern Mexico in the region of Sonora, *tortillas* are made from wheat rather than from the more familiar corn flour (*masa*) of the south. Wheat *tortillas* are usually larger than those made from corn and appear to be lightly dusted with white flour. As you might expect, they taste very different.

Good Mexican food takes full advantage of the lusty flavors of the chilies, tomatoes, herbs, and spices that grow so well in the sunshine-filled climate of the country. And when it comes to dessert, the Mexicans prefer frankly sweet confections that encourage their already singing tastebuds to consider an encore. The succulent melons in the fruit mosaic and a spongecake glazed with a dark, sugary icing provide such harmony.

CHILE CON QUESO
(HOT CHEESE AND TOMATO DIP WITH CHILIES)

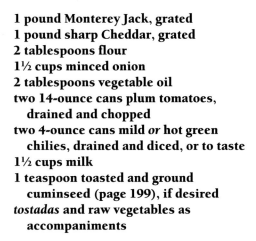

1 pound Monterey Jack, grated
1 pound sharp Cheddar, grated
2 tablespoons flour
1½ cups minced onion
2 tablespoons vegetable oil
two 14-ounce cans plum tomatoes, drained and chopped
two 4-ounce cans mild *or* hot green chilies, drained and diced, or to taste
1½ cups milk
1 teaspoon toasted and ground cuminseed (page 199), if desired
tostadas and raw vegetables as accompaniments

IN A BOWL COMBINE THE CHEESES AND FLOUR. IN A heavy saucepan cook the onion in the oil over moderate heat, stirring, for 3 to 5 minutes, or until soft. Add the tomatoes and chilies and cook for 5 minutes, or until the liquid is almost evaporated. Add the milk and bring just to a boil.

Reduce the heat to moderately low and add the cheese mixture in batches, letting each batch melt before adding the next. Cook, stirring, for 3 to 5 minutes, or until heated through. Transfer the dip to a chafing dish, fondue pot, or heatproof serving bowl set over a brazier. Sprinkle with the cuminseed and serve immediately with the *tostadas* and vegetables. Serves 16 as an hors d'oeuvre.

FAJITAS WITH PEPPERS AND RED ONIONS
(GRILLED MARINATED SKIRT STEAK WITH PEPPERS AND RED ONIONS)

8 garlic cloves, or to taste
½ teaspoon salt
⅓ cup fresh lime juice
10 tablespoons vegetable oil
1 tablespoon toasted and ground cuminseed (page 199)
2 to 3 fresh *jalapeño* peppers, minced (wear rubber gloves), or to taste
freshly ground pepper to taste
5 pounds skirt steak
5 large red, yellow, and green bell peppers, cut into strips
2 large red onions, halved lengthwise and cut into strips
¼ cup minced fresh coriander leaves
32 warm flour *tortillas* (recipe follows) *or* packaged *tortillas*
fresh tomato *salsa* and chunky *guacamole* (recipes follow) as accompaniments

+ WITH A MORTAR AND PESTLE MASH 6 OF THE GARLIC cloves and the salt to a paste. In a glass baking dish combine the paste, lime juice, 6 tablespoons of the oil, cuminseed, *jalapeños*, and pepper. Add the steak and let marinate at room temperature, turning twice, for 2 hours. *The steak can be marinated and kept refrigerated, covered, overnight.*

Prepare a charcoal grill.

In a large skillet cook the bell peppers and onions with salt and pepper to taste in the remaining 4 tablespoons oil over moderate heat, stirring occasionally, until tender. Add the remaining 2 garlic cloves, minced, and cook, stirring, for 2 to 3 minutes. Remove from the heat and add the coriander. Toss to combine and keep warm on a platter.

Drain the steak and pat dry. Grill for 3 to 4 minutes on each side for medium-rare meat. Transfer it to a cutting board and let it stand for 3 minutes. Cut diagonally into pieces and transfer with any accumulated juices to the platter. Wrap the steak and vegetable mixture in the *tortillas* and serve with the *salsa* and *guacamole*. Serves 16.

FLOUR TORTILLAS

6 cups all-purpose flour
¾ cup lard, chilled and cut into bits
1 tablespoon salt
2 cups warm water

IN A BOWL BLEND 2 CUPS OF THE FLOUR, ¼ CUP OF THE lard, and 1 teaspoon of the salt until the mixture resembles meal. Add ⅔ cup of the water and toss until incorporated. Form into a ball and knead on a lightly floured surface for 2 to 3 minutes, or until smooth. Make 2 more batches of dough in the same manner. Chill the batches separately, wrapped in plastic wrap, for 3 hours. *The dough can be made ahead and kept refrigerated, wrapped in plastic wrap, overnight.*

Have ready thirty-six 9-inch squares of wax paper and dust them with flour. Divide 1 batch of dough into 12 pieces and form each piece into a ball. Roll each ball into an 8-inch round on a wax paper square and trim the edge using an inverted 8-inch plate or bowl as a guide. Make *tortillas* with the remaining batches of dough.

Heat a griddle over high heat until hot. Invert a *tortilla* onto it and after 5 seconds carefully peel off the paper. Cook, turning, for 1 to 2 minutes, or until slightly puffed and flecked with golden brown spots. Transfer the cooked *tortillas* to a plate or dish towel. Cook the remaining *tortillas* in the same manner.

The cooked tortillas can be made 3 days ahead and kept refrigerated or frozen, stacked between sheets of wax paper and wrapped in plastic wrap. Let them thaw in the refrigerator and reheat in one layer on baking sheets, covered with foil, in a preheated 350° F. oven for 1 to 2 minutes, or until heated through. Makes 36 *tortillas.*

FRESH TOMATO SALSA

6 cups seeded and chopped tomato
1½ cups minced scallion
3 to 4 fresh *jalapeño* peppers *or serrano* peppers, minced (wear rubber gloves), if desired
6 tablespoons fresh lime juice
⅓ cup minced fresh coriander leaves
salt and freshly ground pepper to taste

☺ + IN A BOWL COMBINE ALL THE INGREDIENTS AND chill them, covered, for up to 2 hours. Drain the *salsa* before serving. Makes about 8 cups.

CHUNKY GUACAMOLE

8 ripe small California avocados, peeled and pitted
6 garlic cloves, mashed to a paste
¼ cup fresh lemon juice
1 to 2 fresh *jalapeño* peppers, minced (wear rubber gloves), if desired
salt and freshly ground pepper to taste
3 tablespoons minced fresh coriander leaves

☺ + IN A BOWL MASH THE AVOCADOS COARSELY WITH THE back of a silver fork. Stir in the garlic, lemon juice, *jalapeños,* and salt and pepper, and chill the *guacamole,* the surface covered with plastic wrap to prevent darkening, for at least 1 hour. *The guacamole can be made ahead and kept refrigerated, the surface covered with plastic wrap, overnight. Just before serving, stir in the coriander.* Makes about 5½ cups.

CORN AND ROASTED RED PEPPER RELISH

❧

1 large onion, minced
2 tablespoons unsalted butter
6 cups cooked fresh corn (about 8 to
    10 ears) *or* three 10-ounce packages
    frozen corn, thawed
1½ cups white-wine vinegar
⅓ cup water
⅔ cup sugar, or to taste
1½ teaspoons cuminseed, toasted
    (page 199)
1 bay leaf
salt and freshly ground pepper to taste
3 large red bell peppers, roasted
    (procedure on page 199) and diced

☺+ IN A LARGE SAUCEPAN COOK THE ONION IN THE
butter over moderate heat, stirring, until softened.
Add the corn and cook, stirring, for 3 minutes. Add
the vinegar, water, sugar, cuminseed, bay leaf, and
salt and pepper and bring to a boil. Simmer the
mixture, covered, for 15 minutes. Add the bell peppers and simmer for 5 minutes.

Transfer the mixture to a colander, reserving the cooking liquid, and discard the bay leaf. Return the cooking liquid to the saucepan and boil it
over moderately high heat until reduced to 1 cup.
In a large bowl toss the vegetables with the reduced
liquid and let the relish cool. Chill it, covered, for at
least 2 hours. *The relish can be made ahead and kept
refrigerated, covered, overnight.* Serves 16.

HOT MILK SPONGECAKE WITH PENUCHE ICING

❧

4 large eggs
1¾ cups sugar
2 cups cake flour (not self-rising)
2 teaspoons baking powder
¼ teaspoon salt
1 cup hot milk
¾ stick (6 tablespoons) unsalted butter,
    cut into bits and softened
1½ teaspoons vanilla
penuche icing (recipe follows)

☺+ PREHEAT THE OVEN TO 350° F. BUTTER AND FLOUR A
10-inch round cake pan, 2 inches deep.

In the bowl of an electric mixer beat the
eggs and sugar until combined well. Sift in the
flour, baking powder, and salt and beat the mixture
until smooth. Add the milk, butter, and vanilla and
beat until the batter is combined well.

Pour the batter into the cake pan and bake
in the middle of the oven for 50 minutes to 1 hour,
or until a cake tester inserted in the center of the
cake comes out clean. Let the cake cool in the pan
for 10 minutes and invert it onto a rack set over a
shallow baking pan to cool completely. *The cake
can be made 1 day ahead and kept in a cool place in an
airtight cake container.*

Working quickly, pour the icing over the
cake, smoothing the top and sides with a spatula.
Let the icing cool. Makes one 10-inch cake.

**QUIVIRA DRY CREEK VALLEY
ZINFANDEL '86**

PENUCHE ICING

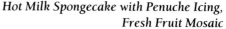

1½ cups firmly packed dark brown sugar
½ cup granulated sugar
1 tablespoon light corn syrup
½ stick (¼ cup) unsalted butter, cut
   into bits
½ cup heavy cream
1 teaspoon vanilla

☺ IN A HEAVY SAUCEPAN BRING THE SUGARS, CORN SYRUP, butter, and cream to a boil over moderate heat, stirring and washing down any sugar crystals clinging to the sides with a brush dipped in cold water until the sugar is dissolved. Boil the mixture, undisturbed, until it reaches the soft-ball stage, or a candy thermometer registers 238° F.

    Remove the saucepan from the heat and stir in the vanilla. Let the icing cool for 5 to 10 minutes, or until it is thickened. Stir gently for 1 to 2 minutes, or until the icing reaches spreading consistency. Pour it over the cake immediately.

FRESH FRUIT MOSAIC

2 papayas or 1 mango, peeled and cut
   into 1-inch pieces
2 cantaloupes, scooped into balls
   with a melon-ball cutter
1 honeydew melon, scooped into balls
   with a melon-ball cutter
½ watermelon, scooped into balls
   with a melon-ball cutter
½ cup sugar, or to taste
⅓ cup fresh lime juice, or to taste
2 teaspoons grated lime zest

☺ + IN A SERVING BOWL COMBINE THE FRUITS AND sprinkle with the sugar, lime juice, and lime zest. Toss the fruit gently and chill it, covered, for at least 2 hours. Serves 16.

Hot Milk Spongecake with Penuche Icing,
Fresh Fruit Mosaic

A HARVEST PATIO DINNER

CAESAR SALAD

GRILLED DUCK WITH MUSTARD AND BASIL

STUFFED TOMATOES PROVENÇALE

BAKED POLENTA WITH PARMESAN

**DEVIL'S FOOD CAKE WITH
CHOCOLATE ICING**

Just when you begin to feel that you really must put the barbecue grill away for the season, the weatherman promises a warm weekend. Why not host a last-minute dinner party for a few close friends and enjoy the patio one more time? Tell your guests to don their favorite toasty sweaters and, as they arrive, lead them to the patio for cocktails before the sun gives up its last light. As a special treat, gather everyone around a crackling fire as you return indoors!

The Fall season calls for robust meals full of strong, true flavors. To this end our menu begins with garlicky Caesar salad and ends with rich chocolate cake. The duck, our entrée, also is a source of full-bodied flavor. We recommend that you take advantage of the still-available outdoor grill but, if you prefer, the duck can be cooked on the stove in a grill pan. Sprinkle the sectioned pieces with herbs and spices the night before so that they have ample time to absorb all the good flavors. Boning the breasts may be a little tricky, but if you work slowly, using your fingers as well as a flexible, sharp knife, you will have success. Duck carcasses, by the way, freeze well and will add rich body to stocks; toss them in with some chicken or turkey bones—you will taste the difference.

The polenta, too, can be made the day before the party. The secret to smooth, creamy polenta is to stir the cornmeal mixture diligently as it slowly cooks. No shortcuts here, please. Stand at the stove for the full 15 to 20 minutes and give your stirring arm a good workout.

We highly recommend making the devil's food cake the day before, since it mellows with a little age. Cover the layers with plastic wrap and refrigerate them until an hour or so before serving. Then, make the chocolate icing and assemble the cake. It will be ready to serve when you are.

CAESAR SALAD

3 garlic cloves
¾ teaspoon salt
6 tablespoons olive oil
5 slices of homemade-type white bread,
   crusts discarded and the bread cut into
   ½-inch cubes
2 tablespoons fresh lemon juice
1 teaspoon Worcestershire sauce
2 heads of romaine, torn into bite-size
   pieces
½ cup freshly grated Parmesan
salt and freshly ground pepper to taste
drained flat anchovy fillets, if desired

PREHEAT THE OVEN TO 350° F.

In a mortar with a pestle mash the garlic to a paste with the salt. Stir in 2 tablespoons of the oil and force the garlic mixture through a fine sieve into a bowl.

In a jelly-roll pan bake the bread cubes in the middle of the oven for 10 minutes. Toss them with the garlic mixture until well coated. Return the croutons to the pan and bake for 3 minutes, or until golden. Let them cool in the pan on a rack.

In a salad bowl drizzle the remaining 4 tablespoons oil, lemon juice, and Worcestershire sauce over the romaine and sprinkle it with the Parmesan, croutons, and salt and pepper. Serve the salad with the anchovies. Serves 6.

GRILLED DUCK WITH MUSTARD
AND BASIL

3 ducks, each 5 pounds
1 tablespoon coarse salt
1½ tablespoons minced fresh thyme *or*
   1½ teaspoons dried, crumbled
¾ teaspoon ground allspice
freshly ground pepper to taste
5 tablespoons unsalted butter, softened
2¾ tablespoons Dijon-style mustard
2 tablespoons minced fresh basil
1 teaspoon minced shallot
½ teaspoon minced garlic
1 cup fresh bread crumbs

CUT THE LEGS FROM THE DUCKS, KEEPING THE THIGHS attached to the drumsticks. Working the knife down either side of the breastbone, cut off each side of the breast meat in one piece. (You will have 4 pieces from each duck: 2 whole legs with thighs and 2 boneless breasts.)

Score the skin on the duck pieces in a cross-hatch pattern ¼ inch deep. In a small bowl combine the salt, thyme, allspice, and pepper and sprinkle the mixture over the pieces. In a large bowl chill the pieces, covered, for at least 12 hours. *The duck can be prepared 1 day ahead up to this point and kept refrigerated.*

In a bowl combine well 4 tablespoons of the butter, 2 teaspoons of the mustard, the basil, shallot, and garlic and chill the mixture, covered, for 15 minutes. Transfer the mixture to a sheet of wax paper and roll the paper around it to form a log. Chill the herb butter until firm.

Prepare a charcoal grill with an oiled rack.

In a nonstick skillet cook the bread crumbs in the remaining 1 tablespoon butter over moderately low heat, stirring occasionally, for 5 minutes, or until golden. Stir in the remaining mustard.

Pat the duck pieces dry. Grill the leg pieces skin side down, turning, for 30 minutes, or until a meat thermometer inserted in the center of a leg registers 160° F. After 10 minutes, add the breasts skin side down and grill them, turning, for 12 minutes for medium-rare meat, or until springy to the touch.

Divide the duck legs among heated serving plates and top them with the crumb mixture. Transfer the breasts to a cutting board and let them stand for 5 minutes. Holding a knife at a 45° angle, slice the breasts thinly across the grain. Fan several slices around each leg and tuck slices of the herb butter among them. Serves 6.

STUFFED TOMATOES PROVENÇALE

6 tomatoes, cored
1 onion, diced
2 tablespoons olive oil
2 garlic cloves, minced
¼ cup fine dry bread crumbs
3 tablespoons minced parsley leaves
⅓ cup chopped brine-cured olives
cayenne to taste
salt and freshly ground pepper to taste

CUT OFF THE TOP THIRD OF EACH TOMATO, RESERVING it, and scoop out the pulp, discarding the seeds. Sprinkle the tomato shells with salt and invert them onto a rack to drain.

Preheat the oven to 350° F.

Chop the pulp and reserved tops. In a skillet cook the onion in the oil over moderately low heat, stirring, until softened. Add the garlic and cook, stirring, for 1 minute. Add the chopped tomato and cook, stirring occasionally, for 10 minutes, or until almost all the liquid is evaporated. Stir in the remaining ingredients.

Mound the mixture in the tomato shells and bake them in an oiled baking pan in the middle of the oven for 10 minutes, or until heated through. Serves 6.

BAKED POLENTA WITH PARMESAN

7½ cups water
2¼ teaspoons salt
2¼ cups yellow cornmeal (not stone-ground)
5 tablespoons unsalted butter, cut into bits
freshly ground pepper to taste
¾ cup freshly grated Parmesan

PREHEAT THE OVEN TO 400° F.

In a heavy saucepan bring the water to a boil and add the salt and cornmeal carefully in a very slow stream, whisking constantly. Cook the cornmeal over moderately low heat, stirring constantly with a wooden spoon, for 15 minutes, or until it is smooth and thick. Stir in 4 tablespoons of the butter and the pepper and pour into a buttered 8-inch-square flameproof baking pan. Sprinkle the top with the Parmesan and dot with the remaining butter. *The polenta can be made 1 day ahead up to this point and kept chilled, covered.*

Bake the polenta in the middle of the oven for 25 minutes, or until the edges are bubbling. Broil the polenta 4 inches from the heat for 3 minutes, or until it is browned lightly. Serves 6.

Grilled Duck with Mustard and Basil,
Stuffed Tomatoes Provençale

DEVIL'S FOOD CAKE WITH CHOCOLATE ICING

1½ sticks (¾ cup) unsalted butter,
 softened
1½ cups sugar
1½ teaspoons vanilla
3 large eggs, beaten well
3 ounces unsweetened chocolate, melted
 and cooled
2½ cups sifted cake flour
1¼ teaspoons baking soda
1 teaspoon salt
1½ cups buttermilk
2 tablespoons ice water

FOR THE ICING:
16 ounces semisweet chocolate,
 melted and cooled
1 cup sour cream at room temperature
½ teaspoon vanilla

PREHEAT THE OVEN TO 350° F.

Line the bottoms of 3 buttered 8-inch round cake pans with wax paper and butter the paper. In a large bowl cream the butter and beat in the sugar, a little at a time, and the vanilla. Beat the mixture until it is light and fluffy. Add the eggs and chocolate and combine well.

Into a large bowl sift the flour, baking soda, and salt and add alternately with the buttermilk to the chocolate mixture. Combine the batter until smooth. Add the ice water and stir 3 or 4 times, or until just combined. (The batter will be thick.)

Divide evenly among the prepared pans and smooth the tops. Bake the layers in the middle of the oven for 25 to 30 minutes, or until a cake tester inserted in the center of each cake comes out clean. Let the layers cool in the pans on racks for 10 minutes. Turn them out onto the racks, peel off the paper, and let them cool completely. *The layers can be made 1 day ahead and kept refrigerated, covered with plastic wrap.*

Make the icing: In a bowl beat together the chocolate, the sour cream, a pinch of salt, and the vanilla until the icing is combined well. The icing should be very glossy. If the sour cream is too cold the icing will become too firm; if this happens, beat in 1 to 2 tablespoons hot water to soften the icing.

Arrange 1 layer on a cake plate and spread it with a thin layer of the icing. Add another layer and spread it with a thin layer of icing. Add the remaining layer and spread the remaining icing over the top and sides. Makes one 8-inch cake.

**MONT ST. JOHN NAPA VALLEY
CABERNET SAUVIGNON '82**

MENU

A SOUTHERN THANKSGIVING

**CREAMED SMOKED OYSTERS
ON CORN STICKS**

**ROAST TURKEY WITH PECAN
AND RICE STUFFING**

SPICED PEARS

PICKLED OKRA

RED PEPPER JELLY

**RUM-GLAZED SWEET POTATO, APPLE,
AND CHESTNUT GRATIN**

GREEN BEANS WITH BACON

CAULIFLOWER SLAW

PUMPKIN PIE

AMBROSIA

SERVES EIGHT

Join us south of the Mason-Dixon Line for a Thanksgiving meal as inviting as a paneled front door opening off a wide veranda. The South, trusted keeper of some of our most treasured traditions, cooks with a keen memory of what has gone before and a clear eye on what is good today. We have assembled a Thanksgiving feast with all the trimmings of a good old-fashioned Southern meal as well as a smart nod to current culinary trends.

In the earliest days, colonists and Native Americans alike indulged in the plentiful oysters available for the picking in the shallow coastal waters. From Maryland to South Carolina to the Gulf Coast, the succulent gems of the sea were devoured with glee by rich and poor. Entrepreneurs soon discovered oysters could be packed in barrels and kept alive for shipping inland, especially in the cold months, and they soon became an expected treat on holiday tables from Kentucky to Mississippi. We serve them here—smoked and easy to find in any supermarket—bathed in a quick cream sauce. Spoon them over corn sticks, another Southern favorite, baked in special pans with corn

cob indentations. Neither the oysters nor the corn sticks take well to advance preparation, but as both are fast and easy to make, you should have little trouble serving them as a first course.

The rest of the meal, with the exception of the green beans, demands early planning and so, when the family is gathered around the holiday table, there will be little for you to do but transfer everything from the kitchen to the table—we hope with a lot of help from eager hands.

Condiments, which add splashes of color and sharp, strong flavor to a meal, are essentially American and common throughout the South. All three of ours taste wonderful with the mild turkey and honey-sweetened gratin. Spiced pears, made with firm, tasty Bartletts, should be prepared weeks before serving to give the flavors time to mellow. If you do not have a canning kettle, you can safely prepare the pears 5 or 6 days before Thanksgiving and keep them in the refrigerator. This is also true of the pickled okra, although in both instances the flavor will be better if each is canned in the early Fall when the produce is best. The red pepper jelly is very easy to make. Just be sure to let the peppers, sprinkled with salt, drain for the full 3 hours before squeezing them dry. They are full of moisture and really must be as dry as can be for good results.

Pecans grow in the deep South and when they are mixed into a rice, mushroom, and herb mixture the result is a stuffing worthy of any turkey. Don't stuff the turkey until just before roasting, but do mix up the stuffing ahead of time. Warm the extra stuffing and serve it as a side dish. The sweet potato and apple gratin can be assembled the day before Thanksgiving, but is best cooked just before serving. The slaw, a crunchy, pretty switch from green salad, does fine if dressed a little ahead of time and left to marinate in the refrigerator or on the counter for an hour or so.

This Thanksgiving dinner is brought to a close with gently spiced pumpkin pie, baked and cooled well in advance of the meal, and sweet ambrosia, which should also be put together ahead of time. It is a simple mixture of coconut and oranges and tastes just right after a big meal—or you may choose to serve it as a side dish with the main course, which is also quite acceptable.

CREAMED SMOKED OYSTERS ON CORN STICKS

3 tablespoons minced shallot
⅔ cup dry white wine
2 cups heavy cream
2 tablespoons water
two 3¾ ounce cans smoked oysters, drained and rinsed
fresh lemon juice to taste
2 tablespoons minced fresh parsley leaves
salt and white pepper to taste
corn sticks (recipe follows)

In a stainless steel or enameled saucepan boil the shallot and wine over moderately high heat until reduced to about 1 tablespoon. Add the cream and water and return to a boil. Simmer until thick enough to coat a spoon. Add the oysters and simmer, stirring occasionally, for 5 minutes, or until heated through. Stir in the lemon juice, parsley, and salt and white pepper.

The creamed oysters can be made ahead and kept refrigerated, covered, overnight. Reheat, uncovered, over moderate heat.

Halve 8 corn sticks lengthwise and arrange 1 half on each serving plate. Spoon some of the creamed oysters over it and top with the remaining half. Serves 8.

CORN STICKS

1 cup white cornmeal, preferably stone-ground
1 cup all-purpose flour
2 teaspoons baking powder
1 teaspoon salt
1 cup milk
2 large eggs, beaten lightly
½ stick (¼ cup) unsalted butter, melted and cooled
lard *or* vegetable shortening as needed

PREHEAT THE OVEN TO 400° F.

Into a bowl sift the dry ingredients. In another bowl combine the milk, eggs, and butter. Add the egg mixture to the dry ingredients and stir until just combined. Grease two 5-stick corn stick molds with the shortening and heat in the oven for 5 minutes.

Spoon the batter into the molds, filling almost to the top, and bake in the middle of the oven for 15 minutes, or until golden. Invert onto a rack to cool. Makes 10 corn sticks.

ROAST TURKEY WITH PECAN AND RICE STUFFING

FOR THE STUFFING:
3 cups chopped onion
2 cups chopped celery
3 garlic cloves, minced, or to taste
salt and freshly ground pepper to taste
1 stick (½ cup) unsalted butter
½ pound mushrooms, sliced
5 cups cooked rice
1½ cups toasted pecans, chopped coarse
½ cup minced fresh parsley leaves
1 tablespoon dried sage, crumbled
1½ teaspoons dried thyme, crumbled
¼ teaspoon ground mace
¼ teaspoon freshly grated nutmeg, if desired

12- to 15-pound turkey, giblets reserved for making stock
salt and freshly ground pepper to taste
1 stick (½ cup) unsalted butter, softened
4 cups turkey giblet stock (page 198), or chicken broth
¼ cup flour
Worcestershire sauce to taste
Tabasco to taste

MAKE THE STUFFING: IN A LARGE STAINLESS STEEL OR enameled skillet cook the onion, celery, garlic, and salt and pepper in 6 tablespoons of the butter over moderate heat, stirring, until softened. Transfer the mixture to a large bowl.

In the skillet sauté the mushrooms with salt and pepper to taste in the remaining 2 tablespoons butter over moderately high heat, stirring, for 2 to 3 minutes, or until they begin to give off their liquid. Add the mushrooms to the vegetables with the remaining stuffing ingredients and combine well.

Rinse the turkey and pat dry. Season inside and out with salt and pepper. Pack the neck cavity loosely with some of the stuffing and fold the neck skin under the body. Fasten with a skewer. Pack the body cavity loosely with some of the stuffing and truss the turkey.

Transfer the remaining stuffing to a buttered 1½-quart baking dish and reserve it, covered and chilled.

Preheat the oven to 425° F.

Spread the turkey with ½ stick of the butter and roast it on the rack of a roasting pan in the middle of the oven for 30 minutes. Reduce the heat to 325° F. Baste the turkey with the pan juices and drape it with a piece of cheesecloth soaked in 1 cup of the stock and the remaining ½ stick butter, melted and cooled.

Roast the turkey, basting it every 20 minutes, for 2½ to 3 hours more, or until the juices run clear when the fleshy part of a thigh is pricked with a skewer and a meat thermometer inserted in the fleshy part of a thigh registers 180° F. During the last hour of roasting time, bake the reserved stuffing, covered.

Discard the cheesecloth, skewer, and trussing strings and transfer the turkey to a platter. Keep the turkey warm, covered loosely with foil.

Skim off all but ¼ cup of the fat from the pan juices. Add the flour and cook over moderately low heat, stirring, until browned lightly. Add the remaining 3 cups stock in a stream, whisking, and simmer it, stirring occasionally, for 20 minutes. Boil the mixture over moderately high heat until reduced to 2½ cups. Add the Worcestershire sauce, Tabasco, and salt and pepper to taste and simmer the gravy for 5 minutes. Strain the gravy into a heated sauceboat. Serve it with the turkey and stuffing. Serves 8.

SPICED PEARS

3 cups sugar
1 cup white vinegar
3 cinnamon sticks, each 3 inches long
2 teaspoons whole cloves
6 whole allspice
3 pounds Bartlett pears, peeled, halved if
    small or quartered if large, and cored

+ IN A HEAVY STAINLESS STEEL OR ENAMELED SAUCEPAN bring the sugar, vinegar, and spices to a boil, stirring, and boil the mixture for 5 minutes. Add the pears and simmer them, covered with wax paper, for 10 to 15 minutes, or until tender. Spoon the pears into sterilized 1-pint Mason-type jars (procedure on page 199) and pour the syrup over them to within ½ inch of the top of the jars. Seal the jars with the lids.

Put the jars in a water bath canner or on a rack in a deep kettle and add enough hot water to cover the jars by 2 inches. Bring to a boil and process, covered, for 10 minutes. Transfer the jars with canning tongs to a rack and let them cool. The pears can be served immediately or stored in a cool, dark place. Makes 3 pints.

MICROWAVE DIRECTIONS

INGREDIENT CHANGE:
Use 6 or 7 firm-ripe pears to weigh a total of 3 pounds, peeled, cored, and quartered.

DIRECTIONS:
Combine the sugar, vinegar, cinnamon sticks, cloves, and allspice in a microwave-safe 3-quart casserole. Cover with a lid and microwave at high power (100%) for 8 minutes, until boiling. Stir. Add the pears. Microwave, uncovered, at high power (100%) for 7 minutes, until just tender, stirring after 4 minutes. Let the pears cool in the syrup. They can be served immediately or stored in the refrigerator, covered, for up to 1 week. If desired, the pears can be processed and stored as in the conventional cooking recipe above.

PICKLED OKRA

1 pound okra, untrimmed
2 fresh hot green chilies, each
    2½ inches long, halved lengthwise and
    seeded (wear rubber gloves) or
    ½ teaspoon red pepper flakes
4 garlic cloves
2 cups cider vinegar
1 tablespoon dill seeds
1 tablespoon salt
2 teaspoons mustard seeds

+ ARRANGE THE OKRA STEM END UP IN 2 STERILIZED 1-pint Mason-type jars (procedure on page 199) and divide the peppers and garlic between the jars.

In a stainless steel or enameled saucepan bring the remaining ingredients to a rolling boil. Pour the mixture over the okra to within ½ inch of the top of the jars and seal with the lids. Process the jars following the procedure for spiced pears (see opposite). The okra can be served immediately or stored in a cool, dark place. Makes 2 pints.

RED PEPPER JELLY

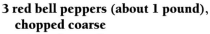

3 red bell peppers (about 1 pound),
    chopped coarse
1 onion, chopped coarse
4 fresh hot red chilies, each
    2½ inches long, chopped coarse
    (wear rubber gloves) or 1 teaspoon
    red pepper flakes
1 tablespoon salt
4½ cups sugar
1¼ cups white vinegar
½ cup fresh lemon juice
6 whole cloves
6 ounces liquid pectin (¾ cup)

IN A FOOD PROCESSOR GRIND IN BATCHES THE BELL peppers, onion, and chilies, transferring the mixture to a large sieve as it is ground. Toss the mixture

with 1½ teaspoons of the salt and let it drain for 3 hours. Squeeze dry gently.

In a heavy stainless steel or enameled saucepan combine the vegetables with the sugar, vinegar, lemon juice, cloves, and remaining 1½ teaspoons salt and bring the mixture to a boil, stirring. Boil for 10 minutes. Add the pectin and boil, stirring, for 1 minute. Pour the jelly into sterilized ½-pint Mason-type glasses and seal with paraffin (procedures on page 199). The jelly can be served immediately or stored in a cool, dark place. Makes four ½-pint glasses.

RUM-GLAZED SWEET POTATO, APPLE, AND CHESTNUT GRATIN

3 pounds sweet potatoes, pricked several
    times with a skewer
3 Golden Delicious apples
¼ cup fresh lemon juice
1 cup halved vacuum-packed roasted
    chestnuts (available at specialty
    food shops)
¾ stick (6 tablespoons) unsalted butter
½ cup firmly packed light brown sugar
½ cup honey
2 tablespoons dark rum
½ teaspoon cinnamon
¼ teaspoon ground ginger
¼ teaspoon ground mace

PREHEAT THE OVEN TO 400° F.

Bake the sweet potatoes in the middle of the oven for 45 minutes to 1 hour, or until tender. Let them cool. Peel the sweet potatoes and cut them diagonally into ¼-inch slices.

Peel the apples and cut them lengthwise into eighths. In a bowl toss the apples with the lemon juice and arrange them with the sweet potato slices in a buttered 14-inch gratin dish. Sprinkle with the chestnuts.

In a stainless steel or enameled saucepan cook the remaining ingredients over moderate heat, stirring, until the sugar is dissolved. Spoon the mixture over the sweet potatoes and apples and bake the gratin in the middle of the oven, basting occasionally, for 30 minutes, or until the apples are just tender and the sweet potatoes are heated through. *The uncooked gratin can be assembled 1 day ahead and kept refrigerated, covered. Bake, uncovered, basting occasionally, for 40 minutes.*

Put the gratin under a preheated broiler about 4 inches from the heat until the edges are browned lightly. Serves 8.

MICROWAVE DIRECTIONS

INGREDIENT CHANGES:
Reduce butter to ¼ cup; reduce honey to ¼ cup. Select 6 evenly sized sweet potatoes to weigh a total of 3 pounds; use medium apples.

DIRECTIONS:
Prick the sweet potatoes as directed. Arrange them, spoke-fashion, on a double layer of paper towels on the oven floor. Microwave at high power (100%), uncovered, for 16 to 18 minutes, until they are just tender, turning the potatoes over after 10 minutes. While the potatoes are cooking cut the apples as directed and toss them with the lemon juice. Cool the potatoes slightly; peel them and slice them diagonally into ¼-inch slices. Combine the butter, brown sugar, ¼ cup honey, rum, cinnamon, ginger, and mace in a microwave-safe 4-cup measure. Microwave, uncovered, at high power (100%) for 2½ minutes, swirling the mixture after 1½ minutes. Arrange the sweet potatoes, apples, and chestnuts as in recipe above in a microwave-safe baking dish about 10 inches square and 2 inches deep. Pour the butter mixture over the potatoes and apples. Microwave, uncovered, at high power (100%) for 10 minutes, basting after 5 minutes. Cover and let stand for 3 minutes.

GREEN BEANS WITH BACON

**¼ pound slab bacon, diced
1 onion, minced
2 pounds green beans, trimmed
1 teaspoon red pepper flakes, or to taste
salt to taste
1 cup boiling water
2 tablespoons unsalted butter, softened
3 tablespoons white vinegar, or to taste
freshly ground pepper to taste**

🕭 IN A LARGE, DEEP SKILLET COOK THE BACON OVER moderate heat, stirring, until golden. Transfer the bacon with a slotted spoon to a plate. Add the onion to the skillet and cook, stirring, until softened. Add the beans, pepper flakes, and salt and sauté over moderately high heat, stirring, for 2 minutes.

Add the boiling water and cover the skillet immediately with the lid. Steam the beans, shaking the skillet occasionally, for 15 minutes, or until just tender. Add the butter, vinegar, and salt and pepper and toss until combined. Sprinkle with the bacon. Serves 8.

MICROWAVE DIRECTIONS

INGREDIENT CHANGES:
Reduce red pepper flakes to ½ teaspoon; use ½ cup cold water; eliminate salt.

DIRECTIONS:
Scatter the bacon on the bottom of a microwave-safe 13- by 9-inch baking dish. Cover the dish with a paper towel. Microwave at high power (100%) for 3½ minutes. Pour off all but 1 tablespoon of the bacon fat. Stir the onion into the dish. Microwave, uncovered, at high power (100%) for 4 minutes. Add the green beans, red pepper flakes, and the ½ cup cold water. Cover the dish and microwave at high power (100%) for 15 minutes, or until the beans are tender, stirring twice. Stir in the butter, vinegar, and pepper.

CAULIFLOWER SLAW

**1 head of cauliflower, trimmed and
    separated into small flowerets
½ head of cabbage, cored and
    shredded fine
2 celery stalks, sliced thin
½ cup sliced radishes
¼ cup minced scallion
2 tablespoons minced fresh parsley
    leaves
½ teaspoon celery seeds
½ cup french dressing (recipe follows),
    or to taste**

🕭 IN A LARGE SAUCEPAN OF BOILING SALTED WATER blanch the cauliflower for 1 minute. Drain it in a colander and refresh it under cold water. In a salad bowl combine the vegetables, parsley, and celery seeds, add the dressing, and toss well. Serves 8.

FRENCH DRESSING

**2 tablespoons white-wine vinegar *or*
    fresh lemon juice
salt and freshly ground pepper to taste
⅓ to ½ cup olive oil, or to taste
Dijon-style mustard *or* dry mustard to
    taste, if desired**

🕭 IN A BOWL COMBINE THE VINEGAR, AND SALT AND pepper. Add the oil in a stream, beating. Beat the mixture until emulsified. For a sharper dressing, add the mustard before adding the oil. Makes ½ cup.

PUMPKIN PIE

½ recipe flaky pie pastry (page 196)
1½ cups canned pumpkin purée
1 cup half-and-half
3 large eggs
⅓ cup firmly packed light brown sugar
⅓ cup granulated sugar
1 teaspoon vanilla
1 teaspoon cinnamon
½ teaspoon ground ginger
½ teaspoon salt
¼ teaspoon freshly grated nutmeg
pinch of ground cloves
lightly whipped cream as an
    accompaniment

ROLL OUT THE DOUGH ⅛ INCH THICK ON A LIGHTLY floured surface and fit the dough into a 9-inch pie plate. Crimp the edge decoratively and chill the shell for 1 hour.

Preheat the oven to 425° F.

In a large bowl combine all the remaining ingredients except the whipped cream until smooth. Pour the mixture into the shell and bake the pie on a baking sheet in the lower third of the oven for 15 minutes. Reduce the heat to 350° F. and bake it for 30 to 35 minutes more, or until a tester inserted in the center comes out clean. Let the pie cool and serve with the whipped cream. Makes one 9-inch pie.

AMBROSIA

6 navel oranges, peeled, pith removed,
    and sliced crosswise
2 cups freshly grated coconut (page 199)
    or 2 cups grated sweetened coconut
⅓ cup sugar, or to taste

☼+ IN A SHALLOW DISH ARRANGE A LAYER OF ORANGE slices and cover them with a layer of coconut. Sprinkle them with some of the sugar. Continue layering in the same manner, ending with a layer of oranges. Garnish the center of each orange slice with some of the coconut. Chill the ambrosia, covered, for at least 2 hours. *The ambrosia can be made ahead and kept refrigerated, covered, overnight.* Serves 8.

**BELVEDERE
RUSSIAN RIVER VALLEY
CHARDONNAY '87**
(*with main course*)

**RENAISSANCE NORTH YUBA SPECIAL
SELECT LATE HARVEST
WHITE RIESLING '85**
(*with dessert*)

A VICTORIAN THANKSGIVING

CLAM HASH CAKES

ROAST TURKEY WITH CORN BREAD, HAM, AND APRICOT STUFFING

CRANBERRY CHUTNEY

PEPPER CORN RELISH

HONEY PEAR CONSERVE

GRATIN OF FOUR ONIONS

SOUFFLÉED YAMS

LEMON PEAS

SPICED APPLE PIE

SERVES EIGHT

Here is a Thanksgiving meal so festive and fancy your guests will be surprised to find that you do not have a bevy of starched and aproned cooks hidden away in the kitchen. Victorian hostesses—the lucky ones, at any rate—relied on skilled staffs to help prepare most meals. We realize only too well that today's hostess rarely has a loyal cook behind the scenes, and so when we assembled our Victorian Thanksgiving, we combined a number of dishes that can be made ahead of time with just a few that require last-minute preparation.

During the weeks leading up to the holiday, make the chutney, relish, and conserve. Make the cornbread stuffing, bake the yams, and line the pie plate with the dough the day before Thanksgiving. The next morning, bright and early if you plan to serve a midday meal, fill the chilled pie shell and bake it while you stuff the turkey. When the pie is done, immediately raise the oven temperature and begin roasting the turkey. Next on the agenda are the clam cakes and onions, both of which can be prepared several hours before serving. The cakes can be cooked ahead of time and then reheated in a moderate oven for about 10 minutes before being served as the first course. While they are being eaten, slip the onions and the soufflé into a hotter oven to cook for a brief 20 minutes or so while you concern yourself with nothing more taxing than the lightly lemon-scented peas.

Roast Turkey; Gratin of Four Onions;
Cranberry Chutney

CLAM HASH CAKES

48 small hard-shelled clams, scrubbed
  or 1 cup drained canned minced clams
1 cup water
½ pound lean sliced bacon, chopped
1 small onion, minced
1 pound russet potatoes, peeled, chopped
  fine, and put in cold water
3 large eggs, beaten lightly
2 tablespoons minced fresh parsley leaves
salt and freshly ground pepper to taste
2 tablespoons unsalted butter
1 to 2 teaspoons drained bottled horseradish
1 teaspoon fresh lemon juice, or to taste

○ IN A KETTLE STEAM THE CLAMS WITH THE WATER,
covered, over high heat, shaking the kettle occasionally, for 7 to 8 minutes, or until most of the
shells have opened. Discard any unopened clams.
Let the clams cool. Remove the meat from the
shells and mince it.

In a skillet cook the bacon over moderate
heat, stirring, until crisp and golden. Transfer it to
paper towels to drain. Reserve the fat.

In the skillet cook the onion in 1 tablespoon
of the fat over moderately low heat until softened
and transfer it to a large bowl. In the skillet cook
the potatoes, drained well and patted dry, in 2 tablespoons of the fat over moderately high heat, stirring, until tender. Transfer them to the bowl and
stir in the bacon, clams, eggs, 1 tablespoon of the
parsley, and salt and pepper. Combine well.

Heat a large griddle or heavy skillet over
moderately high heat until hot and brush with
some of the fat. Drop the clam mixture by scant
¼ cups onto the griddle and with a fork pat it into
neat cakes about ¼ inch thick. Cook them for
1 minute on each side, or until golden.
*The cakes can be made several hours ahead
and kept, covered loosely, on a baking sheet in the refrigerator. Reheat them, uncovered, in a preheated
300° F. oven until hot.*

In a small saucepan melt the butter over
moderately low heat and stir in the horseradish,
lemon juice, and remaining 1 tablespoon parsley.
Drizzle over the clam cakes. Serves 8.

ROAST TURKEY WITH CORN BREAD, HAM, AND APRICOT STUFFING

FOR THE STUFFING:
buttermilk corn bread (recipe follows)
4 cups chopped onion
2 cups chopped celery
3 garlic cloves, minced
salt and freshly ground pepper to taste
⅓ cup vegetable oil
2 cups chopped dried apricots
½ pound sliced smoked ham, such as
  Black Forest or Westphalian,
  chopped fine
½ cup minced fresh parsley leaves
3 tablespoons minced fresh sage *or*
  1 tablespoon dried, crumbled
2 tablespoons minced fresh marjoram *or*
  2 teaspoons dried, crumbled
1 tablespoon minced fresh rosemary *or*
  1 teaspoon dried, crumbled
½ teaspoon freshly grated nutmeg
1 stick (½ cup) unsalted butter, melted
  and cooled

12- to 15-pound turkey, giblets reserved
  for making stock
salt and freshly ground pepper to taste
1 stick (½ cup) unsalted butter, softened
4 cups turkey giblet stock (page 198), *or*
  chicken broth
¼ cup flour

PREHEAT THE OVEN TO 325° F.

Make the stuffing: Crumble the corn bread
coarsely into 2 jelly-roll pans and bake it in the
middle of the oven, stirring frequently, for 30 to 40
minutes, or until dry and deep golden. Let it cool
and transfer to a large bowl.

In a large skillet cook the onion, celery, garlic, and salt and pepper in the oil over moderate
heat, stirring, until softened. Add the mixture to
the corn bread with the remaining ingredients.
Toss gently to combine well and let the stuffing
cool completely. *The stuffing can be made 1 day
ahead and kept refrigerated, covered. Do not stuff the
turkey in advance.*

Increase the heat to 425° F.

Rinse the turkey and pat it dry. Season it inside and out with salt and pepper. Pack the neck cavity loosely with some of the stuffing and fold the neck skin under the body. Fasten with a skewer. Pack the body cavity loosely with some of the remaining stuffing and truss the turkey.

Transfer the remaining stuffing to a buttered 1½-quart baking dish and reserve it, covered and chilled.

Spread the turkey with ½ stick of the butter and roast the turkey on the rack of a roasting pan in the middle of the oven for 30 minutes. Reduce the heat to 325° F. Baste the turkey with the pan juices and drape it with a piece of cheesecloth soaked in 1 cup of the stock and the remaining ½ stick butter, melted and cooled.

Continue to roast the turkey, basting every 20 minutes, for 2½ to 3 hours more, or until the juices run clear when the fleshy part of a thigh is pricked with a skewer and a meat thermometer inserted in the fleshy part of a thigh registers 180° F. During the last hour of roasting, bake the reserved stuffing, covered.

Discard the cheesecloth, skewer, and trussing strings and transfer the turkey to a platter. Keep it warm, covered loosely with foil.

Skim off all but ¼ cup of the fat from the pan juices. Add the flour and cook the mixture over moderately low heat, stirring, for 5 minutes. Add the remaining 3 cups stock in a stream, whisking, and simmer the mixture, stirring occasionally, for 20 minutes, or until reduced to 2½ cups. Season the gravy with salt and pepper and strain it into a heated sauceboat, pressing hard on the solids. Serve the gravy with the turkey and the stuffing. Serves 8.

BUTTERMILK CORN BREAD

1 cup yellow cornmeal
1 cup all-purpose flour
4 teaspoons baking powder
¼ teaspoon baking soda
½ teaspoon salt
¼ cup plus 1 teaspoon chilled
  vegetable shortening
1 cup buttermilk
1 large egg, beaten lightly

PREHEAT THE OVEN TO 425° F.

In a bowl combine well the dry ingredients and add ¼ cup of the shortening, cut into bits. Blend until the mixture resembles coarse meal. Stir in the buttermilk and the egg and stir until combined but still slightly lumpy.

In an 8-inch-square baking pan heat the remaining 1 teaspoon shortening in the oven for 5 minutes. Tilt the pan to coat the bottom and sides well with the shortening and pour in the batter. Bake the corn bread in the middle of the oven for 20 to 25 minutes, or until the top is golden and a skewer comes out clean. Let the corn bread cool in the pan for 5 minutes.

JOSEPH PHELPS VINEYARDS
EARLY HARVEST
JOHANNISBERG RIESLING '88
(with first course)

BYRON VINEYARDS
SANTA BARBARA COUNTY
PINOT NOIR '87
(with main course)

CRANBERRY CHUTNEY

½ cup cider vinegar
2¼ cups firmly packed light brown sugar, or to taste
¾ teaspoon curry powder
½ teaspoon ground ginger
½ teaspoon cinnamon
¼ teaspoon ground cloves
¼ teaspoon ground allspice
1½ cups water
2 lemons, zest grated, pith discarded, fruit cut into sections
2 navel oranges, zest grated, pith discarded, fruit cut into sections
1 apple, peeled, cored, and chopped coarse
6 cups cranberries, picked over
½ cup golden raisins
½ cup chopped dried peaches
½ cup chopped walnuts

IN A LARGE SAUCEPAN BRING TO A BOIL THE VINEGAR, sugar, spices, and water, stirring until the sugar is dissolved. Add the zests, fruit sections, and apple and simmer, stirring, for 10 minutes. Add 3 cups of the cranberries, the raisins, and the peaches and simmer, stirring occasionally, for 30 to 40 minutes, or until thickened.

Stir in 2 cups of the remaining cranberries and simmer, stirring, for 10 minutes. Stir in the remaining 1 cup cranberries and the walnuts and simmer, stirring, for 15 minutes. Transfer the mixture to a bowl and let it cool. Chill, covered, overnight. *The chutney can be made 2 weeks ahead and kept refrigerated, covered.*

Alternatively, before cooling, spoon the hot chutney into 3 sterilized 1-pint Mason-type jars (procedure on page 199), filling the jars to within ¼ inch of the top. Wipe the rims with a dampened cloth and seal with the lids. Put the jars in a water bath canner or on a rack in a deep kettle and add enough hot water to cover the jars by 2 inches. Bring to a boil and process, covered, for 10 minutes. Transfer the jars with canning tongs to a rack and let them cool. Store the jars in a cool, dark place. Serve at room temperature. Makes 3 pints.

MICROWAVE DIRECTIONS

INGREDIENT CHANGES:
Reduce water to ½ cup. Add 2 tablespoons cornstarch dissolved in 2 tablespoons water.

DIRECTIONS:
Place the vinegar, sugar, spices, and the ½ cup water in a microwave-safe 3-quart casserole. Cover and microwave at high power (100%) for 6 minutes, or until boiling. Add the lemons, oranges, apple, raisins, peaches, and 3 cups of the cranberries. Microwave at high power (100%) for 12 minutes, or until the mixture reaches full boil, stirring once during the cooking. Stir in the dissolved cornstarch, remaining 3 cups cranberries, and nuts. Microwave at high power (100%) for 8 minutes, or until thickened. Let it cool and chill as directed.

The following relish and conserve recipes can be made 1 week ahead and kept chilled, covered. Or, you may follow the procedure in the preceding cranberry chutney recipe for canning.

PEPPER CORN RELISH

5½ cups cooked fresh corn (about 8 ears) *or* frozen corn, thawed
1 green bell pepper, chopped
1 red bell pepper, chopped
1 large onion, chopped
2 carrots, chopped
1½ cups sugar
1 teaspoon dry mustard
½ teaspoon celery seeds
¼ teaspoon turmeric
1⅓ cups cider vinegar

 IN A SAUCEPAN COMBINE THE VEGETABLES, SUGAR, and seasonings. Stir in the vinegar gradually and bring to a boil, stirring until the sugar is dissolved. Simmer, stirring occasionally, for 25 to 30 minutes, or until the vegetables are just tender and the liquid is thickened. Transfer to a bowl and let cool. Chill, covered, overnight. Makes about 3½ pints.

MICROWAVE DIRECTIONS

INGREDIENT CHANGE:
Use frozen corn only.

DIRECTIONS:
Place the carrots, sugar, spices, and vinegar in a microwave-safe 3-quart casserole. Microwave, uncovered, at high power (100%) for 15 minutes, or until the carrots are tender-crisp. Stir in the *thawed* corn, peppers, and onion. Microwave at high power (100%) for 20 minutes, stirring once halfway through the cooking. Let the relish cool and chill as directed.

HONEY PEAR CONSERVE

**4 pounds Anjou pears, peeled, cored, and
    cut into 1-inch pieces
¾ cup fresh lemon juice
1 cup honey, or to taste
2 teaspoons cinnamon
½ teaspoon ground cloves
½ cup dried currants**

IN A SAUCEPAN COOK THE PEARS, LEMON JUICE, honey, and spices over moderate heat. Stir until it begins to simmer. Simmer, stirring occasionally, for 35 minutes, or until thickened. Add the currants and simmer, covered partially, stirring occasionally, for 15 minutes. Transfer to a bowl and let it cool. Chill, covered, overnight. Makes 2 pints.

MICROWAVE DIRECTIONS

INGREDIENT CHANGE:
Add 1½ tablespoons cornstarch dissolved in 2 tablespoons water.

DIRECTIONS:
In a microwave-safe 3-quart casserole combine the lemon juice, honey, and spices until blended. Stir in the pears and currants. Cover and microwave at high power (100%) for 25 minutes, or until simmering, stirring 2 times during the cooking. Stir in the dissolved cornstarch and microwave at high power (100%) for 5 minutes, or until thickened. Let the conserve cool and chill as directed.

GRATIN OF FOUR ONIONS

**½ pound shallots, chopped
1 large yellow onion, halved lengthwise
    and sliced thin
2 bunches of leeks, dark green tops
    discarded, halved lengthwise, washed
    well, and chopped
2 garlic cloves, minced
3 tablespoons unsalted butter
1-pound bag frozen pearl onions
2 cups béchamel sauce (page 196)
salt and freshly ground pepper to taste
¼ cup minced fresh parsley leaves
1 tablespoon fine dry bread crumbs**

IN A LARGE SKILLET COOK THE SHALLOTS, YELLOW onion, leeks, and garlic in the butter over moderately low heat, stirring, until softened. Add the pearl onions and cook, stirring, until they are just tender. Stir in the béchamel sauce and bring to a boil. Simmer, stirring, for 5 minutes. Season with salt and pepper and stir in the parsley. *The onions can be made several hours ahead up to this point and kept at room temperature, covered loosely.*
Preheat the oven to 475° F.
Spoon the mixture into a buttered 1½- to 2-quart shallow baking dish and sprinkle with the crumbs. Bake in the middle of the oven for 15 to 20 minutes, or until bubbling around the edges and golden on top. Serve immediately. Serves 8.

MICROWAVE DIRECTIONS

INGREDIENT CHANGES:
Increase flour in béchamel sauce to 3 tablespoons.

DIRECTIONS:
Place butter in a microwave-safe 3-quart casserole and microwave at high power (100%) for 1 minute, or until melted. Add the shallots, onion, leeks, garlic, and *thawed* pearl onions. Cover with wax paper and microwave at high power (100%) for 25 minutes, or until softened, stirring once during the cooking. Stir in the béchamel and microwave at high power (100%) for 10 minutes, or until heated through. Continue with recipe as directed.

SOUFFLÉED YAMS

**4 large yams *or* sweet potatoes (about
    4 pounds)**
salt and freshly ground pepper to taste
2 tablespoons unsalted butter
½ cup milk *or* heavy cream
2 large eggs, separated
pinch of cream of tartar

PREHEAT THE OVEN TO 375° F.

Prick the yams with a fork and bake on a baking sheet in the middle of the oven for 1 hour, or until very tender. Let them cool until they can be handled. Halve, scrape the pulp into a bowl, and discard the skins. *The yams can be made 1 day ahead up to this point and kept refrigerated, covered.*

Increase the heat to 475° F.

Let the yams come to room temperature. Mash and season them with salt and pepper. In a small saucepan heat the butter and milk over moderately low heat until the butter is melted. Stir the mixture into the yams and stir in the egg yolks.

In a bowl beat the egg whites with a pinch of salt until frothy. Add the cream of tartar and beat until the whites hold stiff peaks. Fold into the yam mixture. Spoon into a buttered 1½- to 2-quart shallow baking dish. Smooth the top and score it lightly. Bake the yams in the middle of the oven for 15 to 20 minutes, or until puffed and browned lightly around the edges. Serve immediately. Serves 8.

LEMON PEAS

1 cup salted water
three 10-ounce packages frozen peas
2 tablespoons unsalted butter, softened
salt and freshly ground pepper to taste
grated zest of 1 lemon

◯ IN A LARGE SAUCEPAN BRING THE WATER TO A BOIL, add the peas, and return to a boil, breaking up the peas with a fork. Simmer, covered, for 3 to 4 minutes, or until heated through. Drain well. Transfer the peas to a heated serving dish and toss them well with the butter and salt and pepper. Sprinkle with the lemon zest. Serves 8.

MICROWAVE DIRECTIONS

INGREDIENT CHANGE:
Reduce water to ⅓ cup.

DIRECTIONS:
Place the water and *thawed* peas in a microwave-safe 1-quart casserole. Cover and microwave at high power (100%) for 12 minutes. Drain and continue with recipe as directed.

SPICED APPLE PIE

shortening pie dough (recipe follows)
⅓ cup raisins
2 tablespoons dark rum
¾ cup plus 2½ tablespoons sugar
3 tablespoons flour
½ teaspoon cinnamon
¼ teaspoon freshly grated nutmeg
¼ teaspoon ground ginger
¼ teaspoon salt
½ teaspoon freshly grated lemon zest
**2½ pounds (about 6) Granny Smith
    apples, peeled, cored, and sliced thin**
1 teaspoon fresh lemon juice
**2 tablespoons cold unsalted butter,
    cut into bits**
1 tablespoon milk *or* half-and-half

DIVIDE THE DOUGH INTO 2 PIECES, ONE SLIGHTLY LARGER than the other. Chill the larger piece, wrapped in wax paper. Roll out the smaller piece ⅛ inch thick on a floured surface and fit it into a 9-inch pie plate, preferably ovenproof glass. Trim the edge, leaving a ½-inch overhang. Chill the shell.

In a small saucepan bring the raisins and rum to a simmer. Remove the mixture from the heat and let it stand for 15 minutes, or until the raisins have absorbed the rum.

In a large bowl stir together ¾ cup plus 2 tablespoons of the sugar, the flour, spices, salt, and lemon zest. Add the apple slices and raisins and toss to coat well. Mound in the shell, sprinkle with the lemon juice, and dot with the butter.

Preheat the oven to 425° F.

Roll the larger piece of dough into a 13- to 14-inch round on a floured surface and drape it over the filling. Trim the top crust, leaving a 1-inch overhang. Fold the overhang under the bottom crust, pressing the edge to seal it, and crimp decoratively. Make slits in the top for steam vents. Brush the top with the milk and sprinkle with the remaining ½ tablespoon sugar.

Bake on a baking sheet in the lower third of the oven for 15 minutes. Reduce the heat to 375° F. and bake for 40 minutes more, or until bubbly and golden. Transfer to a rack to cool. Serve warm or at room temperature. *The pie can be made 1 day ahead and kept at room temperature.* Makes one 9-inch pie.

SHORTENING PIE DOUGH

2⅓ cups all-purpose flour
½ teaspoon salt
¼ cup cold vegetable shortening,
  cut into bits
¼ cup ice water

◐+ IN A BOWL STIR TOGETHER THE FLOUR AND SALT AND blend in the shortening until the mixture resembles coarse meal. Add the ice water, or enough to make a soft but not sticky dough, tossing with a fork, and form into a ball. Flatten slightly and dust with flour. Chill, wrapped in wax paper, for 1 hour.

Spiced Apple Pie

We promise. No one will miss the turkey. For a light Thanksgiving that celebrates the good foods most available in the late Fall, plan on serving this easy menu. With a deliberately soft tread, we have sidestepped tradition but not the spirit of the holiday. The shopping list for our meatless feast includes squash, apples, sweet potatoes, chestnuts, Brussels sprouts, and cranberries, but all arrive at the table in unfamiliar guises.

Begin the meal with a thoroughly modern curried soup of butternut squash and tart Granny Smith apples. It can be made 24 hours ahead of time and reheated just before garnishing. This is followed by a satisfyingly filling kasha and cheese loaf served with a dark, earthy *shiitake* mushroom sauce. The loaf, which requires a good, long cooking time in a moderate oven, is simple to assemble; and the sauce can be made hours beforehand and heated just prior to serving.

The sweet potato galette is so easy and so absolutely delicious you will probably invent opportunities for serving it again and again, even during the hectic weeks before Christmas. It can be assembled three hours before it is cooked, which, by the way, is done first on top of the stove for a few minutes and then, covered with foil and nicely weighted, in a very hot oven for 20 minutes to render it delectably crispy. The kasha loaf and the galette are offset with a quick sauté of chestnuts and Brussels sprouts. Brussels sprouts, so often unjustly maligned, are just wonderful when cooked fresh. Late Fall, after the frost, is the peak of their season.

Finally, the meal is concluded with a pretty dessert of pears poached in a red cranberry syrup and served with whole cranberries. The chilled fruit can be made the day before Thanksgiving and so becomes the ideal dessert for the host or hostess who dislikes fussing with anything in the kitchen after the main course has been served.

CURRIED BUTTERNUT SQUASH AND APPLE SOUP

❧

1 large onion, sliced
1 celery stalk, including the leaves,
    sliced
1 Granny Smith apple, peeled, cored, and
    chopped
1 tablespoon minced gingerroot
2 tablespoons vegetable oil
1½ tablespoons curry powder
2½- to 3-pound butternut squash, peeled,
    seeded, and cut into 2-inch pieces
5 cups vegetable stock (page 198)
cheesecloth bag containing 1 bay leaf,
    a strip of lemon zest, and 4 whole cloves
salt and freshly ground pepper to taste
fresh lemon juice to taste
minced fresh coriander leaves and plain
    yogurt *or* sour cream for garnish

In a heavy saucepan cook the onion, celery, apple, and gingerroot in the oil over moderate heat for 5 to 7 minutes, or until softened. Add the curry powder and cook for 2 minutes. Add the squash, stock, cheesecloth bag, and salt and pepper and simmer the mixture for 30 minutes. Discard the cheesecloth bag.

In a food processor purée the mixture. Strain it into a saucepan and add the lemon juice. Bring to a simmer and serve in heated bowls. Garnish with the coriander and yogurt. Serves 6.

MICROWAVE DIRECTIONS

INGREDIENT CHANGE:
Reduce stock to 4 cups.

DIRECTIONS:
Place the onion, celery, gingerroot, oil, and curry powder in a microwave-safe 4-quart casserole. Cover and microwave at high power (100%) for 4 minutes, or until softened. Add the squash, apple, the 4 cups stock, the cheesecloth bag, and salt and pepper. Cover and microwave at high power (100%) for 25 to 28 minutes, or until the squash is tender when pierced with a fork. Remove the cheesecloth bag and continue with the recipe as directed.

KASHA, MUSHROOM, AND CHEESE LOAF WITH SHIITAKE SAUCE

❧

½ ounce dried *shiitake, porcini, or cèpes*
1 cup coarse kasha
1½ cups minced onion
1 cup minced celery
2 tablespoons vegetable oil
1 cup chopped fresh *shiitake or* oyster
    mushrooms
2 garlic cloves, minced
1 cup ground unsalted roasted cashews
3 large eggs, beaten lightly
¼ pound Italian Fontina, grated
⅓ cup freshly grated Parmesan
½ cup minced fresh parsley leaves
½ teaspoon dried thyme, crumbled
½ teaspoon dried marjoram, crumbled
salt and freshly ground pepper to taste
shiitake sauce (page 132)

In a small bowl let the dried mushrooms soak in boiling water to cover for 30 minutes, or until softened. In a saucepan cook the kasha according to the package instructions and transfer to a bowl.

In a skillet cook the onion and celery in the oil, covered, over moderate heat, stirring occasionally, for 7 minutes. Add the fresh mushrooms and cook for 5 minutes, or until most of the liquid is evaporated. Add the garlic and cook, stirring, for 1 minute. Add the mixture to the kasha and let cool.

Preheat the oven to 350° F.

Drain the dried mushrooms and discard the tough stems. Mince the mushrooms and add them to the kasha mixture with the remaining ingredients (except the sauce). Combine well.

Line an oiled loaf pan, 9 by 5 by 3 inches, with parchment paper and oil the paper. Spoon the kasha mixture into the pan and rap the pan to expel air bubbles. Smooth the top. Bake in the middle of the oven, covered with foil, for 50 minutes to 1 hour, or until a skewer inserted in the center comes out clean. Let it stand on a rack for 10 minutes.

Run a knife around the edge of the pan. Invert a platter over the pan and invert the loaf onto it. Discard the paper and cut the loaf into 1-inch slices. Serve the kasha with the sauce. Serves 6.

SHIITAKE SAUCE

1 ounce dried *shiitake*
1½ tablespoons vegetable oil
½ cup minced shallot
¼ pound fresh *shiitake*, sliced
¾ cup Sercial Madeira
4 cups vegetable stock (page 198)
4 teaspoons arrowroot combined with
    2 tablespoons cold water

+ IN A BOWL LET THE DRIED MUSHROOMS SOAK in boiling water to cover for 30 minutes, or until softened. Drain, discard stems, and slice thin.

In a saucepan heat the oil over moderately high heat until hot. Add the shallot and sauté until softened. Add the fresh mushrooms and sauté, stirring, for 1 to 2 minutes, until most of the liquid is absorbed. Add the dried mushrooms and sauté for 1 minute. Add the Madeira, bring to a boil, and boil until reduced to ½ cup. Add the stock, bring to a boil, and boil until reduced to 3 cups.

Bring the sauce to a boil and stir in the arrowroot mixture. Simmer, stirring, for 3 minutes, or until thickened. Makes about 3 cups.

MICROWAVE DIRECTIONS

INGREDIENT CHANGES:
Use 2 tablespoons cornstarch in place of arrowroot; reduce stock to 3 cups; use 1 cup hot water.

DIRECTIONS:
To soak mushrooms, combine dried mushrooms and the 1 cup hot water in a 2-cup measure. Microwave at high power (100%) for 2 minutes, or until boiling. Let the mushrooms stand for 15 minutes, drain, and rinse.

Microwave oil and shallot in a 4-cup measure at high power (100%) for 3 minutes. Add fresh mushrooms and cook for 4 minutes. Add the Madeira, 2¾ cups stock, and the dried mushrooms and cook for 8 minutes. Dissolve cornstarch in remaining ¼ cup stock. Quickly stir into mushroom mixture. Microwave at high power (100%) for 3 minutes, stirring halfway through the cooking. Makes about 3 cups.

CRISPY SWEET POTATO GALETTE

3 tablespoons unsalted butter
1½ pounds sweet potatoes, peeled and
    cut into ⅛-inch slices
freshly grated nutmeg to taste
salt and freshly ground pepper to taste

PREHEAT THE OVEN TO 450° F.

Coat the bottom of a nonstick 10-inch ovenproof skillet with 1 tablespoon of the butter, melted. Arrange half the sweet potato slices in the skillet, overlapping them in one layer. Sprinkle the potatoes with the nutmeg and salt and pepper, and dot them with 1 tablespoon of the remaining butter. Top the butter with the remaining slices, overlapping them in one layer, sprinkle the potatoes with the nutmeg and salt and pepper, and dot them with the remaining 1 tablespoon butter. *The galette can be made 3 hours ahead up to this point and kept refrigerated, covered with plastic wrap.*

Cook the galette, covered with foil and weighted with a heavy ovenproof saucepan, over moderate heat for 5 minutes from the time the butter begins to sizzle. Bake it, still covered and weighted, in the middle of the oven for 10 minutes. Remove the saucepan and foil carefully and bake the galette in the upper third of the oven for 10 minutes more, or until tender.

Invert a platter over the skillet and invert the galette onto it. Cut it into wedges. Serves 6.

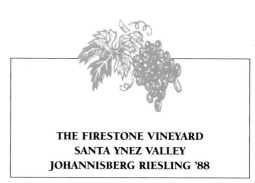

**THE FIRESTONE VINEYARD
SANTA YNEZ VALLEY
JOHANNISBERG RIESLING '88**

GLAZED CHESTNUTS AND BRUSSELS SPROUTS

🍃

1 pound Brussels sprouts, trimmed
3 tablespoons unsalted butter, softened
1 pound cooked chestnuts (procedure on page 199)
1 teaspoon sugar, or to taste
salt and freshly ground pepper to taste

IN A LARGE SAUCEPAN OF BOILING SALTED WATER cook the Brussels sprouts over moderately high heat for 12 to 15 minutes, or until tender. Drain them and transfer to a large bowl. Add 1½ tablespoons of the butter to the Brussels sprouts, stir well, and keep warm, covered.

In a nonstick skillet sauté the chestnuts in the remaining 1½ tablespoons butter over moderately high heat, stirring, until heated through. Add the sugar and salt and pepper and cook, tossing, until glazed. Add to the Brussels sprouts and combine well. Serves 6.

MICROWAVE DIRECTIONS

INGREDIENT CHANGE:
Reduce water to ¼ cup hot (tap) water.

DIRECTIONS:
Combine the Brussels sprouts and the ¼ cup water in a microwave-safe 12-inch quiche or pie pan. Cover with microwave-safe plastic wrap vented on one side and microwave at high power (100%) for 5 to 8 minutes, or until just tender. (Timing will depend on the size of sprouts. If size varies greatly, place larger sprouts toward perimeter of dish.) Drain the sprouts; add the butter, sugar, and chestnuts. Microwave at high power (100%) for 3 to 4 minutes, or until the chestnuts are heated through. Toss to coat and add salt and pepper to taste.

CRANBERRY POACHED PEARS

🍃

2 cups cranberries, thawed if frozen
2 cups water
cheesecloth bag containing 3 whole cloves, 3 whole allspice, 2-inch cinnamon stick, and 3-inch strip of orange zest
2 cups sugar
3 firm ripe Bosc pears, peeled, halved, and cored
1 tablespoon cranberry liqueur, if desired
vanilla frozen yogurt *or* ice cream as an accompaniment, if desired

◑+ IN A SAUCEPAN BRING THE CRANBERRIES, WATER, and cheesecloth bag to a boil and simmer for 15 minutes, or until the cranberries burst. Add the sugar and simmer, stirring occasionally, for 5 minutes, or until the syrup is clear. Let the cranberry mixture cool and chill, covered, for at least 1 hour or overnight.

Discard the cheesecloth bag and drain the cranberries in a fine sieve, reserving the syrup. Chill the cranberries until ready to use.

Arrange the pears cut side down in a skillet just large enough to hold them in one layer. Add enough of the reserved syrup to cover them and bring to a simmer. Simmer the mixture, covered with a round of wax paper, for 6 to 8 minutes, or until the pears are just tender.

Transfer the pears with a slotted spoon to a serving dish and chill them for 1 hour. Transfer the poaching syrup to a bowl and chill it for 1 hour, or until it is thickened slightly. *The dessert can be made 1 day ahead up to this point and kept refrigerated, covered.*

Drizzle the pears with the liqueur and garnish them with the cranberries. Pour some of the poaching syrup over each serving and serve with the frozen yogurt. Serves 6.

MENU

A BABY SHOWER TEA

MUSTARD TARRAGON STUFFED EGGS

**HAM CORNETS WITH APPLE
HORSERADISH FILLING**

TEA SANDWICHES IN A BREAD BASKET

LAYERED WALNUT YOGURT TERRINES

BITTERSWEET CHOCOLATE LEAF COOKIES

LIME-MARINATED FRUIT KEBABS

SERVES TWENTY

Set aside a few hours one afternoon to return to gentler times when the low table in the drawing room or the glass-topped one on the terrace was laid for tea. Arrange fresh flowers in glorious sprays of color bursting from tall vases and prepare a late afternoon repast of the foods we rarely find the time or opportunity to make or eat. We think you will agree that such a gracious party is the perfect way to honor the mother-to-be.

A tea demands nothing especially heavy or filling. The food ought to be pretty, light, colorful, and appetizing, able to be eaten out of hand or from small plates with only forks. The most complicated dish on our menu is the yogurt terrine, which requires advance planning to give the yogurt time to drain and firm up and at least 3 hours—or as long as 2 days—to set. For twenty guests, you will need two terrines. Make the recipe twice rather than doubling the ingredients. It is far more manageable this way, and any more than 2 pounds of yogurt in

one sieve will not drain properly. You could make the two terrines simultaneously for optimum efficiency, however.

The sandwich bread can be baked the day before the party, or earlier if you want to freeze it. This loaf will have to be made twice, too, so that you will end up with two hollowed-out bread shells in which to stack the tiny sandwiches. We have devised two different types of tea sandwiches. Several hours before the party, assemble them, and then, to keep the bread from drying, lay them on baking sheets and cover them with damp but well-wrung tea towels.

The delicate leaf-shaped cookies are made from a firm dough that does not spread very much in the oven and so holds its shape. They are then coated with chocolate and will keep in a tightly lidded tin for 2 or 3 days. These cookies are just delightful and look very pretty indeed, but do not expect the chocolate to keep its shine. Only tempered chocolate does that.

*Tea Sandwiches in a
Bread Basket*

MUSTARD TARRAGON STUFFED EGGS

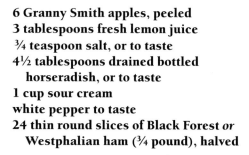

12 hard-cooked large eggs
⅓ to ½ cup mayonnaise, or to taste
1½ to 2 tablespoons Dijon-style mustard
2 teaspoons tarragon vinegar
1 tablespoon minced fresh tarragon
   leaves plus 24 sprigs for garnish
1 tablespoon minced red onion

HALVE THE EGGS LENGTHWISE. REMOVE THE YOLKS and force them through a sieve into a bowl. Add the mayonnaise, mustard, vinegar, salt and pepper to taste, and stir until smooth. Transfer to a pastry bag fitted with a ¼-inch star tip.

Sprinkle ⅛ teaspoon of the minced tarragon in each egg white cavity and pipe in some egg yolk mixture. Garnish with the onion and tarragon sprigs. Makes 24 stuffed halves.

HAM CORNETS WITH APPLE HORSERADISH FILLING

6 Granny Smith apples, peeled
3 tablespoons fresh lemon juice
¾ teaspoon salt, or to taste
4½ tablespoons drained bottled
   horseradish, or to taste
1 cup sour cream
white pepper to taste
24 thin round slices of Black Forest *or*
   Westphalian ham (¾ pound), halved

GRATE COARSE 4½ APPLES, AND RESERVE THE remaining 3 halves in a small bowl of cold water with the lemon juice.

In a sieve toss the grated apple with the salt and drain for 10 minutes. Press gently to remove excess moisture. In a bowl toss the grated apple with the horseradish, sour cream, and white pepper.

Cut the reserved apple halves lengthwise into 48 thin slices. Arrange 1 slice in the center of each ham slice half. Spoon 2 teaspoons of the filling onto each apple slice and roll the ham into cone shapes. Makes 48 cornets.

TEA SANDWICHES IN A BREAD BASKET

2 round loaves of homemade white bread
   (recipe follows), each 2½ pounds and
   8 inches in diameter

FOR THE CURRIED CHICKEN SANDWICHES:
3 to 4 teaspoons curry powder, or to taste
4 teaspoons vegetable oil
½ teaspoon light brown sugar
4 teaspoons cider vinegar
2 cups minced cooked chicken
½ cup minced celery
1 cup mayonnaise
6 tablespoons minced fresh coriander
   leaves
salt and freshly ground pepper to taste

FOR THE SMOKED SALMON AND CUCUMBER
SANDWICHES:
1 stick (½ cup) unsalted butter, softened
3 tablespoons snipped fresh dill
2 to 3 teaspoons fresh lemon juice
salt and freshly ground pepper to taste
2 cups thinly sliced cucumber
½ pound thinly sliced smoked salmon

watercress sprigs and cucumber rose for
   garnish, if desired

INSERT THE TIP OF A SHARP THIN LONG KNIFE INTO THE side of 1 loaf just above the bottom crust. Push the knife into the bread until it reaches but does not pierce the opposite side. Without enlarging the slit, work the sharp edge of the knife as far to one side as possible. Remove it and turning the blade to the other side reinsert it into the slit. Work the knife as far to the other side as possible. Remove it and repeat the procedure from the opposite side of the bread through a second slit.

About 3 inches from the bottom, cut off the top of the loaf and reserve it for another use (such as making bread crumbs). Holding the knife tip straight down, cut around the circumference of the bread about ¼ inch inside the crust until the knife reaches but does not pierce the bottom crust.

With your hands ease out the center piece of bread in one piece. Halve it, cutting downward, and freeze the halves, wrapped tightly in foil or plastic wrap, for at least 1 hour or up to 2 hours (this makes it easier to slice). Reserve the bread shell, wrapped. Repeat the procedure with the remaining loaf.

Lay each bread half curved side up on a work surface and with a serrated knife cut it carefully into 8 thin slices.

Make the curried chicken sandwiches: In a small skillet cook the curry powder in the oil over moderately low heat, stirring, for 3 minutes. Stir in the sugar and vinegar and let the mixture cool to lukewarm. In a bowl toss with the chicken, celery, all but 2 tablespoons of the mayonnaise, 2 tablespoons coriander, and salt and pepper to taste. *The chicken filling can be made 1 day ahead and kept refrigerated, covered.*

Spread about ⅓ cup of the chicken filling on each of 8 bread slices and top with 8 more slices. Cut each sandwich into 4 wedges. Spread the remaining 2 tablespoons mayonnaise on the curved edges and dip the curved edges in the remaining 4 tablespoons coriander.

Make the smoked salmon and cucumber sandwiches: In a small bowl cream the butter, dill, lemon juice, and salt and pepper to taste. *The dill butter can be made 1 day ahead and kept refrigerated, covered. Let soften before using.*

Spread one side of the remaining 16 bread slices with the dill butter. On 8 of them arrange the cucumber in one layer, overlapping slightly, and top with the smoked salmon. Top with the remaining bread slices and cut each sandwich into 4 wedges. Arrange all the sandwiches in the reserved bread shells and garnish with the watercress and cucumber rose.

The sandwich baskets can be made 3 hours ahead and kept covered with a dampened tea towel and plastic wrap. Makes 64 tea sandwiches.

ROUND SANDWICH LOAF

**1 package active dry yeast
  (2½ teaspoons)
3 tablespoons sugar
1 cup lukewarm water
1 cup milk plus additional milk for
  brushing
2½ teaspoons salt
2 tablespoons unsalted butter
5 to 6 cups all-purpose flour**

IN A SMALL BOWL PROOF THE YEAST WITH A PINCH OF the sugar in ¼ cup of the water for 15 minutes, or until foamy. In a saucepan heat the milk, the remaining sugar, the remaining ¾ cup water, the salt, and butter over moderate heat, stirring, until the sugar and salt are dissolved. Let the mixture cool to lukewarm.

In a large bowl combine the yeast mixture and milk mixture. Add 2 cups of the flour and whisk until smooth. Stir in enough of the remaining flour to form a soft but not sticky dough and knead it on a floured surface for 8 to 10 minutes, or until smooth and elastic. Put the dough in a buttered bowl and turn to coat it with the butter. Let the dough rise, covered with plastic wrap, in a warm place for 1¼ hours, or until double in bulk.

Punch down the dough and knead it on a floured surface for 20 seconds. Fit the dough into a buttered 8-by-2-inch springform pan and let it rise, covered loosely with plastic wrap, in a warm place for 30 minutes, or until it just rises above the rim of the pan.

Preheat the oven to 400° F.

Brush the loaf with the additional milk and bake it in the middle of the oven for 30 minutes. Remove the bread from the pan and put it on a baking sheet. Bake the loaf for 5 minutes more, or until it sounds hollow when tapped. Let the bread cool completely on a rack.

The loaf can be made ahead and frozen, wrapped tightly in plastic wrap. Let it thaw in the refrigerator. Makes a 2½-pound round loaf.

LAYERED WALNUT
YOGURT TERRINE

two 1-pound containers plain yogurt
1 envelope unflavored gelatin
¼ cup cold water
½ cup crème fraîche *or* heavy cream
2 teaspoons salt
3 tablespoons walnut oil (available at
    specialty food shops and some
    supermarkets)
white pepper to taste
⅓ cup plus 1 tablespoon minced scallion
    including the green top
⅓ cup plus 1 tablespoon peeled, seeded,
    and minced tomato
1 tablespoon minced walnuts
toasted French bread rounds as an
    accompaniment

IN A LARGE SIEVE LINED WITH A DOUBLE THICKNESS
of rinsed and squeezed cheesecloth set over a
bowl let the yogurt drain, covered and chilled,
for 8 hours.

In a bowl let the gelatin soften in the water
for 10 minutes. In a saucepan heat the gelatin mixture, crème fraîche, and salt over moderately low
heat, stirring, until the gelatin is dissolved. In a
large bowl combine this with the yogurt, walnut
oil, and white pepper.

Line an oiled loaf pan, 7½ by 3½ (across the
top) by 2 inches, with enough plastic wrap to extend about 2 inches over the long sides. Spread one
third of the yogurt mixture in the pan and sprinkle
with ⅓ cup of the scallion. Top with half the remaining yogurt mixture and sprinkle with ⅓ cup
of the tomato. Spread the top of the terrine with the
remaining yogurt mixture.

Cover the terrine with the overhanging
plastic wrap and chill for 3 hours, or until firm
enough to unmold. *The terrine can be made 2 days
ahead up to this point and kept refrigerated, covered.*

Invert the terrine onto a platter and discard
the plastic wrap. Garnish the terrine with the walnuts and remaining scallion and tomato. Serve at
room temperature with the bread rounds. Serves
8 to 10.

BITTERSWEET CHOCOLATE
LEAF COOKIES

9 tablespoons unsalted butter, softened
9 tablespoons sugar
¾ cup sliced blanched almonds, ground
    fine
2 large eggs, beaten lightly
1 teaspoon almond extract
1½ cups sifted all-purpose flour
18 ounces fine-quality bittersweet
    chocolate, chopped

PREHEAT THE OVEN TO 300° F.

In a bowl with an electric mixer cream the
butter and sugar until light and fluffy. Beat in the
almonds, eggs, almond extract, and flour and beat
until just combined.

Lay a 4¼-inch-long leaf-shaped metal stencil (or homemade heavy cardboard stencil) on a
well-buttered baking sheet. With a metal spatula
spread 1 heaping tablespoon of the dough over the
stencil. Press it smoothly and evenly through the
stencil onto the sheet, scraping off the excess. Lift
the stencil straight up, leaving the cookie on the
sheet. Wipe the stencil clean and make more cookies with the remaining dough in the same manner.

Bake the cookies in the middle of the oven
for 10 to 15 minutes, or until the edges are just
golden. Transfer the cookies to racks to cool.

In a bowl set over barely simmering water
melt half the chocolate, stirring, and transfer it to
a flat plate. Working with 1 cookie at a time, lay it
flat side down on the chocolate, coating it. Holding
the leaf near its pointed top, lift the cookie out of
the chocolate at an angle so that the chocolate
drips down to the base, forming ridges like the
veins of a leaf.

Transfer the dipped cookies chocolate side
up to a rack set on a baking sheet and chill them
for 30 minutes, or until the chocolate is hardened.
After coating half the cookies, melt the remaining
chocolate and coat the remaining cookies. *The
cookies can be made up to 3 days ahead and kept
refrigerated in an airtight container.* Makes 48
cookies.

LIME-MARINATED FRUIT KEBABS

**1 lime, zest removed with a vegetable
peeler and both fruit and zest reserved**
½ cup sugar
1 cup water
4 pints strawberries, hulled
10 kiwi fruits, peeled and sliced
**1 pineapple, peeled, cored, and cut into
1-inch pieces**

☺+ IN A FOOD PROCESSOR BLEND ALL THE LIME ZEST, OR
to taste, and sugar for 2 minutes, or until minced
very fine. In a saucepan combine the sugared zest
with the water and bring it to a boil, stirring until
the sugar is dissolved. Simmer for 5 minutes. In a
very large bowl combine the strawberries, kiwi
fruits, and pineapple. Pour the lime marinade over
the fruit and let it cool. Chill the fruit, covered, for
1 to 2 hours, or until cold.

Squeeze the juice from the reserved lime
and stir it into the fruit mixture. Thread the fruit on
wooden skewers. Serves 20.

Below are two "ladies' favorites." The iced ginger
"tea" is probably a bit more unfamiliar and you will
want to have enough on hand should everyone
want to try it. This means that you should make at
least four batches of this brew (ideally, a day or two
beforehand). The white-wine spritzers are easy
enough to make upon request (or by the trayful in a
few minutes). Our recipe makes one drink and is to
be made by the glass.

ICED GINGER "TEA"

**½ cup peeled and thinly sliced
gingerroot**
¼ cup honey, or to taste
7 cups water
2 cups ice cubes
**lemon wedges and mint sprigs for
garnish**

☺+ IN A SAUCEPAN BRING THE GINGERROOT, HONEY,
and water to a boil, stirring, and simmer for 15
minutes. Strain the mixture into a pitcher and chill
it for 30 minutes, or until cold. *The "tea" can be
made 2 days ahead and kept refrigerated, covered.*

Just before serving, stir in the ice cubes and
garnish with the lemon and mint. Serves 6.

WHITE-WINE SPRITZER

¾ cup dry white wine
¼ cup club soda, or to taste
a twist of lemon

☺ IN A TUMBLER FILLED WITH ICE CUBES COMBINE
the wine, the club soda, and the lemon. Makes 1
drink.

ICED GINGER "TEA"

WHITE-WINE SPRITZERS

Fall Gifts

Now is the time for drawing in, for the first cauldron of hot soup and warming stew. The sun may still shine warmly on the burnished leaves and the tangled garden, but by day's end the chill in the air is unmistakable.

The golden days of Autumn inspire us to expect slightly grander entertaining than we experienced in the Summer. Our host may want to light the candles and encourage guests to linger around a well-set table. Whether you are invited for a small dinner party or a larger gathering, consider bringing something from the kitchen as a gift. Our jarred salads and dilled pickles are colorful and easy to tote along with you. Or perhaps you would like to bring along and share our pumpkin-flavored quick bread or chocolate cranberry tart when you are invited for a weekend in the glorious autumnal countryside.

ixed Pickled Mushroom Salad; Hungarian
ickles; Hungarian Mixed Vegetable Salad

Our first three Fall gift recipes are Hungarian preserves that we borrowed from a Hungarian grandmother. Packed in jars, these salads and pickles make lovely surprises when presented to your host. In remote Hungarian villages salad greens must be picked and preserved during the Summer months in order to have "greens" during the Winter. Those of us fortunate to have access to green vegetables all year long will still want to enjoy these recipes for their sweet-sour, unique taste.

HUNGARIAN MIXED VEGETABLE SALAD

1 cucumber, peeled and sliced thin
2½ teaspoons salt
2 red bell peppers, cut into thin strips
1 onion, sliced thin
10 cups finely shredded cabbage
¼ teaspoon freshly ground black pepper
¼ teaspoon sugar
½ cup distilled white vinegar
2 green tomatoes, cut into ½-inch pieces

IN A BOWL TOSS THE CUCUMBER WITH ¼ TEASPOON of the salt. In another bowl toss the bell peppers with ¼ teaspoon of the remaining salt. In a third bowl toss the onion with ¼ teaspoon of the remaining salt. In a large bowl toss the cabbage with ¾ teaspoon of the remaining salt. Let the salted vegetables stand for 1 hour.

In a small saucepan combine the black pepper, the sugar, the vinegar, the remaining 1 teaspoon salt, and ½ cup water and bring the mixture to a boil. Remove the pan from the heat and let the dressing cool. Squeeze the liquid from the salted vegetables, toss the vegetables together in a large bowl, and add the tomatoes. Pour the dressing over the salad, toss the salad well, and let it stand, tossing it occasionally, for 2 hours.

Pack the salad, including the dressing, into a 2-quart jar. The salad keeps, covered and chilled, for several months. Makes about 8 cups.

MIXED PICKLED MUSHROOM SALAD

2 cucumbers, sliced thin
1¼ teaspoons salt
3 green bell peppers, sliced into thin rings
1⅓ cups white-wine vinegar
¾ teaspoon sugar
2 tablespoons fresh lemon juice
2 pounds small white mushrooms, stems discarded and the caps halved
1 bunch of scallions including some of the green part, cut into ¼-inch pieces (about 1 cup)

IN A BOWL TOSS THE CUCUMBERS WITH ¼ TEASPOON OF the salt, in another bowl toss the bell peppers with ¼ teaspoon of the remaining salt, and let the cucumbers and the bell peppers stand for 1 hour.

In a saucepan combine the vinegar, the sugar, the remaining ¾ teaspoon salt, and 2 cups water and bring the mixture to a boil. Remove the pan from the heat and let the mixture cool.

To a large saucepan of boiling water add the lemon juice and the mushrooms, blanch the mushrooms for 2 minutes, or until they are just tender, and drain them in a sieve. Refresh the mushrooms under cold water and drain them well. In a saucepan of boiling water blanch the scallions for 1 minute and drain them in a sieve. Refresh the scallions under cold water and drain them well. Squeeze the liquid from the cucumbers and the bell peppers and in a large bowl toss the salted vegetables with the mushrooms and the scallions.

Pack the salad into two 1-quart jars and divide the vinegar mixture between the jars to cover the vegetables completely. The salad keeps, covered and chilled, for several months. Makes about 8 cups.

HUNGARIAN DILL PICKLES

25 to 30 Kirby cucumbers, each about
  4 inches long, washed well
8 large stalks of fresh dill
6 tablespoons salt
2 slices of homemade-type rye bread

WITH A KNIFE TRIM THE ENDS OF THE CUCUMBERS and make a lengthwise slit through the middle of each cucumber, leaving about 1 inch intact at each end. Make another lengthwise slit perpendicular to the first down the middle of each cucumber, again leaving 1 inch intact at each end. Put 4 of the dill stalks in the bottom of a 1-gallon jar and pack half the cucumbers into the jar, standing them on end. Cover the cucumbers with the remaining 4 dill stalks and pack the remaining cucumbers into the jar tightly, standing them on end.

In a large saucepan combine 2 quarts water with the salt and bring the mixture to a boil. Pour the mixture over the cucumbers to cover them completely and let it cool to lukewarm. Put the bread over the cucumbers, cover the mouth of the jar tightly with a dampened cloth, and let the mixture stand in a warm sunny place, dampening the cloth each day, for 2 days.

Remove the bread, let the pickles stand, dampening the cloth each day, for 2 more days, and remove them from the liquid. Strain the liquid through a fine sieve into a bowl, return the pickles to the jar, cleaned, and pour the strained liquid over them. The pickles keep, covered and chilled, for several months. Makes 25 to 30 pickles.

PUMPKIN CHUTNEY BREAD

This bread, chock full of nuts and raisins, is leavened with baking soda and baking powder rather than yeast, and so falls into the category of quick breads. Wrapped in crinkly colored foil, it becomes a lovely gift.

1¾ cups all-purpose flour
¾ teaspoon salt
1 teaspoon baking soda
½ teaspoon baking powder
1½ teaspoons cinnamon
¼ teaspoon freshly grated nutmeg
⅛ teaspoon ground allspice
⅓ cup vegetable shortening, softened
⅔ cup firmly packed dark brown sugar
2 large eggs, beaten lightly
¼ cup buttermilk
1 cup canned pumpkin purée
⅔ cup bottled mango chutney, large
  pieces chopped
½ cup chopped walnuts
½ cup raisins
cream cheese and mango chutney as
  accompaniments

PREHEAT THE OVEN TO 350° F.

In a bowl combine with a fork the flour, salt, baking soda, baking powder, and spices. In a large bowl stir together the shortening and sugar, add the eggs, and combine. Stir in the buttermilk, pumpkin purée, and chutney and combine well. Add the flour mixture, walnuts, and raisins and stir until just combined.

Spoon into a greased loaf pan, 9¼ by 5¼ by 2¾ inches, and bake in the middle of the oven for 1 hour to 1 hour and 10 minutes, or until a skewer inserted in the center comes out clean.

Let the bread cool in the pan on a rack for 10 minutes. Loosen the edge with a knife and remove the loaf from the pan. Let it cool right side up on the rack for 2 hours. *The bread can be made 1 week ahead and kept refrigerated, wrapped tightly in foil. Or, it can be frozen, wrapped tightly in foil, for 1 month.* Serve warm with the cream cheese and chutney. Makes 1 loaf.

CRANBERRY CHOCOLATE TART

FOR THE PASTRY CREAM:
3 large egg yolks
⅓ cup sugar
2 tablespoons flour
2 tablespoons cornstarch
1 cup scalded milk
2 tablespoons unsalted butter, softened
2 tablespoons dark rum

pâte brisée **(page 196)**
½ cup water
½ cup sugar
1½ cups cranberries, picked over
2 ounces semisweet chocolate, melted

MAKE THE PASTRY CREAM: IN A BOWL BEAT THE EGG YOLKS and sugar with an electric mixer until thick and pale. Gradually add the flour and cornstarch and beat until smooth. Add the milk in a stream, beating, and beat until combined well. Transfer the mixture to a heavy saucepan and bring to a boil, stirring. Simmer, stirring, for 3 minutes and remove from the heat. Beat in the butter and rum. Force the mixture through a fine sieve into a bowl and chill, covered with a buttered round of wax paper, for 1 hour.

Roll out the dough ⅛ inch thick on a floured surface and fit it into a 9-inch tart pan with a removable fluted rim. Crimp the edge decoratively and prick the bottom with a fork. Chill for 30 minutes.

Preheat the oven to 425° F.

Line the shell with wax paper and fill the paper with raw rice. Bake the shell in the lower third of the oven for 15 minutes. Remove the rice and paper and bake for 10 minutes more, or until golden. Let the pie shell cool in the pan on a rack. Remove the rim.

In a stainless steel or enameled saucepan bring the water and sugar to a boil over moderate heat, stirring and washing down any sugar crystals clinging to the sides with a brush dipped in cold water, until the sugar is dissolved. Add the cranberries and simmer, covered, for 3 to 5 minutes, or until they have just burst. Let the mixture cool for 15 minutes.

Spread the chocolate over the bottom of the shell and chill for 15 minutes, or until firm. Top with the pastry cream, spreading evenly. Spoon in the cranberry mixture, covering the pastry cream completely. Chill the tart for 1 hour and let it stand at room temperature for 10 minutes before serving. Makes one 9-inch tart.

ORANGE SQUASH PIE

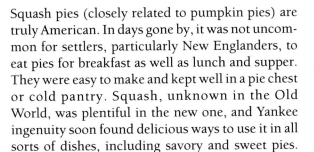

Squash pies (closely related to pumpkin pies) are truly American. In days gone by, it was not uncommon for settlers, particularly New Englanders, to eat pies for breakfast as well as lunch and supper. They were easy to make and kept well in a pie chest or cold pantry. Squash, unknown in the Old World, was plentiful in the new one, and Yankee ingenuity soon found delicious ways to use it in all sorts of dishes, including savory and sweet pies. We have updated ours a bit by adding orange-flavored liqueur.

2½-pound butternut or acorn squash,
    pricked with a knife
1½ recipes *pâte brisée* **(page 196)**
3 ounces large sugar cubes (about ½ cup)
1 navel orange
¼ cup orange-flavored liqueur
3 large eggs, beaten lightly
1 cup heavy cream
1 tablespoon cornstarch
1 tablespoon fresh lemon juice
1 teaspoon ground allspice
½ teaspoon salt

PREHEAT THE OVEN TO 375° F.

On a lightly oiled baking sheet bake the squash for 35 to 40 minutes, or until tender, and let it cool. Peel the squash, seed it, and cut it into pieces. In a food processor or blender purée it in batches and transfer it to a bowl. Chill the squash, covered, until ready to use.

Roll out the dough ⅛ inch thick on a

floured surface and fit it into a 10-inch pie plate. Crimp the edge decoratively. Prick the bottom with a fork and chill the shell for 1 hour.

Preheat the oven to 425° F.

Line the shell with wax paper and fill the paper with raw rice. Bake the shell in the lower third of the oven for 10 minutes. Remove the rice and paper and bake for 10 to 15 minutes more, or until colored lightly. Let it cool on a rack.

Reduce the heat to 350° F.

Rub the sugar cubes across the surface of the orange until orange-colored. In a small saucepan melt the cubes in the liqueur over moderately low heat, stirring. Remove from heat and let the mixture cool.

In a large bowl combine the remaining ingredients with the sugar mixture and squash purée and pour into the shell. Bake in the middle of the oven for 45 minutes, or until set. Let the pie cool on a rack and chill it, covered. Makes one 10-inch pie.

WINE JELLY

Our wine jelly is a delightful treat that complements poultry and game. For a truly "Gourmet" gift why not offer to make the jelly for Thanksgiving? Choose a beautiful mold and present both container and jelly to your hostess for a special gift that will be remembered for years to come.

> 1 tablespoon unflavored gelatin
> ½ cup water
> 1½ cups dry red wine
> ⅓ cup sugar
> 3-inch cinnamon stick
> 4 peppercorns
> 2 whole cloves

☺+ IN A SAUCEPAN SPRINKLE THE GELATIN OVER THE water to soften for 10 minutes. Add the wine, sugar, and spices and cook over moderately low heat, stirring, until the sugar and gelatin are dissolved. Keep hot but not simmering over low heat for 5 minutes to let the flavors blend.

Strain the jelly through a sieve lined with a dampened double thickness of cheesecloth into a 1-quart decorative mold that has been rinsed with cold water but not dried. Let it cool and chill it, covered, for 6 hours, or until set. *The jelly can be made the day before and chilled, covered in the refrigerator, overnight.* Unmold onto a plate to serve. Serves 4.

SPICED CRANBERRY AND ORANGE RELISH

The cloves, ginger, and cinnamon add piquant flavor to this orange-cranberry relish. Serve it with the Thanksgiving turkey or pack it in a pretty jar and take it with you as a gift. It keeps in the refrigerator for up to two weeks.

> ¾ cup water
> 1½ cups sugar
> 2 cups cranberries, picked over
> 2 small navel oranges, cut into 1-inch pieces
> 2 tablespoons minced ginger in syrup (available at specialty food shops)
> ¼ teaspoon ground cloves
> ¼ teaspoon cinnamon

☺ IN A SMALL SAUCEPAN BRING THE WATER AND SUGAR to a boil over moderately low heat, stirring and washing down any sugar crystals clinging to the sides with a brush dipped in cold water, until the sugar is dissolved. Simmer for 5 minutes, remove from heat, and let the syrup cool.

In a large bowl combine the cranberries, oranges, and syrup. In a food processor or blender chop the mixture in batches and transfer it to a bowl. Stir in the remaining ingredients and transfer the relish to a decorative glass container. *The relish can be made 2 weeks ahead and kept refrigerated, covered.* Serve as a condiment with poultry and game. Makes about 2 cups.

PICKLED PUMPKIN BALLS

You may never have seen these spicy little pickled balls before, but they are so easy to make you will want to include them in your regular Autumn repertoire. They make a smashing gift, too, packed in a crock or jar. Serve them with crackers and cheese with before-dinner cocktails or as an accompaniment to turkey or ham.

> 1 pumpkin, halved, seeded, and strings
>   removed
> 1⅔ cups sugar
> ¾ cup cider vinegar
> ½ cup water
> 1 cinnamon stick, broken into pieces
> 6 whole cloves
> 6 whole allspice
> 4 strips of lemon zest, each 2 inches long

+ WITH A 1-INCH MELON BALL CUTTER, SCOOP OUT enough balls from the flesh of the pumpkin to measure 2 cups.

In a saucepan bring the remaining ingredients to a boil over moderate heat, stirring and washing down any sugar crystals clinging to the sides with a brush dipped in cold water, until the sugar is dissolved. Cook the mixture, undisturbed, for 5 minutes.

Add the pumpkin balls and simmer for 15 minutes, or until just tender. Transfer the balls with a slotted spoon to 2 sterilized ½-pint Mason-type jars (procedure on page 199). Reduce the syrup over high heat to 1 cup and pour it and the spices over the balls. Let them cool and chill, covered, for at least 3 hours. *The pumpkin balls can be made 1 week ahead and kept refrigerated, covered.* Makes 1 pint.

MARINATED GOAT CHEESE

The slightly sour, wickedly salty flavor of goat cheese never tastes better than when a firm round of the cheese is marinated in olive oil and herbs. When it is packed in rustic crocks or sturdy glass jars with plain screw-on lids, it makes an attractive gift, one that evokes images of a cool, stone farmhouse deep in the countryside of France.

> 1 garlic clove, sliced
> 2 tablespoons minced fresh parsley
>   leaves
> 2 tablespoons snipped fresh chives
> 1 tablespoon minced fresh basil leaves *or*
>   ½ teaspoon dried, crumbled
> ½ teaspoon dried thyme, crumbled
> ½ teaspoon freshly ground pepper
> 1 small bay leaf
> 1 cup olive oil, heated
> ½-pound piece of Boucheron *or* other
>   French goat cheese, rind removed
> Melba toast *or* French bread as an
>   accompaniment

+ IN A HEATPROOF BOWL COMBINE THE SEASONINGS. Pour the oil carefully over them and let it cool. Add the cheese, making sure it is completely covered by the oil, and let it stand, covered, in the refrigerator for 3 days. Before serving, remove the cheese from the refrigerator and bring it to room temperature. Transfer the cheese with a slotted spoon to a plate and serve it with the Melba toast or bread. Serves 4 as a first course or 8 as an hors d'oeuvre.

APPLE BUTTER

Fruit butters are marvelous put-ups. They taste rich and thick, and, because they contain no dairy butter or cream, they keep for a long time in the refrigerator and can be enjoyed by almost anyone on a restricted diet. Apple butter makes a terrific hostess gift especially when accompanied by a loaf of freshly baked bread wrapped in a checkered napkin.

> **6 pounds Granny Smith *or* other tart
>   apples, unpeeled, cored, and sliced**
> **2½ cups apple cider**
> **2 cups firmly packed light brown sugar**
> **2 strips of lemon zest, each 2½ inches
>   long**
> **1 tablespoon cinnamon**
> **1 teaspoon ground allspice**
> **½ teaspoon ground cloves**
> **½ teaspoon salt**

IN A LARGE SAUCEPAN COOK THE APPLES IN THE CIDER over moderate heat, stirring occasionally, for 30 minutes, or until tender. Purée them through the medium disk of a food mill into another saucepan and add the remaining ingredients.

Cook the mixture over very low heat, stirring occasionally, for 2½ to 3 hours, or until very thick. Discard the lemon zest and spoon the mixture into 4 sterilized ½-pint Mason-type jars (procedure on page 199), filling them to within ¼ inch of the top. Wipe the rims with a dampened cloth and seal the jars with the lids.

Put the jars in a water bath canner or a rack in a deep kettle and add enough water to cover the jars by 2 inches. Bring to a boil and process, covered, for 10 minutes. Transfer the jars with canning tongs to a rack and let them cool. Let the apple butter mellow in a cool, dark place for at least 1 week. Makes about 2 pints.

SMITH COLLEGE FUDGE

Fudge is one of those peculiarly American concoctions whose origin is vague. Some say a baker in Philadelphia spoilt a chocolate cake and came up with fudge; others attribute the first fudge to college girls who allegedly mixed it up over the gas lamps in their dormitories. This may have happened at Smith, or, as others claim, Wellesley—or it may not have happened at all. Regardless, fudge provides chocolate lovers with a mouthful of silky texture and rich flavor. Pack it in tins or pretty cardboard boxes if you plan to give it as a gift.

> **1 cup granulated sugar**
> **1 cup firmly packed light brown sugar**
> **¼ cup molasses**
> **½ cup light cream *or* half-and-half**
> **2 ounces unsweetened chocolate,
>   chopped coarse**
> **½ stick (¼ cup) unsalted butter, cut into
>   bits**
> **1½ teaspoons vanilla**

☺+ IN A HEAVY 2-QUART SAUCEPAN COOK THE SUGARS, molasses, cream, and chocolate over moderate heat, stirring, until the sugar is dissolved and the chocolate is melted. Cook, undisturbed, until a candy thermometer registers 238° F.

Remove the saucepan from the heat and stir in the butter and vanilla. Let the mixture cool for 5 minutes. Beat the fudge with a wooden spoon until it begins to lose its gloss. Pour it into a buttered 9-inch square baking pan and let it cool for 15 minutes, or until it begins to harden. Cut the fudge into 1-inch squares and let it cool completely.

The fudge can be made 2 weeks ahead and stored in a cool place in an airtight container lined with wax paper, separating the layers with wax paper. Makes about 1½ pounds.

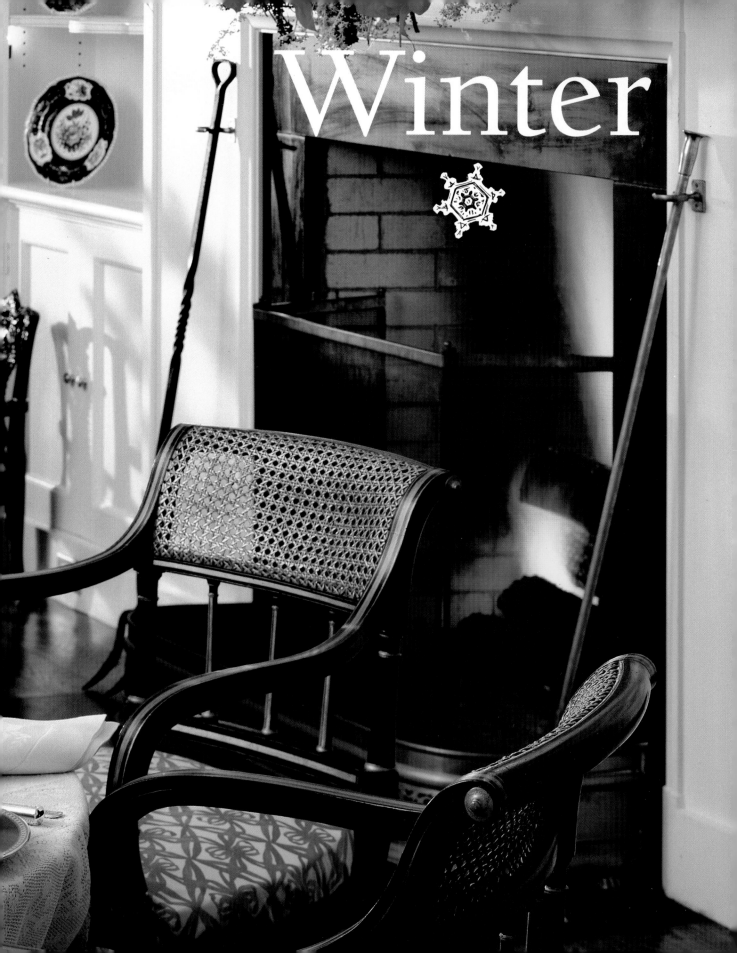

Winter

QUIET SNOWY MORNINGS, ROSY-CHEEKED children, and warming cups of hot chocolate are some of the best things about Winter. Equally wonderful are the parties marking the beginning of the frosty season. Christmas, Hanukkah, and New Year's all beg for lavish, stylish entertaining, on large and intimate scales alike. Now is the time of year when we take Grandmother's white linen tablecloth from the trunk in the attic, arrange shiny sprigs of holly in a silver bowl, and replace half-burned candles with long tapered ones. Winter is the time when we take to the kitchen for hours of uninterrupted baking so that the welcoming, enticing aromas of cinnamon, nutmeg, and chocolate greet everyone coming in from the cold and fill the house with lovely reminders of the holidays.

The menus in this section are tailored for the December holidays, though they may also be called upon later in the Winter. Here are three different approaches to Christmas, including: our country Christmas, which draws upon many of the winning traditions of the South with a glazed smoked ham and cider mustard sauce entrée; a very traditional feast, modeled after an English Christmas dinner with roast prime ribs of beef and Yorkshire pudding; as well as a leaner lighter approach to December 25 featuring roast turkey breast with lemon thyme, where nothing in the meal is especially rich or difficult. Traditional foods, lightened accordingly for the 1990s, make the *latkes* party cheerfully casual. Equally casual and cheerful, but requiring more advance planning, is our New Year's open house, which is preceded by a chic and intimate New Year's Eve supper for two.

All the menus are planned to let you make the most efficient use of the kitchen and your time. Look upon the microwave oven as a helpful friend. If all burners are occupied, use it to melt the butter or steam the vegetables. In other words, let the microwave reach its optimum degree of usefulness by thinking of it as a handy appliance. It is also a good idea to check your other equipment. Do you have tins with snugly fitting lids to keep baked goods fresh? Make sure you have the right-sized pans, the correct number of pots with covers, and a good meat thermometer. The more organized you are, the more smoothly the preparation and the party will go.

When the festivities begin, keep your checklists handy, set timers, and, if need be, tape notes above the kitchen sink. And should you run out of ice cubes, break the water pitcher, or discover that the dog has eaten the cheese puffs, smile. The more relaxed you are, the more fun everyone else will have. After all, isn't that the point? Happy holidays.

AN ENGLISH CHRISTMAS DINNER

OYSTER BISQUE

ROAST PRIME RIBS OF BEEF

INDIVIDUAL YORKSHIRE PUDDINGS

BRAISED ENDIVE AND CELERY

SHOESTRING POTATOES

WATERCRESS AND BEET SALAD

PEAR MINCEMEAT PIE

GINGER ICE CREAM

STILTON

SERVES EIGHT

When Father Christmas visits the British Isles, the jolly old elf brings with him a sackful of tradition influenced by years of baronial celebrating. What this means for us is a vast wealth of cozy, merry customs from which to pick and choose.

For this menu we have selected dishes that highlight the best of the traditional English groaning board while maintaining a sense of America's love for convenience. The meal begins with a creamy oyster bisque that requires cooking just before serving, but cooking of such a gentle, effortless sort, you won't mind at all. If you can, buy the oysters from a fishmonger you trust to shuck them as close to purchase time as possible, and to reserve the liquor for you—this way the oysters will be fresh. Or, better yet, shuck them yourself.

Several hours before you concern yourself with the soup, prepare the roast. An English-style Christmas is unimaginable without rare, juicy roast beef (called a joint in the U.K.) accompanied by Yorkshire pudding. The pudding batter must be mixed 3 hours before baking, which makes it a convenient side dish.

The other three side dishes stray a bit from tradition but are so inviting they beg to be served with the roast beef and Yorkshire pudding. First is the braised endive and celery. We braise Belgian endive, those small white, tightly wrapped leafy vegetables with the delightfully bitter taste, to eliminate just enough of the bitterness. The shoe-string potatoes are, indeed, a bit of a chore to cut up and deep-fry, but with a food processor or *mando-line*, the cutting is quick and easy. Once fried, the potatoes can sit for 2 or 3 hours and then can be popped into the same oven from which you have just removed the roast to quickly reheat them while the beef rests before it is carved.

Finally when preparing the beets for the watercress and beet salad, be sure to leave an inch or so of the stem on the bulb to keep a lot of rosy color from leaching into the cooking water. (Some leaching is inevitable.) Boil the unpeeled vegeta-bles for about 40 minutes and then run cold water over them to halt cooking. When they are well drained and cool enough to handle, peel them with a knife or simply slip off the jackets. Your fingers will turn crimson, but never mind—'tis the season.

Our mincemeat pie is a far cry from the heavy, rich mincemeat of old, which had to be made weeks or months ahead of time. Of course, there was good reason for this forethought: Mince-meat began as a method of preserving meat. Nowa-days it usually contains only fruits and nuts macer-ated in liquor—no meat at all. For our pie, coarsely ground pears are tossed with grated orange and a host of spices, raisins, and walnuts, happily doused with brandy and then left to soak for a mere week. The result? A deliciously light version of mince-meat with just enough sweetness and brandy to taste like Christmas. Our ginger ice cream, which complements the crystallized ginger in the mince-meat, adds a rich and creamy accompaniment. An impressive round of Stilton served with plain bis-cuits concludes our English feast.

OYSTER BISQUE

1 cup minced celery
¼ cup minced shallot
½ stick (¼ cup) unsalted butter
5 cups milk
1 cup heavy cream
1 quart oysters, shucked (procedure on page 160), the liquor strained and reserved
4 large egg yolks
salt and white pepper to taste
paprika for garnish

In a kettle cook the celery and shallot in the butter over moderately low heat, stirring, for 10 minutes, or until they are soft. Stir in the milk, cream, and reserved oyster liquor and bring the mixture just to a simmer.

In a bowl beat the egg yolks lightly and add 1 cup of the milk mixture in a stream, whisking. Whisk this mixture into the remaining milk mix-ture and add the oysters and salt and white pepper. Simmer the soup, stirring, until thickened slightly and the edges of the oysters have curled. Do not let it boil. Transfer the soup to a heated tureen and sprinkle with the paprika. Serves 8.

ROAST PRIME RIBS OF BEEF

12-pound roast of beef
salt and freshly ground pepper to taste

HAVE THE BUTCHER TRIM THE SHORT RIBS FROM THE roast and reserve for another use. Bring the roast to room temperature and rub in the spices.

Preheat the oven to 425° F.

Roast the meat on the rack of a roasting pan in the middle of the oven for 30 minutes. Reduce the heat to 350° F. and roast for 2 hours more for medium-rare meat. Transfer to a heated platter, reserving the pan drippings, and let it stand for 20 minutes, covered loosely with foil. Serves 8.

INDIVIDUAL YORKSHIRE PUDDINGS

¾ cup milk at room temperature
¾ cup water at room temperature
3 large eggs
1½ teaspoons salt
1⅓ cups all-purpose flour
¼ cup roast beef pan drippings

IN A FOOD PROCESSOR BLEND THE MILK, WATER, EGGS, and salt for 15 seconds. With the motor running, add the flour, a little at a time, and blend on high for 2 minutes. Transfer the batter to a bowl and let stand, covered at room temperature, for 3 hours.

Preheat the oven to 450° F.

Pour 1½ teaspoons of the pan drippings into each of eight 4½- by 1-inch pie pans. Put the pans on 2 baking sheets and heat in the oven for 10 minutes, or until smoking.

Return the batter to the food processor and blend for 10 seconds. Divide among the pie pans and bake in the lower third of the oven for 20 minutes. Reduce the heat to 350° F. and bake for 10 minutes more. Remove the puddings from the pans and serve immediately. Serves 8.

BRAISED ENDIVE AND CELERY

4 Belgian endive, split lengthwise
4 celery hearts, split lengthwise
¾ stick (6 tablespoons) unsalted butter
3 tablespoons chicken broth
3 tablespoons fresh lemon juice
salt and freshly ground pepper to taste
minced fresh parsley leaves for garnish

IN A LARGE HEAVY SKILLET COOK THE ENDIVE AND celery in the butter over moderately high heat, turning, until golden. Add the broth, lemon juice, and salt and pepper and cook the vegetables, covered with a buttered round of wax paper and the lid, for 15 to 20 minutes, or until tender. Transfer the vegetables with a slotted spoon to a heated dish and pour the liquid over them. Garnish with the parsley. Serves 8.

SHOESTRING POTATOES

4 large Idaho potatoes, peeled
vegetable shortening for deep frying
salt to taste

ADJUST THE MAIN BLADE AND CROSS-CUTTING BLADE OF A *mandoline* to about ⅛ inch and cut the potatoes lengthwise into strips. Or with a sharp knife cut them lengthwise into ⅛-inch slices and cut the slices into ⅛-inch shoestring strips. As they are cut, drop the potatoes into a large bowl of water. Let stand in the water, changing it 2 or 3 times, or until it is clear, for at least 1 hour.

Drain the potatoes and pat dry well with paper towels. In a deep fryer heat enough shortening to 375° F. to measure 3 inches. Fry the potatoes, a handful at a time, for 3 minutes, or until golden, transferring with a skimmer to baking sheets lined with paper towels to drain. Sprinkle with salt.

The potatoes can be made 3 hours ahead and reheated in a preheated 350° F. oven with the door ajar for no more than 10 minutes. Serves 8.

WATERCRESS AND BEET SALAD

¼ cup white-wine vinegar
1 tablespoon Dijon-style mustard
salt and freshly ground pepper to taste
¾ cup walnut oil (available at specialty
food shops and some supermarkets)
1 pound beets, cooked (procedure
follows)
3 bunches of watercress, rinsed well and
coarse stems removed

 IN A BOWL BEAT THE VINEGAR, MUSTARD, AND SALT and pepper and add the oil in a stream, beating until emulsified.

With a ½-inch melon-ball cutter scoop out 2 cups balls from the beets. Divide the watercress among 8 salad plates, arranging it in a wreath shape. Divide the beet balls among the wreaths like berries. Drizzle with the dressing. Serves 8.

TO COOK BEETS

SCRUB THE BEETS AND TRIM THEM, LEAVING THE ROOTS AND ½ inch of the stems attached. Reserve the greens for another use. In a large saucepan of boiling water simmer the beets, covered, for 45 minutes, or until tender. Drain and peel.

BEAUNE CLOS DU ROI '85
(with main course)

WARRE'S 1963 VINTAGE PORT
(with Stilton)

PEAR MINCEMEAT PIE

6 firm Bartlett *or* Anjou pears
juice of 1 lemon
1 orange, quartered and seeded but
    unpeeled
1 cup sugar
½ cup golden raisins
¼ cup minced crystallized ginger
¾ teaspoon ground mace
¾ teaspoon cinnamon
¾ teaspoon ground allspice
1½ cups chopped walnuts
¼ cup brandy
lard pastry dough (page 196) *or* flaky pie
    pastry (page 196)
1 egg white, beaten lightly

PEEL, QUARTER, AND CORE THE PEARS AND PUT THEM
in a large bowl of water acidulated with the lemon
juice. Drain the pears and put them and the orange
through the coarse blade of a food grinder onto a
sheet of wax paper.

Transfer the mixture to a heavy kettle and
add the sugar, raisins, ginger, and spices. Bring the
mixture to a boil, stirring, and simmer, stirring, for
1½ hours, or until it is thick enough for a wooden
spatula to stand in it. Remove the kettle from the heat
and stir in the walnuts and brandy. Chill the mince-
meat, covered, for at least 1 week.

Form two-thirds of the dough into 1 ball
and the remaining dough into a smaller ball. Roll
out the large ball ⅛ inch thick on a floured surface
and fit it into a 9-inch pie pan. Trim the excess,
leaving a 1-inch overhang. Brush the bottom and
sides with the egg white and chill the shell, covered
with plastic wrap, for 1 hour.

Add the dough scraps to the smaller ball
and roll the dough into a rectangle ¼ inch thick
and 12 inches long on a floured surface. Cut out
fourteen ½-inch-wide strips with a pastry wheel
and put the pastry strips on a floured baking

sheet. Chill the strips for 5 to 10 minutes, or until
just firm.

Preheat oven and a baking sheet to 425° F.

Fill the shell with the mincemeat and
moisten the edge with water. Arrange the strips in
a lattice pattern over the top. Press the ends into
the shell and trim the excess. Turn up the overhang and crimp the edge decoratively. Bake the
pie on the baking sheet in the lower third of the
oven, brushing once or twice with the egg white,
for 20 minutes. Reduce the heat to 350° F. and bake
for 30 minutes more, or until golden. Makes one
9-inch pie.

GINGER ICE CREAM

2 cups milk
2 cups sugar
2 cups heavy cream
1 teaspoon ground ginger
8 large egg yolks
12-ounce jar ginger in syrup, drained
    and chopped fine
½ teaspoon vanilla
slices of crystallized ginger for garnish

IN A HEAVY SAUCEPAN SCALD THE MILK, SUGAR, CREAM,
and ground ginger over moderate heat, stirring. In
a large bowl beat the egg yolks until light and thick
and pour in the milk mixture in a stream through a
fine sieve, stirring. Transfer the mixture to another
heavy saucepan and cook it over moderately low
heat, stirring, until it coats the spoon.

Transfer the cooked mixture to a metal
bowl set in a bowl of cracked ice and cover the surface with a round of wax paper. Let it cool. Stir in
the ginger in syrup and the vanilla and chill it, covered, for 2 hours. Freeze the mixture in an ice-
cream freezer according to the manufacturer's
instructions. Garnish the ice cream with the crystallized ginger. Makes about 1 quart.

A COUNTRY CHRISTMAS

SCALLOPED OYSTERS AND EGGPLANT

**GLAZED SMOKED HAM
WITH CIDER MUSTARD SAUCE**

CHEDDAR GRITS PUDDING

PARSLEYED CARROTS

ORANGE AND RED ONION SALAD

BURNT CREAM

**MINIATURE CHOCOLATE, FRUIT,
AND NUT CAKES**

SERVES EIGHT

Our collective memory tells us that country food is simple and hearty, pure and plentiful. Christmas, then, is a holiday when the farmhouse kitchen bustles with activity aimed at producing a meal that will cover the rough-hewn table in the keeping room with festive abundance.

We have taken a few liberties with our menu by mixing this century with the last, the South with the North, and both with the Midwest—but the spirit of America reigns at its culinary best. Scalloped oysters have long been a holiday treat in the South; we have updated the recipe by layering the oysters with eggplant and baking them in the shell.

The oysters are followed by a classic baked ham, diamond-scored and clove-studded. In the days before supermarkets and mass transportation, every farm family slaughtered a hog as soon as the weather turned cold enough to prevent the meat from spoiling. From this prize came the touted hams of America's farmlands. Ours is no exception. As it cooks in a moderate oven, the oysters may be reheated with it minutes before dinner. Into this same oven, and long before the oysters, can go the Cheddar grits pudding, a marvelous dish with a Southern drawl. When buying grits—which, by the way, is cornmeal in a less refined state—do not purchase the instant variety for this recipe. You will find that our combination of coarser grits with finer cornmeal blends so well with Cheddar and a handful of scallions, you will wonder why you have bypassed the grits on the supermarket shelves all these years.

Both the carrots and the salad can be prepared up to certain points well before cooking or assembling, which makes their last-minute preparation simple. The burnt cream, actually the precursor to what we all know as *crème brûlée*, is more demanding, but once cooked it waits for you. The maple topping is a purely American invention, one that speaks of the stately stands of maple trees in New England and the Great Lake States. Finally, our chocolate, fruit, and nut cakes take very kindly to being made days ahead of time, and make as pretty a gift, packed in a pretty tin and tied with a bright ribbon, as they do a sweet on the holiday table. So you might consider making some extras to give a co-worker, your child's teacher, or the choirmistress.

SCALLOPED OYSTERS AND EGGPLANT

1¼- to 1½ pound eggplant, peeled and
    cut into ½-inch rounds
1 teaspoon salt
vegetable oil for brushing the eggplant
½ cup minced scallion
¾ stick (6 tablespoons) unsalted butter
1½ cups soda cracker crumbs
½ cup minced fresh parsley leaves
salt and freshly ground pepper to taste
24 oysters, shucked (procedure follows),
    reserving the bottom shells, plus 1 pint
    additional shucked oysters
Tabasco to taste, if desired
lemon wedges for garnish

IN A LARGE COLANDER SPRINKLE THE EGGPLANT WITH THE salt and let it drain for 20 minutes.

Preheat the broiler.

Pat the eggplant dry and arrange it in one layer on lightly oiled baking sheets. Brush the eggplant with the oil and broil it about 2 inches from the heat, turning once and brushing with oil, for 6 to 8 minutes, or until golden and tender. Quarter the rounds. *The eggplant can be made 1 day ahead and kept refrigerated, covered.*

In a skillet cook the scallion in the butter over moderately low heat, stirring, for 1 minute. Stir in the crumbs and remove the skillet from the heat. Stir in the parsley and season the crumb mixture with salt and pepper.

Preheat the oven to 425° F.

Wash, dry, and lightly butter the reserved oyster shells. Line them with a layer of eggplant and top the eggplant with at least 1 oyster. Season each oyster with a drop of Tabasco and cover the oysters with the crumb mixture. Arrange the shells in a baking pan lined with rock salt or dried beans and bake them in the middle of the oven for 20 minutes. *The oysters can be made 6 hours ahead and kept refrigerated, covered. Reheat in a preheated 325° F. oven for 15 minutes.*

Divide the oysters among serving plates and garnish with the lemon wedges. Serves 8.

TO SHUCK OYSTERS

SCRUB THE OYSTERS WELL WITH A STIFF BRUSH UNDER cold water. Hold each oyster in a kitchen towel in the palm of the hand with the hinged end away from you. Force an oyster knife between the shells at the hinged end, twisting the knife to pop open the shell. Slide the blade against the flat upper shell to cut the large muscle and free the upper shell.

If the shell crumbles and cannot be opened at the hinge, insert the knife between the shells at the curved end, pry the shells open, and sever the large muscle. Break off and discard the upper shell and slide the knife under the oyster to release it from the bottom shell.

GLAZED SMOKED HAM WITH CIDER MUSTARD SAUCE

**11- to 13-pound fully cooked whole
   (bone-in) cured smoked ham**
whole cloves
1 cup firmly packed light brown sugar
4 teaspoons dry mustard
3 tablespoons cider vinegar
**cider mustard sauce (page 162)
   as an accompaniment**

IF THE HAM COMES WITH THE SKIN STILL ATTACHED, remove most of it with a sharp knife, leaving a collar of skin around the shank bone. Trim the fat if necessary, leaving a ⅓-inch layer, and score it into diamonds about ¼ inch deep. Stud the center of each diamond with a clove. Set the ham on the rack of a roasting pan.

Preheat the oven to 325° F.

In a bowl combine well the sugar and dry mustard. Add the vinegar and stir the mixture until it forms a paste. Spread it over the top and sides of the ham. Bake the ham in the middle of the oven, basting occasionally, for 12 minutes per pound. Let it stand, covered loosely, for 10 minutes before carving. Serve the ham with the sauce. Serves 8 with plenty of leftovers.

Glazed Smoked Ham with Cider Mustard Sauce, Parsleyed Carrots

CIDER MUSTARD SAUCE

⅔ cup cider vinegar
½ cup minced shallot
2 tablespoons sugar
2 cups apple cider
1 teaspoon dry mustard
¼ teaspoon dried thyme, crumbled
1½ cups chicken broth
2 tablespoons unsalted butter, softened
2 tablespoons flour
2 tablespoons Dijon-style mustard
salt and freshly ground pepper to taste

 In a heavy saucepan bring the vinegar, shallot, and sugar to a boil, stirring until the sugar is dissolved. Boil until the liquid is evaporated and the glaze remaining in the pan is caramelized, being careful not to let it burn.

Add the cider, dry mustard, and thyme and bring the glaze to a boil, stirring. Boil until reduced to 1 cup. Add the broth and boil until reduced to 2 cups. Knead together the butter and flour and whisk in bits of it until the sauce is thickened slightly. Remove from the heat and whisk in the Dijon-style mustard and salt and pepper.

The sauce can be made 1 day ahead and kept refrigerated, covered. Reheat over moderately low heat and thin with additional vinegar or broth if necessary. Makes about 2 cups.

CHEDDAR GRITS PUDDING

1½ teaspoons salt
1 cup hominy grits (available at
   supermarkets)
½ cup yellow cornmeal, stone-ground
2 tablespoons unsalted butter,
   cut into bits
1 teaspoon sugar
¼ teaspoon cayenne
2 teaspoons baking powder
½ cup milk
4 large eggs, beaten lightly

½ cup thinly sliced scallion, including
   the green tops
¼ pound sharp Cheddar, grated

In a heavy saucepan bring 4 cups water to a boil and add the salt. Whisk in the grits and cornmeal gradually and return to a boil, whisking. Cook, covered, over low heat, stirring occasionally, for 25 minutes, or until very thick.

Preheat the oven to 325° F.

Remove the saucepan from the heat, add the butter, sugar, and cayenne, and stir until the butter is melted. In a large bowl dissolve the baking powder in the milk and beat in the eggs. Add the grits mixture and blend well. Stir in the scallion and 1 cup of the Cheddar.

Spoon into a buttered 2-quart glass baking dish and bake in the middle of the oven for 1 hour. Sprinkle with the remaining ¼ cup Cheddar and bake for 15 to 20 minutes more, or until puffed and golden. Serves 8.

PARSLEYED CARROTS

2 pounds carrots
2 tablespoons unsalted butter
½ teaspoon cinnamon
2 tablespoons white-wine vinegar
¼ cup minced fresh parsley leaves

Halve the carrots crosswise on the diagonal and halve or quarter each piece lengthwise to form tapering pieces, rounding the edges if desired with a vegetable peeler.

In a steamer set over boiling water steam the carrots, covered, for 7 to 8 minutes, or until they are just tender. Plunge them into a bowl of ice water, drain, and pat dry. *The carrots can be prepared 6 hours ahead up to this point and kept refrigerated, covered.*

In a large skillet melt the butter over moderate heat and stir in the cinnamon. Add the carrots and salt and pepper to taste, and cook, stirring, for 1 to 2 minutes, or until the carrots are heated through. Add the vinegar and bring to a boil. Boil, stirring, until the vinegar is evaporated and stir in the parsley. Serves 8.

ORANGE AND RED ONION SALAD

4 navel oranges
2 red onions, sliced thin and separated
    into rings
2 tablespoons white-wine vinegar
1 small garlic clove, minced
½ teaspoon ground cumin
salt and freshly ground pepper to taste
½ cup olive oil
1 head of curly endive (chicory), cut
    crosswise into ½-inch pieces

+ WORKING OVER A BOWL TO CATCH THE JUICE, CUT away the zest and pith of the oranges with a serrated knife. Slice the oranges crosswise and chill them on a large plate, covered, for at least 15 minutes or up to 4 hours. In a bowl of ice water let the onion rings soak for at least 30 minutes or up to 1 hour.

In a blender or bowl whisk together 2 tablespoons of the orange juice, the vinegar, garlic, cumin, and salt and pepper. With the motor running or whisking, add the oil in a stream and blend until emulsified.

Arrange three-fourths of the endive around the edge of a platter and overlap the orange slices on it. Drain the onion rings and pat them dry. Overlap the onions on the oranges. Mound the remaining endive in the center and drizzle the salad with the dressing. Serves 8.

Orange and Red Onion Salad

BURNT CREAM

1⅔ cups sugar
7 tablespoons water
2½ cups milk
1½ cups heavy cream
1½-inch vanilla bean, split
¼ teaspoon salt
4 large whole eggs
5 large egg yolks

PREHEAT THE OVEN TO 325° F.

In a large heavy saucepan bring ⅔ cup of the sugar and 4 tablespoons of the water to a boil over moderate heat, stirring until the sugar is dissolved. Boil the syrup, stirring occasionally, for 5 minutes. Stir in the milk, cream, vanilla bean, and salt and scald the mixture.

In a large bowl stir (do not whisk or beat) the whole eggs and egg yolks until just combined and add the milk mixture in a slow stream, stirring constantly. Strain through a fine sieve into a 1½-quart shallow baking dish.

Set the dish in a larger pan or ovenproof skillet (the smaller the better) lined with a kitchen towel for insulation. Add enough hot water to the pan to reach no more than halfway up the sides of the dish and bake the custard in the middle of the oven for 40 minutes, or until just set. Remove the dish from the pan and let it cool. Chill it, covered, for at least 3 hours. *The custard can be made 1 day ahead up to this point and kept refrigerated, covered.*

In a small heavy saucepan heat the remaining 1 cup sugar and 3 tablespoons water over moderate heat, stirring and washing down any sugar crystals clinging to the sides of the pan with a brush dipped in cold water, until the sugar is dissolved. Bring the syrup to a boil and boil, undisturbed, swirling the pan occasionally, until golden. Let the caramel cool for 15 seconds, or until it stops bubbling furiously.

Pour the caramel immediately over the custard, tilting the dish to cover evenly. Let it stand for at least 20 minutes, or until the caramel is hardened. *The burnt cream can be made 2 hours ahead and left at room temperature.* Serves 8.

MINIATURE CHOCOLATE, FRUIT, AND NUT CAKES

1 cup plus 2 tablespoons all-purpose flour
½ cup granulated sugar
1 teaspoon baking powder
½ teaspoon baking soda
¼ teaspoon salt
¾ cup sweetened flaked coconut
½ cup golden *or* dark raisins or a combination of the two
¼ cup chopped dried apricots
½ cup semisweet chocolate chips
⅓ cup chopped walnuts, toasted lightly if desired
⅓ cup chopped pecans, toasted lightly if desired
1 teaspoon grated orange zest
1 large egg
⅓ cup milk
1 stick (½ cup) unsalted butter, melted and cooled
2 tablespoons cream Sherry
½ teaspoon vanilla
confectioners' sugar glaze (recipe follows)

PREHEAT THE OVEN TO 325° F.

Into a large bowl sift the flour, sugar, baking powder, baking soda, and salt. Add the coconut, dried fruits, chocolate chips, nuts, and orange zest and toss well.

In a bowl beat the egg and milk and beat in the butter, Sherry, and vanilla. Add this mixture all at once to the flour mixture, stirring until just combined. Spoon the mixture into buttered gem tins (2 tablespoons each in size), filling three-fourths full. Bake the cakes in the middle of the oven for 15 to 20 minutes, or until puffed and springy to the touch. Turn the cakes out onto racks to cool.

With the tip of a knife, drizzle the glaze over the cakes. Let them stand for 30 minutes to harden. *The cakes can be made 4 days ahead and kept in layers separated by wax paper in airtight containers.* Makes about 40 miniature cakes.

CONFECTIONERS' SUGAR GLAZE

**1¼ cup confectioners' sugar, plus
additional, if needed
2 to 3 teaspoons fresh lemon juice, plus
additional, if needed**

IN A BOWL WHISK TOGETHER THE CONFECTIONERS' sugar, sifted, and enough of the lemon juice to make a thick but pourable glaze. The glaze should be thin enough to drizzle from the tip of a knife but thick enough to hold its shape on the cakes. If necessary, beat in additional sugar, 1 tablespoon at a time, or additional lemon juice, ½ teaspoon at a time for the desired consistency.

SAINT-VERAN '88
(with first course)

**SIMI WINERY ROSÉ OF CABERNET
SAUVIGNON '88**
(with main course)

OLD BUAL MADEIRA
(with dessert)

Miniature Chocolate, Fruit, and Nut Cakes

A LEANER, LIGHTER
CHRISTMAS DINNER

SCALLOP AND LEEK SOUP

ROAST TURKEY BREAST WITH LEMON THYME

ONION RYE STUFFING

RUSSET POTATO AND RICOTTA CHEESE PIE

STEAMED BROCCOLI RABE

SPICED ANGEL FOOD CAKE WITH
FRESH CRANBERRY SAUCE

| *SERVES EIGHT* |

Celebrate Christmas this year with all the trimmings but without a surplus of dishes heavy with calories. We have devised a menu that showcases a succulent, lean turkey breast and carotene-rich broccoli rabe, as well as a creamy soup and a spicy angel food cake. Streamlined and thoroughly modern, this Christmas dinner can be enjoyed without spending hours in the kitchen.

The soup is the only course that demands much time right before dinner. Be sure the leeks, which tend to be sandy and gritty, are thoroughly washed. One good way to do this is to cut a cross in the bottom of each one and let them soak in a sinkful of cold water for a good 20 minutes or so. Sea scallops, much more available than bay scallops, are often quite large; cut any that are not bite-size in half before adding them to the soup.

Our Christmas turkey is stuffed with a distinctive mixture of rye bread and caraway seeds. The stuffing can be made the day before Christmas. Tuck some of it into the neck cavity of the turkey breast and spoon the rest into a separate dish to heat with the bird. Turkey growers are marketing the large-breasted fowl in all sorts of ways, and whole fresh breasts are readily available all year long. If you prefer more traditional fare, buy a small whole turkey instead.

The potato and cheese pie can be assembled several hours before cooking it for half an hour in the oven with the turkey and stuffing. The low-fat ricotta, smoothed to the consistency of sour cream in a food mill, nicely enriches the potatoes so that no one will miss the large amounts of butter more customary to Christmas potato preparations.

If you cannot locate broccoli rabe, use fresh broccoli in its place. Both taste deliciously fresh when quickly steamed and flavored with garlic-laced oil. And both can be trimmed several hours beforehand and stored in the refrigerator until minutes before dinner, when they are cooked.

We are quite proud of our angel food cake. The light-as-air dessert is often associated with summertime and fresh Summer berries, but we have made it truly seasonal with the addition of cinnamon, ginger, and nutmeg. All three spices are so generously used in Christmas sweets we decided to blend them with the flour to heighten the flavor of the cake. Bake it a day ahead of time or on Christmas morning. It is simple to mix and takes less than an hour in the oven. Served with a quick cranberry sauce, it looks pretty and tastes the way a Christmas cake ought to taste: sweet and indulgent.

SCALLOP AND LEEK SOUP

2½ cups well-washed and minced leek
  (the white part of 4 leeks)
½ cup minced celery
¼ pound mushrooms, minced
2 pounds sea scallops, halved if large
salt and freshly ground pepper to taste
3 tablespoons unsalted butter
½ cup dry white wine
8 cups white fish stock (page 198), *or*
  chicken stock (page 198), *or* canned
  chicken broth
cheesecloth bag containing 12 parsley
  stems, ½ teaspoon dried thyme, 1 bay
  leaf, and 12 peppercorns
2 tablespoons cornstarch
1 cup heavy cream *or* half-and-half
fresh lemon juice to taste
snipped fresh chives for garnish

+ In a large saucepan sweat the vegetables, half the scallops, and salt and pepper in the butter, covered with a round of buttered wax paper and the lid, over moderately low heat for 5 minutes. Add

the wine and simmer the mixture over moderate heat for 1 minute. Add the stock and cheesecloth bag and bring the mixture to a boil. Simmer it, covered, for 20 minutes. Discard the cheesecloth bag.

In a food processor or blender purée the mixture in batches and strain it through a fine sieve into another saucepan. Bring the purée to a boil and boil for 5 minutes, or until reduced to about 7 cups. In a bowl combine the cornstarch and cream.

Return the purée to a boil. Stir the cream mixture and add it to the saucepan, stirring. Simmer, stirring, until thickened slightly. *The soup base can be made 4 hours ahead up to this point and kept in a cool place, covered on the surface with a buttered round of wax paper.*

Add the remaining scallops and salt and pepper to taste and bring the mixture just to a boil. Simmer it for 3 minutes, or until the scallops are opaque. Stir in the lemon juice and garnish the soup with the chives. Serves 8.

MICROWAVE DIRECTIONS

INGREDIENT CHANGES:
Reduce the stock to 5½ cups; use 1 cup half-and-half.

DIRECTIONS:
Combine the leeks, celery, mushrooms, and half the scallops in a microwave-safe 3-quart casserole; place small pieces of butter over the top. Cover and microwave at high power (100%) for 8 minutes. Stir in the wine. Microwave, uncovered, at high power (100%) for 5 minutes. Add 5 cups of the stock and the cheesecloth bag. Cover and microwave at high power (100%) for 9 minutes until boiling. Purée the mixture in a blender or food processor. Pour the purée mixture into a large sieve; press out as much liquid as possible with a wooden spoon. Discard the solids and return the liquid to the casserole. Whisk together the remaining ½ cup stock and the cornstarch; stir into the casserole. Cover and microwave at high power (100%) for 10 minutes until boiling, whisking well after 5 minutes. Remove the casserole from the oven; whisk again. Add the remaining scallops. Cover and microwave at high power (100%) for 3 to 4 minutes, until simmering. Stir in the half-and-half, lemon juice, and salt and pepper to taste. Garnish with the chives.

ROAST TURKEY BREAST WITH LEMON THYME

5- to 6-pound turkey breast, thawed if
 frozen and wishbone removed
1 cup onion rye stuffing (recipe follows)
1 tablespoon unsalted butter
1 tablespoon vegetable oil
2 garlic cloves, minced, or to taste
1 teaspoon grated lemon zest
1 teaspoon dried lemon thyme, crumbled
 (available at specialty food shops)
 or regular thyme
salt and freshly ground pepper to taste
1 onion, quartered
1 celery stalk, cut into 1-inch pieces
1 small carrot, cut into 1-inch pieces
¾ cup dry white wine
3 cups turkey giblet stock (page 198), *or*
 chicken stock (page 198), *or* canned
 chicken broth
2 tablespoons arrowroot

PREHEAT THE OVEN TO 450° F.

Pack the neck cavity of the turkey breast loosely with the stuffing, fold the skin under, and fasten it with a skewer. Pat the turkey dry and coat it all over with the butter and oil. In a small bowl combine the garlic, lemon zest, lemon thyme, and salt and pepper and rub the mixture on the cut side of the turkey.

Arrange the turkey on a rack in a roasting pan and surround it with the onion, celery, and carrot. Put the turkey in the middle of the oven and reduce the heat to 375° F. Bake it for 1¼ to 1½ hours, or until the juices run clear when the breast is pricked with a skewer and a meat thermometer registers 165° F. Transfer the turkey to a platter and keep it warm, covered loosely with foil.

Pour off the fat in the pan and add all but 2 tablespoons of the wine, scraping up the brown bits clinging to the bottom and sides. Add the stock and bring the mixture to a boil. Simmer, stirring occasionally, for 20 minutes, or until it is reduced to 2½ cups. In a small bowl combine the arrowroot and remaining 2 tablespoons wine.

Return the pan juices to a boil and add the arrowroot mixture, stirring. Simmer, stirring, for 5 minutes, or until the gravy is thickened slightly. Add salt and pepper to taste and strain it into a heated sauceboat. Serve with the turkey and stuffing. Serves 8.

ONION RYE STUFFING

1½ cups minced onion
1 cup minced celery
3 tablespoons unsalted butter
3 garlic cloves, minced
1 teaspoon caraway seeds
6 slices rye bread, cubed and toasted
 (about 5 cups)
¼ cup minced fresh parsley leaves
salt and freshly ground pepper to taste
about ½ cup chicken broth

IN A SAUCEPAN COOK THE ONION AND CELERY IN THE butter over moderate heat, stirring, until softened. Stir in the garlic and cook for 2 minutes. Add the remaining ingredients and enough broth to bind the mixture. Let the stuffing cool. *The stuffing can be made 1 day ahead up to this point and kept refrigerated, covered.*

Reserve 1 cup of the stuffing for the neck cavity of the turkey breast. Spoon the remaining stuffing into a buttered baking dish and bake, covered, in the 375° F. oven with the turkey for 15 to 20 minutes, or until the edges are browned. Bake, uncovered, for 15 minutes more. Makes 4½ cups, excluding the turkey stuffing.

RUSSET POTATO AND RICOTTA CHEESE PIE

⅓ cup dry bread crumbs
2 cups cooked and mashed russet *or* other baking potato
15-ounces skim-milk ricotta, forced through the fine blade of a food mill
½ cup sour cream
½ cup snipped fresh chives
2 large eggs, beaten lightly
5 tablespoons freshly grated Parmesan
salt and freshly ground pepper to taste
paprika to taste
1 tablespoon unsalted butter, cut into bits

◐ PREHEAT THE OVEN TO 375° F.

Coat the bottom and sides of a buttered 9-inch pie plate with the bread crumbs. Tap the excess into a bowl and reserve.

In a large bowl combine the potato, ricotta, sour cream, chives, eggs, 4 tablespoons of the Parmesan, and salt and pepper and spoon the mixture into the prepared pie plate. Sprinkle with the reserved bread crumbs, remaining 1 tablespoon Parmesan, and paprika and dot with the butter. *The pie can be made 2 hours ahead up to this point and kept refrigerated, covered.*

Bake in the middle of the oven for 30 to 35 minutes, or until puffed and golden. Serves 8.

MICROWAVE DIRECTIONS

INGREDIENT CHANGES:
Use two 10-ounce potatoes; use light sour cream; use ½ teaspoon paprika; eliminate butter.

DIRECTIONS:
Pierce the potatoes several times with the tines of a fork. Place the potatoes on a double thickness of paper towels in the oven. Microwave, uncovered, at high power (100%) for 10 minutes, until soft. Halve the potatoes; scoop out the flesh into a food processor. Add the ricotta, light sour cream, chives, eggs, and all the Parmesan; process until smooth. Season the mixture with salt and pepper. Prepare a microwave-safe pie plate as directed in

the original recipe; combine the reserved bread crumbs with the ½ teaspoon paprika. Spoon the potato mixture into the pie plate; sprinkle with the bread crumb mixture. Cover the pie with wax paper. Microwave at high power (100%) for 5 minutes. Remove the wax paper. Microwave at medium power (50%) for 10 minutes. Let the pie stand 5 minutes before serving.

STEAMED BROCCOLI RABE

2 pounds broccoli rabe
1 garlic clove, sliced thin
¼ cup olive oil
fresh lemon juice to taste
salt and freshly ground pepper to taste

◐ BREAK OFF THE OUTER LEAVES OF THE BROCCOLI RABE and reserve. Peel the central stems and halve them lengthwise if more than ½ inch thick.

Arrange the reserved leaves and stem pieces on a rack in a steamer and steam them, covered, over boiling water for 4 to 6 minutes, or until bright green and just tender. Transfer the broccoli rabe to a platter and keep it warm.

In a skillet cook the garlic in the oil over moderate heat, stirring, until golden. Strain the oil over the broccoli rabe and season with lemon juice and salt and pepper to taste. Serves 8.

MICROWAVE DIRECTIONS

INGREDIENT CHANGES:
Prepare broccoli rabe as directed but cut stems into 2-inch pieces; add ¼ cup water.

DIRECTIONS:
Place the broccoli rabe and ¼ cup water in a microwave-safe 3-quart casserole (casserole will be full). Cover it with a lid and microwave at high power (100%) for 8 minutes, stirring twice. Drain; let it stand, covered. Combine the oil and garlic in a microwave-safe 1-cup measure. Microwave, uncovered, at high power (100%) for 1 minute. Strain the oil over the broccoli rabe; add lemon juice and salt and pepper to taste.

SPICED ANGEL FOOD CAKE WITH FRESH CRANBERRY SAUCE

1½ cups granulated sugar
1 cup sifted cake flour
1 teaspoon cinnamon
¼ teaspoon ground ginger
¼ teaspoon freshly grated nutmeg
1¼ cups large egg whites (about 10)
2 tablespoons water
1 teaspoon fresh lemon juice
1 teaspoon cream of tartar
1 teaspoon vanilla
½ teaspoon almond extract
sifted confectioners' sugar for garnish
fresh cranberry sauce (recipe follows)

PREHEAT THE OVEN TO 350° F.

In a food processor grind the sugar until fine. In a bowl combine ¾ cup of the sugar with the flour and spices and sift the mixture twice.

In the bowl of an electric mixer beat the egg whites with the water and lemon juice until foamy. Add the cream of tartar and beat until the whites hold stiff peaks. Add the remaining sugar, 1 tablespoon at a time, and beat until just mixed. Fold in the vanilla and almond extract.

Sift one-third of the flour mixture over the whites and fold it in quickly and lightly. Add 2 more batches of the flour mixture in the same manner. Pour the batter into an ungreased 10-inch tube pan, 4 inches deep, with a removable bottom, and run a thin spatula through it to eliminate air bubbles. Smooth the top.

Bake the cake in the middle of the oven for 40 to 45 minutes, or until it springs back when pressed lightly with a finger. Remove the pan from the oven and suspend it upside down on the neck of a bottle. Let it cool.

With a sharp knife, loosen the cake from the sides and center tube of the pan. Tap the bottom firmly on a flat surface to loosen the cake and turn it out of the pan. Dust with the confectioners' sugar.

The cake can be made ahead and kept in an airtight container at room temperature overnight. Serve with the sauce. Makes one 10-inch cake.

FRESH CRANBERRY SAUCE

2 teaspoons cornstarch
2 tablespoons fresh orange juice
2 cups fresh cranberries, picked over
1½ cups sugar
½ cup water
½ teaspoon cinnamon
¼ teaspoon freshly grated nutmeg
1½ teaspoons grated orange zest

+ IN A SMALL BOWL COMBINE THE CORNSTARCH AND orange juice. In a saucepan combine the cranberries, sugar, water, spices, and orange zest and bring to a boil. Simmer the mixture for 3 to 5 minutes, or until the cranberries are tender.

Return the cranberry mixture to a boil and stir in the cornstarch mixture. Simmer the mixture, stirring, for 3 minutes and let the sauce cool. Chill it, covered, until ready to serve. Makes about 3 cups.

MICROWAVE DIRECTIONS

INGREDIENT CHANGES:
Use fresh or thawed frozen cranberries; eliminate water; increase orange juice to ¼ cup.

DIRECTIONS:
Stir together the sugar and cornstarch in a microwave-safe 4-cup measure. Stir in the cranberries, orange juice, cinnamon, nutmeg, and orange zest. Cover with microwave-safe plastic wrap vented at one side. Microwave at high power (100%) for 5½ minutes until the mixture boils, stirring after 3 minutes. Remove the sauce from the microwave oven; stir well. Let it cool to room temperature. Cover and chill the sauce until ready to use. Makes about 2 cups.

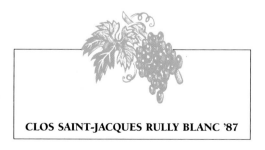

CLOS SAINT-JACQUES RULLY BLANC '87

Spiced Angel Food Cake with
Fresh Cranberry Sauce

Hanukkah Jelly Doughnuts,
Hot Cranberry Apple Cider

A LATKES PARTY FOR HANUKKAH

HOT CRANBERRY APPLE CIDER

MUSHROOM BARLEY SOUP

POTATO LATKES WITH APPLESAUCE AND SOUR CREAM

DILLED CUCUMBER SALAD

HANUKKAH JELLY DOUGHNUTS

When you are thinking of Hanukkah, consider a *latkes* party. It's an easy way to entertain on a night in early Winter when you invite a few friends to share the holiday but do not want a lot of fuss and bother. *Latkes*—potato pancakes—are traditional for Hanukkah because they are cooked in a little oil. This represents the small measure of oil the Jews had centuries ago when they found themselves defending the Temple of Jerusalem with only enough sanctified oil for one night. Miraculously, the oil lasted for eight days, and today Jews around the world celebrate Hanukkah by lighting one candle every night for eight days and also by eating foods fried in oil.

Our meal may center on *latkes*, but it does not otherwise include a lot of fried foods. As *latkes*

often are, ours are served with sour cream and applesauce, but our unique applesauce is sweetened with a syrup flavored with apricot jam. The apples, which should be firm and tart to begin with, are simmered for a brief 15 minutes in the syrup before being puréed in a food processor or blender. Finally, the thickened, reduced syrup is mixed with the apple purée and chilled.

Begin the Hanukkah celebration by welcoming your friends with cups of hot cranberry apple cider. The brew is nonalcoholic, so young guests can enjoy its warm, comforting taste, too. A simple mushroom barley soup precedes the *latkes*, and a chilled cucumber salad accompanies them. Fresh dill and minced scallion give the cucumbers zing; we suggest making them pretty by scoring them with a fork before slicing. Toss the slices with a tarragon-vinegar based dressing and let them marinate in the refrigerator for an hour or so before the guests arrive.

End the meal with jelly doughnuts. Yeast-raised and then deep-fried, the sweet puffs echo the Hanukkah tradition. It is best to fry them not more than an hour or so before the party begins; the fresher doughnuts are, the better they taste.

HOT CRANBERRY APPLE CIDER

4 cups cranberry juice cocktail
4 cups apple cider
a 3-inch cinnamon stick
2 tablespoons honey, or to taste

IN A STAINLESS STEEL OR ENAMELED SAUCEPAN BRING the cranberry juice, cider, and cinnamon stick to a boil and simmer the mixture for 10 minutes. Remove from the heat and stir in the honey. Serves 8.

MUSHROOM BARLEY SOUP

1 ounce imported dried mushrooms
2 cups hot water
1 large onion, minced
½ stick (¼ cup) unsalted butter
1 pound fresh mushrooms, sliced thin
2 tablespoons flour
8 cups vegetable stock (page 198)
½ cup pearled barley
1 bay leaf
½ teaspoon dried thyme, crumbled
salt and freshly ground pepper to taste
2 cups half-and-half, scalded
snipped fresh dill for garnish

IN A SMALL BOWL LET THE DRIED MUSHROOMS SOAK IN the hot water for 30 minutes. Drain them, reserving the water, and chop the mushrooms fine. Strain the water and reserve 1 cup.

In a large saucepan cook the onion in the butter over moderate heat, stirring occasionally, until it is softened. Add the dried and fresh mushrooms and cook them, stirring, until most of the liquid they give off has evaporated.

Add the flour and cook, stirring, for 2 minutes. Add the reserved mushroom water, stock, barley, bay leaf, thyme, and salt and pepper and bring the mixture to a boil. Simmer, covered, for 45 minutes. Add the half-and-half and bring the mixture to a boil. Simmer for 15 minutes, or until the barley is tender. Discard the bay leaf and add salt and pepper to taste. Garnish with the dill. Serves 8.

POTATO LATKES WITH APPLESAUCE AND SOUR CREAM

2½ pounds russet *or* other
   baking potatoes
1 large onion, grated
4 large eggs, beaten lightly
⅓ cup matzo meal
1 teaspoon salt
¼ teaspoon freshly ground pepper
vegetable oil for frying
applesauce (recipe follows) and sour
   cream as accompaniments

PREHEAT THE OVEN TO 200° F.

Peel and grate the potatoes (there should be about 4 cups). Squeeze them with the grated onion in a dish towel to remove as much moisture as possible. In a large bowl combine well with the remaining ingredients, not including the oil or accompaniments.

In a large skillet heat ¼ inch vegetable oil until hot. Drop ¼-cup portions of the potato mixture into the oil in batches, spreading each portion with the back of a spoon to flatten it. Fry the *latkes* for 1 to 2 minutes on each side, or until golden. Transfer the *latkes* as they are cooked to a shallow baking pan lined with paper towels and keep them warm in the oven. Serve with the applesauce and sour cream. Serves 8.

APPLESAUCE

⅔ cup water
½ cup sugar
¼ cup apricot jam
6 McIntosh apples
2 tablespoons fresh lemon juice

☽+ In a heavy saucepan cook all ingredients except the apples and lemon juice over moderately high heat, stirring and washing down any sugar crystals clinging to the sides with a brush dipped in cold water, until the sugar is dissolved. Bring the syrup to a boil and simmer, undisturbed, for 5 minutes. Peel the apples, slice thick, and toss them with the lemon juice.

Add the apples to the saucepan and simmer for 10 to 15 minutes, or until softened. Transfer the apples with a slotted spoon to a bowl and mash them with a fork. Boil the syrup over high heat until thickened and pour it over the purée. Combine well and chill. Makes 3 cups.

DILLED CUCUMBER SALAD

4 cucumbers
1½ teaspoons salt
⅓ cup tarragon vinegar
1½ teaspoons sugar
½ cup minced scallion
3 tablespoons snipped fresh dill
freshly ground pepper to taste

☽+ Score the cucumbers lengthwise with a fork and slice them thin crosswise. In a bowl toss the cucumber with the salt and let it stand, covered, for 30 minutes.

In a stainless steel or enameled saucepan bring the vinegar, sugar, and ⅓ cup water to a boil, stirring until the sugar is dissolved. Let the mixture cool. Drain the cucumber in a colander and rinse under cold water. Drain it well. In a ceramic or glass bowl combine the cucumber, vinegar mixture, and remaining ingredients and chill, covered, for at least 1 hour. Makes about 4 cups.

HANUKKAH JELLY DOUGHNUTS

1 package active dry yeast
  (2½ teaspoons)
1 cup milk, scalded and cooled to warm
3 tablespoons sugar
3½ cups sifted all-purpose flour
½ teaspoon salt
3 tablespoons vegetable oil
1 large egg, beaten lightly
¼ to ⅓ cup strawberry jelly
vegetable shortening for deep frying
fine granulated sugar for coating the
  doughnuts

In a large bowl proof the yeast in the milk with 1 teaspoon of the sugar until foamy. Sift the flour, salt, and remaining sugar into a bowl. Add the oil and egg to the yeast mixture and beat until combined. Add the flour mixture and beat until the dough is smooth and comes away from the sides of the bowl. Let the dough rise, covered, in a warm place for 1½ hours, or until double in bulk.

Roll out the dough ½ inch thick on a well-floured surface and with a 2½-inch cutter cut out rounds. Reroll the scraps and make more rounds. Place 1 teaspoon of the jelly on half the rounds and moisten the edges with water. Cover them with the remaining rounds and pinch the edges together. Put the doughnuts on a floured baking sheet and let them rise, covered with a tea towel, for 30 minutes.

In a deep fryer heat 3 inches of shortening to 360° F. Fry the doughnuts in batches for 2 minutes on each side, or until golden. Drain the doughnuts on paper towels and let them cool. Toss the doughnuts with the sugar. Makes 8 to 10 doughnuts.

AUSTRALIAN RHINE RIESLING '87

MENU

AN INTIMATE
NEW YEAR'S EVE DINNER

BLINI WITH CAVIAR

**FILETS MIGNONS WITH PORCINI AND
SHIITAKE MUSHROOMS**

CELERY ROOT PURÉE

**BABY EGGPLANTS STUFFED WITH
RATATOUILLE**

APPLE GALETTES

SERVES TWO

Why go out on New Year's Eve? Instead, plan a quiet dinner for two with lots of time to savor each course and every bite. Light a cozy fire and greet the new year with this elegant meal, most of which can be made ahead of time. With a little planning, you have only to concern yourself with some easy preparation 30 minutes or so before you dine.

Begin by preheating the oven; the blini, celery root purée, and stuffed baby eggplant—all of which may be made the day or morning before—

are reheated in the same hot oven. The filets mignons require quick cooking in a skillet, and the wine sauce, fortified with an earthy blending of dried and fresh mushrooms, takes only a few minutes longer. After arranging the entrée presentation, place the apricot glazed apple galettes, prepared several hours before, into a reduced oven. They will be ready to dab with sweetened whipped cream or ice cream as you prepare to ring in the new year. Serve them with coffee or, in keeping with the holiday, fine Champagne as the minute hand sweeps past midnight.

BLINI WITH CAVIAR

½ teaspoon active dry yeast
¼ cup milk, scalded and cooled
   to lukewarm
pinch of sugar
1 large egg, separated
⅓ cup all-purpose flour
¼ teaspoon salt
1 tablespoon unsalted butter, melted and
   cooled, plus additional for brushing
softened unsalted butter, fresh black
   or red caviar, and sour cream
   as accompaniments

IN A BOWL PROOF THE YEAST IN THE MILK WITH THE sugar until foamy. In another bowl beat the egg yolk and stir in the yeast mixture, the flour combined with the salt, and the 1 tablespoon melted butter. Let the batter stand, covered with plastic wrap, in a warm place for 3 hours, or until double in bulk.

In another bowl beat the egg white until it holds stiff peaks. Stir down the batter and fold in the egg white.

Heat a griddle over moderately high heat until hot, brush it with melted butter, and drop the batter by tablespoons 2 inches apart onto it. Cook the blini for 1 minute, or until browned on the bottom. Turn them and cook for 30 seconds.

The blini can be made 1 day ahead and kept refrigerated, wrapped in plastic wrap. Reheat on a baking sheet in a preheated 400° F. oven for 5 to 7 minutes, or until heated through.

Spread the blini with the softened butter and top with the caviar and sour cream. Serves 2.

CROZES-HERMITAGE ROUGE '85
(with main course)

PIPER-HEIDSIECK EXTRA SEC
(with dessert)

FILETS MIGNONS WITH PORCINI AND SHIITAKE MUSHROOMS

½ ounce dried *porcini*, or *cèpes*
1 cup hot water
2 teaspoons arrowroot
2 tablespoons heavy cream
1 cup brown stock (page 197)
½ cup Burgundy *or* other dry red wine
¼ cup minced shallot
1 teaspoon tomato paste
¼ teaspoon dried thyme, crumbled
¼ teaspoon peppercorns, crushed
2 filets mignons, each 1 inch thick and
   weighing 6 to 7 ounces
salt and freshly ground pepper to taste
2 tablespoons unsalted butter
1 tablespoon vegetable oil
2 ounces fresh *shiitake* mushrooms,
   sliced
minced fresh parsley leaves for garnish

IN A BOWL SOAK THE DRIED MUSHROOMS IN THE HOT water for 15 to 20 minutes, or until softened. Drain, reserving ½ cup of the liquid. Cut off any stems and slice the mushrooms. In a small bowl combine the arrowroot and cream.

In a saucepan bring the stock, wine, shallot, tomato paste, thyme, peppercorns, and reserved soaking liquid to a boil over high heat and boil until reduced to 1 cup. Stir in the arrowroot mixture and cook for 1 minute, or until thickened.

Pat the filets dry and sprinkle them with the salt and pepper. In a skillet cook them in 1 tablespoon of the butter and the oil over moderately high heat for 3 to 4 minutes on each side for medium-rare. Transfer the filets to a plate and keep warm.

Pour off the fat from the skillet. In the skillet cook the dried and fresh mushrooms in the remaining 1 tablespoon butter over moderately high heat, stirring, for 3 minutes, or until the liquid they give off is evaporated. Strain the wine sauce into the skillet and season with salt and pepper. Simmer the sauce for 1 minute and add any juices that have accumulated on the plate.

Nap the filets mignons with the sauce and garnish with the parsley. Serves 2.

CELERY ROOT PURÉE

¾ **pound celery root, trimmed, peeled, and cubed**
¾ **pound russet potatoes, peeled and cubed**
1 **tablespoon unsalted butter, softened**
2 **to 4 tablespoons milk**
salt and freshly ground pepper to taste

 IN A LARGE SAUCEPAN OF SALTED WATER COMBINE THE celery root and potatoes, bring to a boil, and simmer, covered, for 20 to 30 minutes, or until tender. Drain and put through a ricer into a bowl. Beat in the butter and enough milk to bind the purée. Season with the salt and pepper. *The purée can be made 1 day ahead and kept refrigerated in a buttered gratin dish, covered with foil. Reheat, covered, in a preheated 400° F. oven for 20 minutes, or until hot.* Serves 2.

BABY EGGPLANTS STUFFED WITH RATATOUILLE

2 **baby eggplants, each ¼ pound**
3 **tablespoons olive oil**
½ **cup minced onion**
½ **cup minced red bell pepper**
½ **cup diced zucchini**
1 **cup canned tomatoes, drained and chopped**
¼ **teaspoon dried thyme, crumbled**
¼ **teaspoon dried basil, crumbled**
1 **garlic clove, minced**
salt and freshly ground pepper to taste
2 **tablespoons minced fresh basil leaves**
2 **tablespoons freshly grated Parmesan**

PREHEAT THE OVEN TO 400° F.

Halve the eggplants lengthwise and cut 3 slashes in the flesh of each half. Arrange them cut side down in an oiled baking pan and brush with 1 tablespoon of the olive oil. Bake in the middle of the oven for 10 minutes, or until tender.

Transfer the eggplants to a rack and let them cool. Scoop out the pulp, leaving ¼-inch shells. Chop the pulp and reserve the shells.

In a saucepan cook the onion and red pepper in the remaining 2 tablespoons oil over moderate heat, stirring, for 3 to 4 minutes, or until the onion is softened. Add the zucchini and eggplant pulp and cook, stirring, for 3 minutes. Add the tomatoes, dried herbs, garlic, and salt and pepper and cook the stuffing over low heat, covered, stirring occasionally, for 10 minutes. Stir in the fresh basil.

Mound the stuffing in the eggplant shells and sprinkle the stuffed eggplants with the Parmesan. Bake them in an oiled gratin dish in the middle of the oven for 7 minutes, or until heated through.

The stuffed eggplants can be made 1 day ahead and kept refrigerated, covered. Cook, covered, in a preheated 400° F. oven for 30 minutes, or until heated through. Serves 2.

APPLE GALETTES
(INDIVIDUAL APPLE TARTS)

½ **recipe** *pâte brisée* **(page 196)**
2 **Golden Delicious apples**
2 **tablespoons sugar, or to taste**
2 **tablespoons unsalted butter**

FOR THE APRICOT GLAZE:
½ **cup apricot preserves, strained**
1 **tablespoon Cognac**

+ HALVE THE DOUGH AND ROLL EACH HALF INTO A 7-inch round. Transfer the rounds to a heavy baking sheet and chill them for 30 minutes.

Preheat the oven to 425° F.

Peel and core the apples. Halve them lengthwise and cut them crosswise into very thin slices. Arrange the slices decoratively on the 2 rounds. Sprinkle each tart with 1 tablespoon sugar, or to taste, dot it with 1 tablespoon butter, and crimp the edges decoratively. Bake the tarts in the lower third of the oven for 30 minutes, or until the edges of the apples are browned and the pastry is golden.

While the tarts are baking make the apricot glaze: In a saucepan combine the apricot preserves and the Cognac, bring the mixture to a boil, and simmer it, stirring, for 1 minute.

Transfer the tarts to a rack and brush them lightly with the apricot glaze. Serve the tarts warm or at room temperature. Makes 2 tarts.

Raisin and Currant Cake; Claret Punch;
Roasted Chestnuts

NEW YEAR'S OPEN HOUSE

PICKLED EGGS

GRUYÈRE AND PARMESAN PUFFS

GLAZED VIRGINIA HAM

BEATEN BISCUITS

CHEDDAR BISCUITS

SPINACH AND GOAT CHEESE TART

ROASTED CHESTNUTS

RAISIN AND CURRANT CAKE

SERVES TWENTY-FOUR

Open your home to friends on this first day of the new year. There is no better way to welcome a fresh beginning than by draping a lovely cloth over the table and setting out your most festive serving platters laden with good things to eat. This buffet easily serves 24 people, and if a few of the guests are children, you might be able to stretch that number by two or three. Our menu assures an informal, comfortable day, and since the food is decidedly influenced by the traditions of the South, it evokes all the warmth and hospitality of that region.

Pink-hued pickled eggs, an unexpected and pretty appetizer, begin the meal. They are accompanied by cheese puffs, which are easily made with simple *pâte à chou* dough and flavored with generous additions of grated Gruyère and Parmesan. Both can be made the day before.

Glazed Virginia ham, while not difficult, does require some advance planning. Be sure to buy a ham that has not already been cooked but that *has* been smoke-cured. Soak the ham for a good 24 hours and then scrub off the outside mold with a brush. The mold, which develops during curing, may not look appetizing, but rest assured it is natural to a smoke-cured ham.

Biscuits are the order of the day with Virginia ham, and while the batter for both biscuit recipes should not be mixed much before baking, measure the dry and liquid ingredients well ahead of time so that you can blend them together in a blink. A spinach tart adds a splash of green to the table. Bake the shell the morning before the party and let it cool on a wire rack so that the bottom does not turn soggy. Remember that the finished tart must be room temperature before it is cut into small wedges.

Finally, a raisin and currant cake, reminiscent of a traditional fruit cake but far more modern, ends the feast on a sweet note. This tastes best if permitted to age for a day or so before it is served.

CLARET PUNCH

1 large block of ice
1 seedless orange, peeled and sliced
1 lemon, peeled, sliced, and seeded
1 grapefruit, peeled, sliced, seeded, and
   the slices halved *or* quartered
1 cup Curaçao *or* other orange-flavored
   liqueur
1 cup crème de cassis
½ cup cherry-flavored liqueur
3 quarts chilled claret
1 quart chilled club soda

PUT THE ICE IN A PUNCH BOWL AND ADD THE FRUIT. Pour in the Curaçao, crème de cassis, and cherry-flavored liqueur and combine well. Just before serving, stir in the claret and club soda. Serves 24.

PICKLED EGGS

24 medium eggs
2 pounds beets, trimmed and peeled
1½ cups white vinegar
⅓ cup sugar
2 tablespoons mixed pickling spice
2 pieces of gingerroot, each 1½ inches
   long, peeled
1 teaspoon salt

IN A LARGE SAUCEPAN COOK THE EGGS IN SIMMERING water for 10 minutes. Peel the eggs under cold water and let them cool.

In a saucepan cook the beets in boiling water to cover, covered, for 30 to 40 minutes, or until tender. Transfer the beets with a slotted spoon to a bowl and reserve them for another use.

To the liquid in the saucepan add the remaining ingredients and cook the mixture over moderate heat for 5 minutes. Put the eggs in a bowl and strain the beet liquid over them to cover.

Chill the eggs, turning occasionally, for 24 hours. Transfer them with a slotted spoon to paper towels to drain and pat dry. Serves 24.

GRUYÈRE AND PARMESAN PUFFS

light *pâte à chou* (recipe follows)
⅓ cup grated Gruyère
⅓ cup minced Gruyère
⅓ cup freshly grated Parmesan
salt and white pepper to taste
egg wash made by beating 1 egg with
   1 tablespoon milk

PREHEAT THE OVEN TO 425° F.

In a bowl fold together the dough, the cheeses, and salt and pepper. Transfer the mixture to a pastry bag fitted with a ½-inch plain tip. Pipe 1-inch mounds onto a buttered baking sheet, leaving

1 inch between the mounds. Brush the mounds with the egg wash.

Bake the mounds in the middle of the oven for 10 minutes. Reduce the heat to 400° F. and bake for 10 minutes more. Transfer the puffs to a rack and let them stand for 10 minutes.

The puffs can be made 1 day ahead and kept refrigerated or frozen, covered with plastic wrap and foil. Reheat, uncovered, on a baking sheet in a pre-heated 400° F. oven for 5 to 7 minutes if cold or 7 to 10 minutes if frozen, or until heated through. Serve warm. Makes 48 puffs.

LIGHT PÂTE À CHOU

1 cup water
¼ cup unsalted butter, cut into pieces
¼ teaspoon salt
1 cup all-purpose flour
3 to 5 large eggs

IN A HEAVY SAUCEPAN BRING THE WATER, BUTTER, AND salt to a boil over high heat. Reduce to moderate heat and add the flour. Beat the mixture with a wooden paddle until it leaves the sides of the pan and forms a ball.

Transfer the mixture to a bowl and with an electric mixer at high speed beat in 3 of the eggs, 1 at a time, beating well after each addition. The batter should be stiff enough to just hold soft peaks. If it is too stiff, break 1 or 2 more of the eggs into a bowl, beat lightly, and add enough to thin the batter to the proper consistency. To store, rub the surface of the dough with butter and let it cool.

The dough can be made 3 days ahead and kept refrigerated, wrapped in plastic wrap. To use, warm over very low heat, stirring constantly, until tepid. Makes about 2½ cups.

GLAZED VIRGINIA HAM

12- to 14-pound Virginia ham
whole cloves
2 cups firmly packed light brown sugar
1 cup fine stale bread crumbs
1 tablespoon dry mustard
2¼ cups sweet Sherry
beaten biscuits and cheddar biscuits
(page 184) as accompaniments

IN A PAIL OF COLD WATER SOAK THE HAM FOR 24 HOURS. Scrub off the spices and mold and rinse the ham. Put the ham in a kettle with water to cover and bring it to a boil over moderately high heat. Reduce the heat to low and cook at a bare simmer for 4 to 4½ hours, or until the flat bone at the butt of the ham is very loose.

Transfer the ham to a cutting board and trim off the skin and excess fat, leaving a ½-inch layer. Remove the loose bone. Score the fat in diamond shapes about ¼ inch deep and stick a whole clove in the center of each diamond.

Preheat the oven to 375° F.

In a bowl combine the sugar, bread crumbs, mustard, and ¼ cup of the Sherry to make a thick paste. Spread this on the ham.

Put the ham on a rack in a baking pan and pour in the remaining 2 cups Sherry. Bake the ham in the middle of the oven, basting 4 or 5 times, for 30 minutes, or until well glazed.

Transfer the ham to a cutting board and let it cool. Slice half the ham thinly and transfer the remaining ham to a platter. Arrange the slices around it and serve with the biscuits. Serves 24.

BEATEN BISCUITS

½ cup lard, cut into bits
4 cups all-purpose flour
¾ teaspoon salt
¼ teaspoon sugar
¼ teaspoon baking soda
1 cup cold water
softened unsalted butter as an
   accompaniment

○ IN A BOWL COMBINE THE LARD AND DRY INGREDIENTS and blend in the water to make a stiff dough. Turn the dough out onto a smooth surface and beat it with a wooden mallet, folding often, for 25 minutes, or until blisters appear.

Preheat the oven to 400° F.

With lightly floured hands form the dough into 1-inch balls. Arrange them on a buttered baking sheet and flatten them slightly. With a fork, prick the top of each round in 4 places, one row beneath the other.

Bake the biscuits in the middle of the oven for 20 minutes, or until colored lightly. Split them and spread with butter. Makes about 36 biscuits.

CHEDDAR BISCUITS

1 cup sifted cake flour (not self-rising)
1 cup yellow cornmeal
1 tablespoon baking powder
¾ teaspoon salt
½ stick (¼ cup) unsalted butter, chilled
   and cut into bits
⅔ cup finely cubed sharp Cheddar
½ cup milk

○ PREHEAT THE OVEN TO 400° F.

Into a bowl sift together the dry ingredients and cut in the butter until the mixture resembles meal. Add the Cheddar and milk and combine to just form a dough.

Roll out the dough ½ inch thick on a

floured surface and with a 1½-inch cutter cut out rounds. Reroll the scraps and cut out more rounds. Arrange them on a lightly buttered baking sheet and bake in the middle of the oven for 12 to 15 minutes, or until puffed and golden. Serve warm or at room temperature. Makes about 24 biscuits.

SPINACH AND GOAT CHEESE TART

pâte brisée (page 196)
3 tablespoons minced scallion
3 tablespoons unsalted butter
1½ cups cooked chopped spinach
¼ teaspoon freshly grated nutmeg
¼ teaspoon salt
¼ teaspoon freshly ground pepper
¼ pound cream cheese, softened
¼ pound Boucheron (French goat cheese)
3 large eggs, separated, plus 1 additional
   egg white
½ cup heavy cream
⅓ cup fresh bread crumbs

ROLL OUT THE DOUGH ⅛ INCH THICK ON A FLOURED surface. Drape it over the rolling pin and fit it into a 9-inch tart pan with a removable fluted rim. Press the dough firmly into the pan and trim off the excess, leaving a ½-inch overhang. Fold the overhang over the rim, pressing onto the sides of the shell. Prick the shell with a fork and chill it for 1 hour.

Preheat the oven to 400° F.

Line the shell with wax paper and fill the paper with raw rice. Bake the shell in the middle of the oven for 10 minutes. Remove the rice and paper and bake for 10 to 15 minutes more, or until colored lightly. Cool on a rack.

Reduce the heat to 375° F.

In a skillet sauté the scallion in 2 tablespoons of the butter over moderately high heat, stirring, until soft. Stir in the spinach, nutmeg, salt, and pepper and cook, stirring, for 5 minutes. Transfer to a large bowl and add the cheeses. Add the egg yolks, 1 at a time, and the cream and combine well. In a large bowl beat the egg whites with a pinch of salt until they hold stiff peaks and fold into the spinach mixture.

Pour the filling into the shell and dot the top with the remaining 1 tablespoon butter. Sprinkle the tart with the bread crumbs and bake in the middle of the oven for 25 minutes, or until puffed and browned. Remove the tart from the pan and cool it on a rack. Serve cut carefully into very thin wedges. Serves 24.

ROASTED CHESTNUTS

2 pounds chestnuts

PREHEAT THE OVEN TO 400° F.

With a sharp knife score each chestnut ¼ inch deep all around. Put them in one layer in 2 baking pans and roast in the middle of the oven for 20 minutes, or until the shells are just opened. Holding the chestnuts in a pot holder, peel off both layers of skin with a knife while the nuts are still hot, returning them to the oven if necessary, to keep them warm. Makes about 60 chestnuts.

RAISIN AND CURRANT CAKE

1½ sticks (¾ cup) unsalted butter
¾ cup sugar
3 large eggs
1¾ cups all-purpose flour
¾ teaspoon baking soda
½ teaspoon cinnamon
¼ teaspoon freshly grated nutmeg
¼ teaspoon salt
½ cup golden raisins
½ cup dried currants
⅓ cup dark raisins
3 tablespoons sweet Sherry
3 to 4 tablespoons milk
confectioners' sugar for garnish

PREHEAT THE OVEN TO 350° F.

In a large bowl cream the butter and sugar for 10 minutes, or until the mixture is fluffy. Beat in the eggs, 1 at a time.

Into a bowl sift the flour, baking soda, spices, and salt. In a small bowl combine ½ cup of the flour mixture with the dried fruits. Fold the flour mixture and raisin mixture into the butter mixture alternately with the Sherry and 3 tablespoons of the milk. Add enough additional milk so the batter drops from a spoon.

Transfer the batter to a buttered and floured loaf pan, 8½ by 4½ by 2½ inches, and bake in the middle of the oven for 30 minutes. Reduce the heat to 325° F. and bake for 1 hour more, or until puffed and well browned. Let the cake cool in the pan for 30 minutes. Turn it out onto a rack and let it cool. Sift confectioners' sugar over the top. Makes 1 large loaf cake.

CLARET PUNCH

Peanut Butter Sauce; Butterscotch Rum Sauce; Melba Sauce

Winter Gifts

A rush of holidays — Hanukkah, Christmas, and New Year's — usher in Winter and provide opportunity after opportunity for entertaining so that the season passes with a whirl of parties. It is the time you think about giving gifts to friends, family members, and co-workers, as well as party givers. We can think of no better way to wish someone a joyful holiday than with a gift you make yourself.

Here we have ideas for sweet sauces, baked goods, candies, and other festive treats. Shop early in the Fall for pretty jars, tins, and boxes in all sizes and shapes to have them ready to pack with your homemade goodies. Buy yards of red, green, and white ribbon to tie around the jars and tins, and sheets of colorful tissue paper to line the bottoms of the boxes. Include a jolly cookie cutter with cookies or a colorful card with the recipe clearly printed on it. Wrap the ribbon around candy canes and cinnamon sticks when you tie the bow on the package, or attach tiny Christmas balls, bells, or sprigs of holly. And remember, even a small tin is remembered and appreciated all year long.

There is nothing more appealing than a gift of a sweet sauce. Each of our sauces below can be made 1 week ahead and chilled, in an airtight container, in the refrigerator.

PEANUT BUTTER SAUCE

¼ cup firmly packed light brown sugar
2 tablespoons light corn syrup
2 tablespoons unsalted butter
½ cup smooth peanut butter
½ cup heavy cream
1½ teaspoons vanilla

 IN A SMALL, HEAVY SAUCEPAN COMBINE THE BROWN sugar, the corn syrup, and the butter and bring the mixture to a boil, stirring until the sugar is dissolved. Add the peanut butter, whisking, and whisk the mixture until it is smooth. Whisk in the cream and the vanilla, simmer the sauce for 2 minutes, and thin it to the desired consistency with hot water. Serve the sauce warm. Makes 1½ cups.

BUTTERSCOTCH RUM SAUCE

1 cup firmly packed light brown sugar
¼ cup light corn syrup
½ stick (¼ cup) unsalted butter
½ cup heavy cream
1½ teaspoons vanilla
¼ teaspoon fresh lemon juice
1½ tablespoons dark rum, or to taste
½ cup coarsely chopped pecans, toasted

IN A SMALL, HEAVY SAUCEPAN COMBINE THE BROWN sugar, the corn syrup, the butter, and a pinch of salt, cook the mixture over moderate heat, stirring and washing down any sugar crystals clinging to the sides with a brush dipped in cold water, until the sugar is dissolved, and boil it, undisturbed, for 12 minutes, or until a candy thermometer registers 280° F. Remove the pan from the heat and stir in the cream, vanilla, lemon juice, rum, and pecans. Serve the sauce warm or at room temperature. Makes about 1⅓ cups.

MELBA SAUCE

2 cups fresh raspberries *or* two
    10-ounce packages frozen raspberries
    in light syrup, thawed, juice included
½ cup red-currant jelly
¼ cup sugar, or to taste
1 tablespoon *eau-de-vie de framboise*

 + IN A SAUCEPAN COMBINE THE RASPBERRIES, THE jelly, and the sugar, bring the mixture to a boil over moderately high heat, crushing the raspberries with the back of a spoon, and simmer it, stirring occasionally, for 15 minutes, or until it is thickened. Force the mixture through a fine sieve into a bowl, pressing hard on the solids. Transfer the sauce to the pan, cleaned, and boil it, stirring occasionally, for 5 minutes, or until it is thickened to the desired consistency. Stir in the *eau-de-vie de framboise* and chill the sauce, covered, for at least 2 hours before serving it. Makes about 1⅓ cups.

CHOCOLATE RAISIN BOURBON BALLS

1 cup golden raisins
¼ cup bourbon
8½-ounce package chocolate wafers, crumbled
¼ cup unsweetened cocoa powder

+ IN A SMALL BOWL MACERATE THE RAISINS IN THE bourbon, stirring occasionally, for 1 hour. In a food processor grind the raisin mixture and wafers until the mixture forms a ball on top of the blade.

Form into marble-size balls and roll in the cocoa. Keep the confections in an airtight container for 1 day to allow them to mellow. *The balls can be made 2 weeks ahead and kept in an airtight container lined with wax paper, separating the layers with wax paper.* Makes 55 confections.

RUM CHOCOLATE TRUFFLES

Truffles are a lovely gift. Layer them between sheets of wax paper in tins or boxes and remind your hostess to keep them chilled. If you use tissue paper to line the tin, the cocoa coating will smear.

> **2 cups semisweet chocolate chips**
> **½ stick unsalted butter, cut into bits**
> **½ cup heavy cream**
> **¼ to ⅓ cup dark rum, or to taste**
> **unsweetened cocoa powder**

☺ + IN A SAUCEPAN HEAT THE CHOCOLATE, BUTTER, cream, and rum over moderately low heat, stirring, until smooth. Transfer the mixture to a bowl and chill, covered, for 3 hours, or until firm.

Put the bowl in a larger bowl of ice and cold water. With cocoa-dusted fingers, form the mixture into 1-inch balls and roll them in cocoa. Chill the truffles on a baking sheet lined with wax paper for 1 hour, or until firm.

The truffles can be made 2 weeks ahead and kept refrigerated in an airtight container lined with wax paper, separating the layers with wax paper. Makes about 60 truffles.

WALNUT PENUCHE

Penuche is also known as brown sugar fudge and is firmer than classic chocolate fudge. Be sure to pack it in airtight tins or the fudge will lose its texture.

> **1 cup granulated sugar**
> **1 cup firmly packed light brown sugar**
> **1 cup light cream**
> **1 tablespoon dark rum**
> **2 cups broken or halved walnuts**

☺ + IN A HEAVY SAUCEPAN BRING THE SUGARS AND CREAM to a boil over moderate heat, stirring and washing down any sugar crystals clinging to the sides with a brush dipped in cold water. Reduce the heat and simmer, undisturbed, until a candy thermometer registers 238° F.

Remove the mixture from the heat and let it cool for 5 minutes. Add the rum and beat until thickened. Sprinkle a buttered 8-inch-square shallow pan with the walnuts and pour in the mixture. Shake the pan to distribute the mixture evenly. Let it cool completely and cut into 1-inch squares.

The penuche can be made 2 weeks ahead and stored in a cool place in airtight containers lined with wax paper, separating the layers with wax paper. Makes 64 squares.

POPCORN BALLS

Try wrapping these simple popcorn balls in bright-colored cellophane or in the colored plastic wrap now available in supermarkets. Twist the tops of the package, secure them with thin lengths of ribbon tied with a loop, and hang the balls on the tree.

> **¾ cup molasses**
> **¾ cup sugar**
> **½ cup light corn syrup**
> **1 tablespoon cider vinegar**
> **3 tablespoons unsalted butter, cut**
>   **into bits**
> **½ cup water**
> **14 cups salted popcorn, kept warm in a**
>   **200° F. oven**

IN A SAUCEPAN COOK THE MOLASSES, SUGAR, CORN SYRUP, vinegar, butter, and water over moderate heat, stirring and washing down any sugar crystals clinging to the sides with a brush dipped in cold water, until the sugar is dissolved. Boil over moderately high heat until a candy thermometer registers 290° F.

In a buttered heatproof bowl pour the syrup evenly over the popcorn, tossing to coat well. Let it stand until just cool enough to handle.

Working quickly with buttered hands, form the popcorn into 3-inch balls and put them on a lightly oiled jelly-roll pan. (If the mixture becomes too hard to work with, heat it in a preheated 200° F. oven for 10 minutes, or until softened.)

The popcorn balls can be made 3 days ahead and stored, wrapped individually in wax paper, in airtight containers. Makes about 20 popcorn balls.

GINGERBREAD MEN

2 sticks (1 cup) unsalted butter, softened
1 cup firmly packed light brown sugar
1 large egg
1 cup dark molasses
2 tablespoons cider vinegar
5 cups all-purpose flour plus additional
    flour for dusting
2 teaspoons ground ginger
1½ teaspoons baking soda
1¼ teaspoons cinnamon
1 teaspoon ground cloves
½ teaspoon salt
sugar icing (recipe follows), if desired

IN A LARGE BOWL CREAM THE BUTTER AND SUGAR WITH an electric mixer until fluffy. Beat in the egg, molasses, and vinegar. Into a bowl sift the dry ingredients. Stir the dry ingredients into the butter mixture, a little at a time. The dough will be soft.

Quarter the dough, dust it with flour, and wrap each piece in wax paper. Flatten the pieces slightly and chill them for at least 3 hours. *The dough can be made ahead and kept refrigerated, wrapped in wax paper, overnight.*

Preheat the oven to 375° F.

Roll out the dough, 1 piece at a time, ¼ inch thick on a floured surface. Cut out cookies with a 4-inch gingerbread man cutter dipped in flour. Make more cookies with the scraps. Transfer the cookies with a spatula to buttered baking sheets, arranging them 2 inches apart.

Bake the cookies in the middle of the oven for 6 to 8 minutes, or until no imprint remains when touched lightly with a fingertip. Transfer the cookies with the spatula to racks to cool. *The gingerbread men can be made 3 days ahead up to this point and kept in airtight containers.*

Pipe the icing on the cookies using a pastry bag fitted with a small decorative tip. Let the cookies stand for 20 minutes, or until the icing is set. Makes about 50 gingerbread men.

SUGAR ICING

3 cups confectioners' sugar
¼ cup strained fresh lemon juice

 IN A LARGE BOWL SIFT THE SUGAR AND WHISK IN THE lemon juice, whisking until the icing is smooth. Makes enough icing for 50 cookies.

PECAN TASSIES

1½ sticks (¾ cup) unsalted butter,
    softened slightly
3 ounces cream cheese, softened slightly
1 cup all-purpose flour
1 large egg
¾ cup firmly packed light brown sugar
¾ cup chopped and toasted pecans
1 teaspoon vanilla
pinch of salt
sifted confectioners' sugar for garnish

+ PREHEAT THE OVEN TO 350° F.

In a bowl cream 1 stick of the butter and the cream cheese. Stir in the flour and form into a ball. Divide the dough into 24 pieces and press into 24 gem tins (2 tablespoons each in size) to form shells.

In a small bowl beat the egg lightly with the brown sugar and stir in the pecans, remaining ½ stick butter, vanilla, and salt. Divide the pecan mixture among the shells, filling them two-thirds full, and bake in the middle of the oven for 25 minutes, or until the filling is puffed slightly and the pastry is golden. Let the tassies cool on racks and garnish with the confectioners' sugar.

The tassies can be made 3 days ahead and kept in airtight containers in a cool, dry place. Or they can be frozen for 1 month, wrapped tightly in plastic wrap and foil. Makes 24 tassies.

GERMAN SPICE COOKIES

¼ **cup raisins, chopped fine**
2 **tablespoons dark rum**
1½ **sticks (¾ cup) unsalted butter,**
   softened
½ **cup granulated sugar**
¼ **cup firmly packed dark brown sugar**
¼ **cup light cream**
2 **cups all-purpose flour**
½ **teaspoon baking soda**
½ **teaspoon salt**
1 **teaspoon cinnamon**
¾ **teaspoon aniseed, ground in**
   a spice grinder
¼ **teaspoon ground cloves**
2 **ounces semisweet chocolate,**
   chopped fine

IN A SMALL BOWL MACERATE THE RAISINS IN THE RUM for 15 minutes. In a bowl cream the butter and sugars with an electric mixer until fluffy. Add the cream and beat the mixture until it is smooth. Sift in the flour, baking soda, salt, and spices and blend well. Add the chocolate and the raisin mixture and blend well.

On a piece of wax paper form the dough into a log 2 inches in diameter, using the paper as a guide. Chill the dough, wrapped in the wax paper and foil, for 2 hours. *The dough can be made 3 months ahead and frozen, wrapped well in plastic wrap and foil.*

Preheat the oven to 350° F.

Cut the roll into ¼-inch slices and bake the cookies 1 inch apart on ungreased baking sheets in the middle of the oven for 10 to 12 minutes, or until they are just firm to the touch. Transfer the cookies with a metal spatula to racks to cool. *The cookies can be made 3 days ahead and kept in airtight containers.* Makes about 50 cookies.

SCOTCH SHORTBREAD

Buttery, crumbly shortbread is as beloved in Scotland during the Winter holidays as decorated sugar cookies are in the United States. Usually, it is cut into plain-looking squares, which you may choose to dress up a little by crimping the unbaked dough with a fork. Or fashion the dough into festive shapes with cookie cutters. Pack the shortbread in a pretty tin and tie it with a red or green tartan ribbon.

4 **sticks (2 cups) unsalted butter,**
   softened
1 **cup sugar**
4 **cups plus 1 tablespoon all-purpose**
   flour
¼ **teaspoon salt**

PREHEAT THE OVEN TO 275° F.

In a bowl cream the butter and sugar until the mixture is light and fluffy. Stir in the flour and salt and with floured hands knead the dough briefly on a floured surface. The dough will be soft.

Press the dough into a baking pan, 13 by 9 by 2 inches, and prick it at ½-inch intervals with a fork. Bake the shortbread in the middle of the oven for 1½ hours, or until it is pale golden. Turn off the oven, remove the pan, and cut the shortbread into 1-inch squares. Return the shortbread to the oven and let it cool completely.

The shortbread can be made 2 weeks ahead and kept in airtight containers, separating the layers with wax paper. Makes about 10 dozen squares.

EGGNOG PIE WITH PECAN CRUST AND CHOCOLATE CURLS

FOR THE CRUST:
2½ cups ground pecans
½ stick (¼ cup) butter, melted
⅓ cup granulated sugar

1½ tablespoons unflavored gelatin
3 tablespoons brandy
4 large eggs, separated
⅓ cup granulated sugar
1⅓ cups scalded milk
1½ teaspoons vanilla
5½ tablespoons dark rum
1¾ cups chilled heavy cream
2 to 3 tablespoons sifted confectioners'
  sugar
chocolate curls (recipe follows)

MAKE THE CRUST: IN A BOWL BLEND THE PECANS, butter, and sugar. Press the mixture firmly into a 10-inch pie plate and chill it for 30 minutes.

Preheat the oven to 375° F.

Bake the crust in the middle of the oven for 15 minutes, or until it is lightly browned. Let the crust cool on a rack.

In a small bowl soften the gelatin in the brandy for 10 minutes. In another bowl beat the egg yolks with the granulated sugar until the mixture forms a ribbon when the beater is lifted. Add the milk in a stream, stirring. In a heavy saucepan cook the egg mixture over moderately low heat, stirring, until it is thick enough to coat the spoon. Do not let it boil. Remove the egg mixture from the heat and stir in the gelatin mixture, vanilla, and 4 tablespoons of the rum.

Transfer the custard to a bowl set over a larger bowl of ice and cold water and let it cool, stirring occasionally, but do not let it set. In a large bowl beat the egg whites with a pinch of salt until they hold stiff peaks and fold them into the custard. In a chilled bowl beat ¾ cup of the cream until it holds soft peaks and fold it into the custard and egg white mixture.

Mound some of the filling in the crust up to the top and chill it for 20 minutes, or until it is set. Mound the remaining filling on top and chill it for 20 minutes, or until it is set.

In a small, chilled bowl beat the remaining 1 cup cream with the confectioners' sugar and remaining 1½ tablespoons rum until it holds stiff peaks. Spread the whipped cream on the pie and sprinkle it with the chocolate curls. Chill the pie but remove it from the refrigerator at least 30 minutes before serving.

CHOCOLATE CURLS

3 ounces semisweet chocolate,
chopped coarse

IN THE TOP OF A DOUBLE BOILER SET OVER BARELY simmering water melt the chocolate, stirring, until it is smooth. With a metal spatula spread a thin layer of chocolate on the bottoms of 2 or 3 inverted cake pans. Chill the chocolate for 10 to 15 minutes, or until it loses its shine and is solid but still pliable.

Removing 1 cake pan from the refrigerator at a time, put a metal spatula under an edge of the chocolate and push it firmly away from you so that the chocolate curls as it is pushed. Chill the chocolate for several minutes if it becomes too soft to curl. Transfer the curls to wax paper and chill them as they are made.

STEAMED FIG PUDDING WITH RUM BUTTER

Steamed puddings are dense, moist affairs, often served with a liquor-spiked butter such as the rum butter we suggest here, or with sweet, rich hard sauce. Similar to English plum pudding—also known as Christmas pudding—our fig pudding is made with suet. The marble-white beef fat adds richness and distinctive flavor to the puddings, moistening them as they cook in the wet heat as neither vegetable nor dairy fat can. For gift giving, set the steamed pudding in a crockery pudding mold and attach handwritten instructions for reheating it (it must be steamed again). These puddings do very well if made ahead of time, which makes them convenient to prepare for giving.

1 pound dried Smyrna figs, chopped
1¾ cups milk
1½ cups all-purpose flour
2½ teaspoons baking powder
1 teaspoon freshly grated nutmeg
1 teaspoon cinnamon
¾ teaspoon salt
¾ pound suet, ground
1 cup sugar
3 large eggs
1½ cups fresh bread crumbs
3 tablespoons grated orange zest
rum butter (recipe follows)

RINSE A HEAVY SAUCEPAN WITH COLD WATER AND IN IT combine the figs and milk. Bring the mixture just to the boiling point over very low heat and simmer, stirring, for 20 minutes. Let it cool.

Into a bowl sift the flour, baking powder, nutmeg, cinnamon, and salt. In a large bowl cream the suet and sugar until the mixture is fluffy and add the eggs, 1 at a time, beating well after each addition. Stir in the bread crumbs and orange zest. Add the flour mixture alternately with the fig mixture, beating well after each addition.

Pour the batter into a well-buttered 2-quart decorative pudding mold fitted with a lid. Put the mold on a rack in a heavy kettle and add enough hot water to the kettle to reach halfway up the sides of the mold. Cover the kettle and steam the pudding over moderately low heat for 2 hours, adding more water if necessary.

Remove the mold from the kettle and let the pudding cool, covered, for 20 minutes. *The pudding can be made several hours ahead, cooled, and kept refrigerated. Steam for 1 to 1½ hours to reheat.*

Remove the lid, invert a serving plate over the mold, and invert the pudding onto the plate. Serve the pudding warm with the rum butter. Serves 6.

RUM BUTTER

If you give the fig pudding as a gift, you might want to attach a recipe for rum butter with it, as well as a sack of Demerara sugar. Demerara sugar, popular in the British Isles, is coarse-grained golden-colored sugar with a decidedly pleasant, strong flavor. If you cannot locate it, make the butter with granulated white sugar.

1 stick (½ cup) unsalted butter, softened
½ cup Demerara sugar (available at specialty food shops)
2 tablespoons dark rum
1 tablespoon grated orange zest
freshly grated nutmeg to taste

IN A WARM BOWL CREAM THE BUTTER AND SUGAR. BEAT in the rum, 1 tablespoon at a time, orange zest, and nutmeg and beat the mixture until light and fluffy. Makes about 1 cup.

WHITE FRUITCAKE

Traditional fruitcakes are made early in the Fall and drenched in rum or whiskey before they are stored away in dark tins to ripen before Christmas. Our white fruitcake is a simpler, lighter version of such holiday fare. No need to make it long before serving—it can be enjoyed soon after it is taken from the oven and glazed with a sugary white frosting.

⅓ cup dark raisins
⅓ cup golden raisins
⅓ cup diced mixed glacéed fruits
3 glacéed red cherries, halved
3 glacéed green cherries, halved
⅓ cup dark rum
1½ sticks (¾ cup) unsalted butter, softened
¾ cup sugar
pinch of salt
3 large eggs
1 teaspoon vanilla
¼ teaspoon freshly grated nutmeg
2 cups plus 2 tablespoons all-purpose flour
1 tablespoon baking powder
¼ cup chopped walnuts *or* pecans

FOR THE SUGAR GLAZE:
1¼ cups confectioners' sugar
2 tablespoons lemon juice

glacéed cherries and angelica (available at specialty food shops) for garnish, if desired

IN A SMALL BOWL LET THE DRIED AND GLACÉED FRUITS macerate in the rum for a minimum of 6 hours or overnight.

Preheat the oven to 375° F.

In a bowl beat the butter, sugar, and salt with a mixer for 10 minutes. Beat in the eggs, 1 at a time, and beat in the vanilla and nutmeg.

Into another bowl sift 2 cups of the flour and the baking powder. Stir this mixture into the butter mixture in 4 batches. Drain the dried and glacéed fruits in a strainer set over a bowl and add the rum to the batter.

Dry the fruits on paper towels and in a bowl toss them with the remaining 2 tablespoons flour. Shake the fruits in a sieve to rid them of excess flour and fold them into the batter with the nuts.

Pour the batter into a well-buttered baking pan, 12 by 4½ by 3 inches, and bake in the middle of the oven for 10 minutes. Reduce the heat to 325° F. and bake for 40 minutes more, or until the cake is well puffed and golden. Let the fruitcake stand in the pan for 10 minutes and turn it out onto a rack to cool completely. *The fruitcake can be made 3 days ahead up to this point and kept in a cool, dry place, wrapped tightly in plastic wrap.*

Make the sugar glaze: In a bowl whisk together the confectioners' sugar, sifted, the lemon juice, and 1 tablespoon water. Add additional water, if necessary, to make a thick, spreadable glaze.

Set the rack with the cake over a shallow pan. Spread the cake with the glaze and decorate it with the glacéed cherries and angelica. Let the glaze set for at least 1 hour. Makes 1 fruitcake.

CHALLAH

4 teaspoons active dry yeast
1 tablespoon sugar
¾ cup lukewarm water
2 large eggs
2 tablespoons unsalted butter, softened
3½ to 4 cups all-purpose flour
1½ teaspoons salt
egg wash made by beating 1 egg yolk
  with 1 teaspoon water
poppy seeds for garnish

IN A BOWL PROOF THE YEAST WITH THE SUGAR IN THE water until foamy. Beat in the eggs and the butter. Add 3 cups of the flour and the salt and stir until the mixture is combined.

Knead the dough on a floured surface, adding more flour as necessary to form a soft but not sticky dough. Transfer the dough to a buttered bowl and turn it to coat with the butter. Let it rise, covered with plastic wrap and a dish towel, in a warm place for 1½ hours, or until the dough is double in bulk.

Punch down the dough and divide it into 3 equal pieces. On a work surface roll each piece of dough into a 12-inch rope about 1½ to 2 inches in diameter. To braid, start with 2 of the ropes crossed to form an X with the intersection in the middle. (By braiding from the middle, you create the greatest height in the center of the loaf.)

Take the third rope and lay it over the middle of the intersection. Starting at the X point, pull the left rope gently over the middle and pull the right rope over and between the other two. Pull the left rope over and between the other two, then pull the right rope over and between the other two. Continue until completely braided.

Pinch the ends together and tuck them under the loaf. Turn the loaf around and braid the other side, starting with the right rope. Pinch and tuck the ends in the same manner.

Transfer the loaf to a well-greased baking sheet and brush it with the egg wash. Sprinkle the loaf with the poppy seeds and let it rise, covered loosely, in a warm place for 30 minutes, or until it is double in bulk.

Preheat the oven to 375° F.

Bake the loaf in the middle of the oven for 40 to 45 minutes, or until the bottom sounds hollow when tapped. Let the bread cool on a rack.

The loaf can be made 1 day ahead and kept in a cool, dry place, wrapped tightly in plastic wrap. Makes 1 braided loaf.

MULLED CIDER MIX

Scoop some of this heady mix into small plastic or cellophane bags secured with pretty ribbons. Offer an aromatic sackful with a jug of fresh apple cider and perhaps some handsome mugs. Or tie a bag of cider mix on top of any holiday package for an extra touch of thoughtfulness.

8 cinnamon sticks, broken into pieces
2 whole nutmegs, crushed
⅓ cup whole cloves
⅓ cup minced dried orange zest
¼ cup whole allspice

IN A LARGE BOWL COMBINE ALL THE INGREDIENTS. TIE 1-tablespoon batches of the mix in small cheesecloth or muslin bags and tie the bags with string. *The cider mix can be made ahead and kept indefinitely in a tea tin.* One bag makes enough to flavor 1 quart of cider.

To make mulled cider, put the bag in a saucepan with 1 quart cider and bring the cider to a boil over moderately high heat. Simmer slowly, covered, for 20 minutes. Add ¼ cup dark rum, if desired, and simmer for 5 minutes. Discard the bag. Serve the mulled cider hot with a cinnamon stick in each cup.

Basics

PÂTE BRISÉE

1¼ cups all-purpose flour
¾ stick (6 tablespoons) unsalted butter,
    chilled and cut into bits
2 tablespoons vegetable shortening,
    chilled
¼ teaspoon salt
2 to 3 tablespoons ice water

◷+ In a bowl blend the flour, butter, shortening, and salt until the mixture resembles meal. Add the water, tossing with a fork and adding more water if necessary to form a soft but not sticky dough. Form the dough into a ball, dust it with flour, and chill, wrapped in wax paper, for 1 hour. *The dough can be made 2 days ahead and kept refrigerated, wrapped in plastic wrap. Or, it can be frozen for 1 month, wrapped in plastic wrap and foil.* Makes enough dough for 1 single-crust 9-inch pie.

FLAKY PIE PASTRY

2¼ cups all-purpose flour
½ teaspoon salt
½ stick (¼ cup) unsalted butter, chilled
    and cut into bits
½ cup vegetable shortening, chilled and
    cut into bits
¼ cup ice water

◷ In a bowl combine the flour and salt. Add the butter and blend until the mixture resembles coarse meal. Add the shortening and blend until it resembles meal. Add the ice water, tossing with a fork, and add more water if necessary to form a soft but not sticky dough. Form the dough into a ball. *The dough can be used immediately or made ahead and kept refrigerated, wrapped in wax paper, for up to 2 days. Or, it can be frozen for 1 month, wrapped in plastic wrap and foil.* Makes enough for 1 double-crust 9-inch pie or 2 single-crust 9-inch pies.

LARD PASTRY DOUGH

3 cups sifted all-purpose flour
¾ cup lard, chilled and cut into bits
4½ tablespoons unsalted butter, chilled
    and cut into bits
1½ teaspoons salt
⅓ to ½ cup ice water

◷+ In a large bowl blend the flour, lard, butter, and salt until the mixture resembles meal. Add enough water, tossing to incorporate it, to form a dough. Form the dough into a ball and chill it, wrapped in wax paper, for 1 hour. Makes enough dough for 1 double-crust 9-inch pie or 1 single-crust 9-inch pie with a lattice top.

BÉCHAMEL SAUCE

1 tablespoon minced onion
3 tablespoons unsalted butter
¼ cup all-purpose flour
3 cups milk
¼ teaspoon salt
white pepper to taste

◷ In a saucepan cook the onion in the butter over moderate heat, stirring, until it is softened. Stir in the flour and cook the mixture over low heat, stirring constantly, for 3 minutes. Add the milk in a stream, whisking vigorously until the mixture is thick and smooth, and add the salt and white pepper.

Bring the sauce to a boil and simmer it for 10 to 15 minutes, or until it is thickened to the desired consistency. Strain the sauce through a fine sieve into a bowl and cover the surface with a buttered round of wax paper to prevent a skin from forming. Makes about 2¼ cups.

BROWN SAUCE

2 onions, quartered
1 small carrot, quartered
½ cup beef, veal, or pork drippings *or*
    1 stick (½ cup) unsalted butter
½ cup all-purpose flour
8 cups brown stock (recipe follows) *or*
    canned beef broth, heated
3 parsley sprigs
1 bay leaf
pinch of dried thyme, crumbled
1 garlic clove, crushed
1 celery stalk
¼ cup canned tomato purée

IN STAINLESS STEEL OR ENAMELED KETTLE SAUTÉ THE onions and carrot in the drippings over moderately high heat, stirring, until the onions begin to turn golden. Add the flour and cook over low heat, stirring, until the mixture is a rich brown.

Remove the mixture from the heat, add 3 cups of the stock in a stream, stirring, and combine well. Add the herbs, garlic, and celery and cook the mixture over low heat, stirring, until it is thickened. Add 3 more cups of the stock and simmer the sauce, stirring occasionally and skimming the froth, for 1½ hours, or until it is reduced to 3 cups.

Add the tomato purée and simmer the sauce for 5 minutes. Strain the sauce through a fine sieve into a bowl and return it to the kettle. Add the remaining 2 cups stock to the sauce and simmer, skimming any froth, for 15 minutes, or until it is reduced to 4 cups.

The sauce can be made 1 month ahead and frozen in an airtight container. Reheat over moderate heat. Makes about 4 cups.

BROWN STOCK

3 pounds veal or beef bones, sawed into
    2-inch pieces
2 pounds stew beef, cut into 1½-inch
    pieces
2 unpeeled onions, quartered
2 carrots, halved
16½ cups cold water
2 celery ribs, halved
4 unpeeled garlic cloves
6 long parsley sprigs
1 teaspoon salt
½ teaspoon dried thyme, crumbled
1 bay leaf

PREHEAT THE OVEN TO 400° F.

Spread the bones and beef in a flameproof baking pan and roast them in the oven for 25 minutes. Add the onions and carrots and roast the mixture, stirring once or twice, for 30 minutes more, or until it is browned well. Transfer the roasted mixture with a slotted spoon to a stockpot or kettle.

Pour off any fat from the pan and add 2 cups of the water and deglaze the pan over high heat, scraping up the brown bits. Add the water and brown bits mixture to the stockpot with 14 cups of the remaining water and bring the mixture to a boil, skimming the froth. Add the remaining ½ cup water and bring the mixture to a simmer, skimming the froth. Add the remaining ingredients and simmer the stock for 4 hours. If a more concentrated flavor is desired, boil the stock until it is reduced to the desired flavor.

Strain the stock through a fine sieve into a bowl. Let it cool. Chill the stock and remove the fat.

The stock can be made ahead and frozen for 3 months. Makes about 8 cups.

CHICKEN STOCK

**3 pounds assorted chicken wings (halved
    at the joints), necks, backs, and bones
14½ cups cold water
2 onions stuck with 2 whole cloves, halved
4 unpeeled garlic cloves
2 carrots, halved
1 celery rib, halved
1 teaspoon salt
6 long parsley sprigs
12 black peppercorns
½ teaspoon dried thyme, crumbled
1 bay leaf**

IN A STOCKPOT OR KETTLE BRING THE CHICKEN PARTS
and 14 cups of the water to a boil, skimming the
froth. Add the remaining ½ cup water and bring
the mixture to a simmer, skimming the froth. Add
the remaining ingredients and simmer, skimming,
for 3 hours. If a more concentrated flavor is desired, boil the stock until it is reduced to the desired flavor.
    Strain the stock through a fine sieve into a
bowl. Let it cool. Chill the stock and remove the fat.
    *The stock can be made ahead and frozen for 3
months.* Makes about 10 cups.

WHITE FISH STOCK

**3 pounds bones and trimmings of any
    white fish such as sole, flounder, or
    whiting, chopped
3 cups sliced onion
36 long parsley sprigs
6 tablespoons fresh lemon juice
1½ teaspoons salt
10½ cups water
1½ cups dry white wine**

◯ IN A WELL-BUTTERED HEAVY STOCKPOT COMBINE ALL
the ingredients except the water and wine and
steam the mixture, covered, over moderately high
heat for 5 minutes. Add the water and wine and
bring the mixture to a boil, skimming the froth.
Simmer for 20 minutes. Strain the stock through a
fine sieve into a bowl and let it cool.
    *The stock can be made ahead and frozen for 3
months.* Makes about 9 cups.

TURKEY GIBLET STOCK

**neck and giblets (excluding the liver) of a
    12- to 14-pound turkey
4 cups canned chicken broth
1 celery rib, chopped
1 carrot, chopped
1 onion, quartered
1 bay leaf
½ teaspoon dried thyme, crumbled
12 parsley stems
6 whole allspice
4 whole cloves**

IN A LARGE SAUCEPAN BRING THE NECK AND GIBLETS,
broth, celery, carrot, onion, and 4 cups water to a
boil and skim the froth. Add the remaining ingredients and cook at a bare simmer for 2 hours, or until
the stock is reduced to about 4 cups. Strain the
stock through a fine sieve into a bowl, pressing
hard on the solids.
    *The stock can be made 2 days ahead. Let it
cool and keep it refrigerated in an airtight container.
The stock can also be frozen for 3 months.* Makes
about 4 cups.

VEGETABLE STOCK

**3 onions, chopped
2 tablespoons olive oil
white and pale green parts of 2 leeks,
    washed well and chopped
2 carrots, chopped
2 celery ribs, chopped
¼ pound mushrooms, chopped
1 cup potato peelings
12⅓ cups cold water
¼ cup lentils
6 unpeeled garlic cloves
½ teaspoon peppercorns
½ teaspoon dried thyme, crumbled
1 bay leaf
12 parsley sprigs
1 teaspoon salt**

IN A STOCKPOT OR KETTLE COOK THE ONION IN THE OIL
over moderate heat, stirring, until it is golden. Add
the leeks, carrots, celery, mushrooms, potato peelings, and ⅓ cup of the water and simmer the mix-

ture, covered, stirring occasionally, for 5 minutes. Add the remaining 12 cups water and the remaining ingredients and bring the mixture to a boil. Simmer, uncovered, for 2 hours. Strain the stock through a fine sieve into a bowl and let it cool. Chill the stock and remove the fat.

The stock can be made ahead and frozen for 3 months. Makes about 9 cups.

TO COOK CHESTNUTS

PREHEAT THE OVEN TO 450° F.

With a sharp knife cut an X on the round side of each chestnut. Arrange the cut chestnuts in a jelly-roll pan, add ¼ cup water, and bake them in the oven for 10 minutes, or until the shells open. Shell and peel the chestnuts while they are hot.

In a deep skillet arrange the chestnuts in one layer and add water to cover. Simmer the chestnuts for 45 minutes, or until they are tender. Drain the chestnuts and pat them dry.

TO GRATE FRESH COCONUT

PREHEAT THE OVEN TO 400° F.

Choose a coconut without cracks and containing liquid. Pierce the eyes with an ice pick or skewer, drain the liquid, and reserve for another use.

Bake the coconut in the oven for 15 minutes. Break it with a hammer and remove the flesh from the shell, levering it out carefully with the point of a sharp knife. Peel off the brown membrane with a vegetable peeler and cut the meat into small pieces.

In a blender or food processor grind the pieces, a few at a time. One large coconut yields about 4 cups grated coconut.

TO TOAST AND GRIND CUMINSEED

IN A DRY SMALL SKILLET TOAST THE CUMINSEED OVER moderate heat, swirling the skillet, for 3 to 4 minutes, or until the cuminseed turns several shades darker and starts to pop. If desired, pulverize the cuminseed in a spice or coffee grinder. Each teaspoon of whole cuminseed will yield 1¼ teaspoons toasted and ground cuminseed.

TO ROAST PEPPERS

USING A LONG-HANDLED FORK, CHAR THE PEPPERS over an open flame, turning, for 2 minutes, or until the skins are blackened. (Or broil them under a preheated broiler about 2 inches from the heat, turning every 5 minutes, for 15 minutes, or until the skins are blistered and charred.)

Transfer the peppers to a bowl and let them steam, covered, until they are cool enough to handle. Keeping the peppers whole, peel them starting at the blossom end, cut off the tops, and discard the seeds and ribs. Wear rubber gloves when working with chili peppers.

TO CLEAN MUSSELS

SCRUB THE MUSSELS WELL IN SEVERAL CHANGES OF water. Scrape off the beards and rinse the mussels. If the mussels are exceptionally dirty, let them soak in water to cover, with ⅓ cup salt and 1 tablespoon cornmeal per gallon of water, for 2 hours to help disgorge any sand. Drain the mussels and rinse them.

TO STERILIZE JARS AND GLASSES

WASH THE JARS IN HOT SUDS AND RINSE THEM WITH scalding water. Put the jars in a kettle and cover them with hot water. Bring the water to a boil, covered, and boil for 15 minutes from the time steam emerges from the kettle. Remove the kettle from the heat and let the jars stand in the hot water. Just before filling the jars, invert them onto a tea towel to dry. Fill the jars while they are still hot. Sterilize the lids for 5 minutes.

TO SEAL JARS AND GLASSES WITH PARAFFIN

SHAVE A BAR OF PARAFFIN INTO THE TOP OF A DOUBLE boiler set over simmering water and melt it. When ready to seal the jars, wipe off anything that may have stuck to the rim. Pour an ⅛-inch layer of paraffin over the contents of the jar, swirling to cover completely, and let it set. Repeat with a second layer of paraffin.

Index

Page numbers in *italics* indicate color photographs

(M) indicates a microwave recipe

Table Setting Acknowledgments

Any items in the photographs not credited are privately owned.
All addresses, except where noted, are in New York City.

Front Jacket

Curried Butternut Squash and Apple Soup for a Vegetarian Thanksgiving: Tetard "Trianon" silver flatware; Peill "Diana" water goblets and wineglasses—Cardel, Ltd., 621 Madison Avenue. Flowers from Zezé, 398 E. 52nd Street. All other accessories and furniture from Kentshire Galleries, 37 E. 12th Street.

Frontispiece

Fajitas with Peppers and Red Onions; Flour Tortillas; Chunky Guacamole; Fresh Tomato Salsa (page 2): See credits for A South-of-the-Border Birthday below.

Spring Opener

Table Setting (pages 10 and 11): China—J. Garvin Mecking, 72 East 11th Street. Flatware—Pavillon Christofle, 680 Madison Avenue. Champagne flutes—Lenox, Inc., Lawrenceville, NJ. Place mats and napkins—D. Porthault, Inc., 18 E. 69th Street. Butter knives, salt and pepper shakers—James II Galleries, Ltd., 15 E. 57th Street. Chairs—Stair & Company, Inc., 942 Madison Avenue.

An Easter Brunch

Table Setting (page 14): Dinner plates by Lynn Chase Designs Inc.—The Naked Zebra, 279 Greenwich Avenue, Greenwich, CT. Dinner forks and knives—Tiffany & Company, 727 Fifth Avenue. Salad forks—S. Wyler & Son, 941 Lexington Avenue. Glasses—The Pottery Barn, 117 East 59th Street. Tablecloth (fabric available through decorator)—Cowtan & Tout, 979 Third Avenue. Iron gates—Yale R. Burge, 305 East 63rd Street.

An Elegant Easter Dinner

Crown Roast of Lamb; Saffron Rice Timbales; Gingered Carrots (page 18): Platter and sideboard—Stair & Company, Inc., 942 Madison Avenue. Carving knife and fork and sauceboat—James Robinson, Inc., 15 East 57th Street.

Asparagus with Scallion and Parsley (page 22): Hot water plate—Stair & Company, Inc., 942 Madison Avenue.

Passover Seder

Herbed Roast Chicken, Baked Tomatoes with Parsley Basil Stuffing (page 25): Herend platters—Cardel, Ltd., 621 Madison Avenue.

Passover Spongecake with Citrus Glaze (page 28): Bernardaud cake plate and cake knife—Cardel, Ltd., 621 Madison Avenue. Matzah cover—Moriah, 699 Madison Avenue.

An Anniversary Dinner

Watercress, Pear, and Grape Salad with Chrysanthemum Petals (page 33): Salad bowl and salad plates—Waterford Wedgwood, 713 Madison Avenue. Georgian House serving pieces—Fortunoff, 68 Fifth Avenue.

A Christening Luncheon

Lemon Cake with Lemon Meringue Frosting (page 34): Cake stand; cake knife; Champagne flutes; child's flatware in case; wine rinser (filled with candy)—James II Galleries, 15 E. 57th Street. Plates—courtesy of Bergdorf Goodman, 754 Fifth Avenue. Tablecloth and napkins—Françoise Nunnallé, (212) 246-4281.

Spring Gifts

Hamantaschen, Chocolate-Dipped Fruit Balls (pages 40 and 41): Plates by Dorothy Hafner from Tiffany & Company, 727 Fifth Avenue.

Summer Opener

Table Setting (pages 48 and 49): Dinner plates by Mottahedeh—Cardel Ltd., 621 Madison Avenue. Flatware (made to order)—Gorham, P.O. Box 6150, Providence, RI 02940. Napkins—Françoise Nunnallé Fine Arts, 105 West 55th Street (by appointment only). Cruet set—James II Galleries, Ltd., 15 East 57th Street.

A Memorial Day Picnic

Red Cabbage Coleslaw, Sesame Chicken Wings (page 52): "Stars & Stripes" cotton fabric (for tablecloth and napkins)—available through decorator from Grey Watkins Ltd., 979 Third Avenue.

A Small Wedding Luncheon

Table Setting (page 60):"Clothilde" cotton fabric (tablecloths)—available through decorator from Brunschwig & Fils, 979 Third Avenue. Cotton seersucker napkins by Brook Hill—special order from Bergdorf Goodman, 754 Fifth Avenue. Vintage sterling flatware—F. Gorevic & Son, 635 Madison Avenue. Silverplate pail—Keesal & Mathews, 1244 Madison Avenue. Silverplate punchbowl—Wolfman Gold, 116 Greene Street.

Poached Whole Salmon in Aspic; Tarama-Filled Eggs; Steamed Mussels in Aspic (page 64): Tray—F. Gorevic & Son, Inc., 635 Madison Avenue.

Turkey Ballottine, Duchesse Potatoes (page 66): Tray—Gorevic & Son, Inc., 635 Madison Avenue.

Graduation Day Buffet

Strawberry Kiwi Bowl, Palmiers (page 70): Trays, serving spoon, and demitasse spoons—Pavillon Christofle, 680 Madison Avenue. Bowl—Cardel, Ltd., 621 Madison Avenue. Decanter—Baccarat, Inc., 625 Madison Avenue. Tumblers, coffeepot, and sugar bowl—S. Wyler, Inc., 941 Lexington Avenue. Mottahedeh plates, cups, and saucers—The Metropolitan Museum of Art, Gift Shop, Fifth Avenue at 82nd Street.

Composed Salad with Chive Dressing; Cheeses; French Bread (page 74): Crystal serving plate—Cardel, Ltd., 621 Madison Avenue. Salad servers and cheese knife—Pavillon Christofle, 680 Madison Avenue. Marble cheese server—Bridge Kitchenware Corporation, 214 East 52nd Street. Papier-mâché basket—James II Galleries, Ltd., 15 East 57th Street.

Independence Day Buffet

Cornmeal Puffs; Smoked Salmon Cream; Clams Steamed on the Grill (page 80): Wine goblets by Simon Pearce. Salt and pepper grinders—Frank McIntosh at Henri Bendel, 712 Fifth Avenue. Cachepots and bread basket—Eigen Arts, 150 Bay Street, Jersey City, NJ 07302. Tile floor—Country Floors, Inc., 15 E. 16th Street.

Orange-Flavored Chicken Breasts with Bacon, Vegetable Brochettes (page 84): Earthenware platter, Earthenware 13-inch buffet plates—Wolfman • Gold & Good Company, 484 Broome Street.

Fall Opener

Table Setting (pages 100 and 101): Flatware—Pavillon Christofle, 680 Madison Avenue. Wineglasses—Simon Pearce, 385 Bleecker Street. Linen napkins—Frank McIntosh at Henri Bendel, 712 Fifth Avenue. Open salts, wine cooler—James II Galleries, Ltd., 15 E. 57th Street. Table base—Howard Kaplan Antiques, 827 Broadway. Garden Chairs—Newel Art Galleries, Inc., 425 East 53rd Street.

A South-of-the-Border Birthday

Fajitas with Peppers and Red Onions; Flour Tortillas; Chunky Guacamole; Fresh Tomato Salsa (page 104): All merchandise from Pan American Phoenix, 153 E. 53rd Street.

Hot Milk Spongecake with Penuche Icing, Fresh Fruit Mosaic (page 109): All merchandise from Pan American Phoenix, 153 E. 53rd Street.

A Harvest Patio Dinner

Grilled Duck with Mustard and Basil, Stuffed Tomatoes Provençale (page 112): Céralene dinner plate—Baccarat, Inc., 625 Madison Avenue.

A Southern Thanksgiving

Table Setting (page 114): Photographed at Kentshire Galleries, 37 E. 12th Street. Flowers from Zezé, 398 E. 52nd Street. Dinner plates, relish dishes, furniture, and accessories from Kentshire Galleries.

A Victorian Thanksgiving

Roast Turkey with Corn Bread, Ham, and Apricot Stuffing; Gratin of Four Onions; Cranberry Chutney (page 122): Platter, sauce tureens, and ladles—James Robinson, Inc., 15 East 57th Street. Royal Worcester/ Spode vegetable dish—Cardel, Ltd., 621 Madison Avenue.

Spiced Apple Pie (page 129): Amish quilt—Judith and James Milne Inc., 506 East 74th Street.

A Baby Shower Tea

Tea Sandwiches in a Bread Basket (page 134): Silverplate tray—F. Gorevic & Son, 635 Madison Avenue. Champagne flutes and leaf plates—Keesal & Mathews, 1244 Madison Avenue.

Winter Opener

Table Setting (pages 148 and 149): Wedgwood dinner plates; Rosenthal soup bowls—Cardel, Ltd., 621 Madison Avenue. Puiforcat flatware, wineglasses, water goblets, and Champagne glasses—Baccarat, Inc., 625 Madison Avenue. Candlesticks—Bardith Ltd., 31 East 72nd Street. Saltcellar and salt spoons—F. Gorevic & Son, Inc., 635 Madison Avenue. Glass piggins—James II Galleries, Ltd., 15 East 57th Street. Tablecloth—J. Garvin Mecking Antiques, 72 East 11th Street. Napkins—Françoise Nunnallé Fine Arts, 105 West 55th Street (by appointment only). Chairs—Stair & Company, Inc., 842 Madison Avenue. Fabric (available through decorator)—Cowtan & Tout, 979 Third Avenue. Topiary—Mädderlake, 478 Broadway.

An English Christmas Dinner

Table Setting (page 152): Photographed at Kentshire Galleries, 37 E. 12th Street. "Winter Game Birds" porcelain dinner plates by Chase Ltd.—Scully & Scully Inc., 506 Park Avenue. Solid silver flatware, ca. 1920—F. Gorevic & Son, 635 Madison Avenue. Flowers and potted cypress plants—Zezé, 398 E. 52nd Street. All other accessories and furniture from Kentshire Galleries.

A Country Christmas

Table Setting (page 158): Wedgwood salad plates, Val St. Lambert wineglasses and water goblets—Cardel, Ltd., 621 Madison Avenue. Flatware, saltshakers, and pepper shakers—Towle Manufacturing Company, 260 Merrimac Street, Newburyport, MA. Candy dishes—F. Gorevic & Son, Inc., 635 Madison Avenue. Linen napkins—Léron, Inc., 750 Madison Avenue. Quilt—George Schoellkopf, 1065 Madison Avenue. Chairs—Raymond B. Knight, Antiques, 113 Birch Hill Road, Locust Valley, NY. Mantelpiece and spark guard—Wm. H. Jackson Company, 3 East 47th Street. Christmas tree decorations—Vincent Lippe, 225 Fifth Avenue.

Orange and Red Onion Salad (page 163): Fabric (available through decorator)—Brunschwig & Fils, Inc., 979 Third Avenue.

A Latkes Party for Hanukkah

Hanukkah Jelly Doughnuts, Hot Cranberry Apple Cider (page 172): Bowl, candlesticks, and napkins—Frank McIntosh at Henri Bendel, 712 Fifth Avenue. Glasses—Wolfman Gold, 116 Greene Street.

An Intimate New Year's Eve Dinner

Table Setting (page 176): Dinner plates; flatwear; wineglasses; saltshaker and pepper shaker; candlesticks; sweet-meat tree; wine cooler—Tiffany & Company, 727 Fifth Avenue. Chairs (available through decorator)—Louis Maslow & Son, Inc., 979 Third Avenue. Screen (available through decorator)—Charles R. Gracie & Sons, Inc., 979 Third Avenue.

New Year's Open House

Raisin and Currant Cake; Claret Punch; Roasted Chestnuts (page 180): Wood box and cake server—James II Galleries, 15 E. 57th Street. Silver nut bowl—F. Gorevic & Son, 635 Madison Avenue. Fabric on wall (available through decorator)—Clarence House, 211 E. 58th Street.

Winter Gifts

Peanut Butter Sauce; Butterscotch Rum Sauce; Melba Sauce (pages 186 and 187): Christmas boxes, bags and labels—The Gifted Line, 2656 Bridgeway, Sausalito, CA 94965, tel. (415) 332-4488. Embossed brass Mason jar lids—Chapelle Designers, Box 9252, Newgate Station, Ogden, UT 84409.

Back Jacket

Hanukkah Jelly Doughnuts and Hot Cranberry Apple Cider: See credits for A Latkes Party for Hanukkah above.

Orange-Flavored Chicken Breasts with Bacon, Vegetable Brochettes: See credits for Independence Day Buffet above.

Tea Sandwiches in a Bread Basket: See credits for A Baby Shower Tea above.